Georgian Court

Georgian Court

An Estate of the Gilded Age

M. Christina Geis, R.S.M.

Philadelphia
The Art Alliance Press
London and Toronto: Associated University Presses

© 1982 by Associated University Presses, Inc.

Associated University Presses, Inc.
440 Forsgate Drive
Cranbury, NJ 08512

Associated University Presses Ltd
25 Sicilian Avenue
London SC1A 2QH, England

Associated University Presses
P.O. Box 39, Clarkson Pstl. Stn.
Mississauga, Ontario
Canada LSJ 3X9

SECOND PRINTING 1991

Library of Congress Cataloging in Publication Data

Geis, M. Christina, 1919–
    Georgian Court, an estate of the gilded age.

    Bibliography: p.
    Includes index.
    1. Georgian Court College—Buildings—History.
I. Title
LD7251.L343G39   378.749′48   81-65875
ISBN 0-87982-043-8   AACR2

PRINTED IN THE UNITED STATES OF AMERICA

Contents

GEORGIAN COURT

Acknowledgments

The original idea for this book occurred to me during the Summer Seminar of 1976 sponsored by the National Endowment for the Humanities, entitled "Institutional Patronage and Architecture as Symbolic Form" and directed by Professor Egon Verheyen of the Johns Hopkins University, Baltimore, Maryland. In 1979 a grant-in-aid from the New Jersey Historical Commission helped further the completion of the work.

I wish to express particular gratitude to Professor Donald J. McGinn of the English Department of Georgian Court College, not only for his invaluable encouragement and support but also for his many helpful suggestions in the preparation of the manuscript. I am also indebted to Samuel H. Graybill, Jr., for permission to use material from his dissertation "Bruce Price, American Architect, 1845–1903," Yale University, 1957, as a basis for the content of Part II. He also kindly shared time and references.

My further obligation extends to local residents who guided me to sources of information or supplied me with newspaper clippings, items of information, or photographs. These include Gene L. Hendrickson, Mary Hurlburt, Jane Westhall, Ziegfried Steele, Claribel Young, Hope Downs, and Ellen Yates Wolf.

I take this opportunity to thank Vincent Hart, photographer, for the cheerful and generous disposal of his time. For original photographs of Georgian Court and of the Gould family, I am indebted to George H. Moss, Jr., director of the Moss Archives, Rumson, New Jersey. Robert LaBurt and George H. Boynton of Tuxedo Park Associates made it possible for me to take photographs at Tuxedo Park, New York.

Three men who had once lived on the estate shared recollections: George A. Bishop of Lakewood, son of William Bishop, the butler for the Goulds; G. Frank Langford of Marco Island, Florida, son of George P. Langford, English butler and overseer of supplies for the Gould residences; and Peter Gascoyne of Lakewood, Colorado, son of Peter Gascoyne, superintendent of the gardens and greenhouses under the Goulds.

Expert and cheerful assistance has been provided by Sister Anita Talar, librarian, and all the reference librarians of Farley Memorial Library, Georgian Court College. Likewise I am indebted to the staffs of the Archives of American Art both in New York City and in Washington, D.C., the Ocean County College and County Libraries in Toms River, and the Lakewood Public Library. Mrs. Benjamin Sylvester, archivist at Choate Rosemary Hall, Wallingford, Connecticut, provided information and correspondence relative to the muralist Robert Van Vorst Sewell.

Finally, I wish to acknowledge the helpful criticisms of James W. Hyres and Paul G. Amelchenko, architects, who shared their valuable expertise. I am grateful to individual Sisters of Mercy: Sister Mary Giovanni McDonough, archivist, who supplied me with necessary papers; Sister Mary Celeste McCone, who gave me valuable newspaper clippings; Sister Mary Phyllis Breimayer, who traveled out of state with me in search of reference material; Sister Mary Demetria McDade and Sister Carolyn Martin, who made excellent suggestions; Sister Mary Stephanie Sloyan, who searched for newspaper items; and Sisters Mary Blaise Miller and Mary Stanislaus Zita, who assisted in the typing of the manuscript.

Prologue

In the 1880s the charming little town of Lakewood in the pines area of South Central New Jersey was a well-known health resort and winter paradise for the wealthy. After all, no one could enjoy Newport or Bar Harbor during the winter, and Palm Beach was just too far from the metropolitan social scene. But for visitors from New York and Philadelphia this town could be reached in a matter of hours by the New Jersey Southern Railroad, built in 1863, or by coach.[1] Thus the formality of Fifth Avenue or Rittenhouse Square could be quickly exchanged for the rustic beauty of the pine woods and the invigorating country air.

To the early settlers, however, the town gave promise of industrial enterprise, not carefree playground. About 1786 one of the first structures in the area, the Three Partners Saw-Mill, was erected by the Skidmores, John, George, and Henry, on the South Branch of the Metedeconk River and was quickly surrounded by the shanties of the woodsmen. By the early nineteenth century bog iron deposits were discovered in the South Jersey pines, and furnaces were erected to convert the iron into usable products. About 1814, in partnership with William Irwin, Jesse Richards, son of William Richards of the thriving Batsto iron village, built a furnace near the mill site. The builders changed the name of the sawmill community to Washington's Furnace. Taking over the operation of the furnace in 1833, Joseph W. Brick, a former Richard's employee and a more capable businessman, rebuilt it and renamed it the Bergen Iron Works. The waterpower needed to run the iron furnaces or the sawmill that preceded them, usually obtained by damming the cedar swamp streams, caused them to broaden out into pretty lakes, two of which are located near the center of the town. By 1844 a community of about two hundred people dwelt on the shores of the two lakes in the vicinity of what is now Main Street and Clifton Avenue.

After Brick's death in 1847 his property was inherited by his five children, one of whom, Riley A. Brick, took over the management of the thriving business. Six-team wagons regularly hauled products of the blast furnace over to Furnace Dock, now Cedar Bridge, in the Laurelton section of the present Brick Township. There they were loaded into scows that carried them down the Metedeconk River to Bay Head, where they were transferred to schooners for the trip to New York. The Bergen Iron Works community prospered and grew in numbers. On 4 July 1865 the citizens honored the memory of Joseph W. Brick by changing the name of the town to Bricksburg. On the same occasion, it is reputed, a friend of the family, Henry M. Alexander, named the larger of the two lakes Carasaljo—a contraction of the names of Brick's three daughters, Caroline, Sarah, and Josephine ("Carrie," "Sal," and "Jo")—and the smaller lake Manetta after Brick's wife, although her name was Margaret.[2] That same year Riley A. Brick built a tavern on what is now the north side of Main Street, between Lexington and Clifton Avenues, and called it the Bricksburg House. Publicizing the virtues of the site, he encouraged the first visitors from New York.

By the mid-1860s, when better iron deposits were discovered elsewhere, especially in Pennsylvania, the Bricksburg enterprise gradually declined. In February 1866 Robert Campbell, Riley A.

Brick, and other interested citizens incorporated the Bricksburg Land and Improvement Company and launched a plan for the development of the town. Streets were laid out by Samuel Shreave, a civil engineer, and the sale of lots was advertised in the New York City newspapers. Major William J. Parmentier, a Civil War veteran, was named the first agent of the Land Company.

The town is situated at the bottom of a depression in the Pine Plain—a hole in the bed of the ancient sea—where an encircling ridge of pine and deciduous trees forms a natural shelter. Hence the temperature in winter was advertised as averaging about twelve degrees higher than in New York. In 1879 Charles H. Kimball, a New York banker, discovered the health-giving climate and the mild temperatures of Bricksburg. While on a visit to an old school friend, Sarah A. Bradshaw, he experienced an improvement in a respiratory problem. He conceived the idea that, with sufficient backing and the addition of a fine hotel, the village in the pines could be made a popular resort.

Upon his return to New York, Kimball interested another banker, his friend Samuel D. Davis. When the two bankers again visited Bricksburg, they secured the support of Sarah's husband, Captain Albert M. Bradshaw, Civil War veteran, local real estate dealer, and the most influential man in town. They and other interested men acquired all the stock of the Bricksburg Land and Improvement Company as well as the Bricksburg House, and pledged themselves to the promotion of the town. Realizing the potential liability of a name like Bricksburg for a resort spot, they secured the change of name through a vote of the citizens and an act of the legislature. On 20 March 1880 the Post Office officially recognized the town as "Lakewood." As a means of capitalizing on the beauty of the stands of pines and the sparkling waters, roads and paths were laid out around the lakes for riding, cycling, driving, and walking. In the center of the town, wooden sidewalks lined the streets for the comfort of the strollers. Rows of picturesque shops provided necessities and luxuries. By April 1880 the greatly enlarged Bricksburg House, renamed the "Laurel House" after the flowers that grow among the pines, opened its doors to the first guests. The appointments of this luxurious hotel rivaled those of the best hotels in New York.

During the "season," approximately mid-October to May, people of wealth flocked to the town. The "Romantic Laurel House," as it became known, was host to the Vanderbilts, the Rockefellers, the Astors, the Tilfords, the Rhinelanders, the Arbuckles, the Jamisons, and scores of others prominent in the social and business worlds. The jurist Oliver Wendell Holmes, one of its first visitors, recited his famous poems before the roaring fireplace. Rudyard Kipling, who came in 1889 and several times thereafter, held the children spellbound with his stories. In his *American Notes* of 1891 Kipling mentioned "peaceful, pleasure-loving Lakewood," and he also included a reference to the town in *Captains Courageous*, 1897. Mark Twain, America's beloved humorist, enlivened many a winter evening with his wit. Other early guests were the authors William Cullen Bryant and Albion W. Tourgée, and the publishers Henry Oscar Houghton and George H. Mifflin.

During the next two decades almost one hundred sumptuous hostelries were built to accommodate the crowds. In 1891 Nathan Strauss's Lakewood Hotel between Clifton and Lexington Avenue, encompassing fourteen acres, was ready with rooms for seven hundred guests. It was surrounded by a quarter of a mile of palm-decked sun parlors. In the days of Richard Croker this hotel became the unofficial headquarters for Tammany Hall. Nearby, in "The Little White House,"—a three-story cottage owned by Oscar Strauss, Nathan's diplomat brother—lived Grover Cleveland between his two terms as president of the United States. His daughter Ruth, for whom the Baby Ruth candy bar was later named, was the admiration of Lakewood sidewalk society. In 1908 the Lakewood Hotel stayed open an extra month after the season to enable this former president to pass his dying days peacefully.[3]

Also in 1891 the famous Laurel-in-the-Pines Hotel, a "palace fit for kings," designed by the noted firm of Carrère and Hastings, was ready for sojourners. Numbered among its guests were persons prominent in the sports and entertainment worlds, as well as glittering names from the social register. It was there in 1916 that Charles Evans Hughes learned that he had lost the presidency to Woodrow Wilson.

Visitors to Lakewood enjoyed the pine-scented air, the beautiful tree-lined streets, and the charm of horse-drawn sleighs on fresh snow. During the daytime the vacationers could choose from among ice-skating, iceboating, or skate-sailing on the lovely lakes, the thrill of the fox hunt in season, or golf when weather permitted. They could linger under the romantic "Kissing Bridge," sip tea in the picturesque tea houses, or simply take a leisurely stroll along the lake shores. In the evenings the air resounded with the music of many orchestras and the laughter of dancers and merrymakers.

By the 1890s Lakewood was a resort of the rich and famous. The newspapers recorded the arrivals of the capitalists John D. Rockefeller, Russell Sage, and George Jay Gould, of the publishers Joseph Pulitzer and Charles Scribner, of the lawyers Elihu

Root and Clarence Blair Mitchell, and of the express magnate James C. Fargo. In addition, politicians, writers, artists, reformers, sportsmen, and socialites found the town attractive.

Some of the wealthy visitors also fell in love with Lakewood and built comfortable "cottages" for extended visits or year-round use. Charles Lathrop Pack, rehabilitator of parks and forests, built an estate on Forest Avenue. Close by, Jasper Lynch built Lynx Hall. Among the others who built were Arthur B. Claflin, Franklin L. Willock, Shepherd K. De Forest, George Fales Baker, and Francis P. Freeman, an associate of Cornelius Vanderbilt. Attracted by his liking for golf, John D. Rockefeller purchased the Ocean County Hunt and Country Club property and remodeled the clubhouse for a comfortable seasonal retreat.

During these "gay nineties" years when economic princes went on veritable spending sprees of building, from brownstones in the city to marble palaces in the resorts, it was not enough to outdo one's social peers in the town house. The comfortable country house also must reflect the owner's vast wealth. Along the eastern seaboard foremost among these patrons of the architects were the Vanderbilt heirs. In 1892 William K. Vanderbilt's Marble House at Newport, Rhode Island, designed by Richard Morris Hunt, dazzled the townsfolk with its splendor. A few years later his brother, Cornelius II, commissioned the same architect to design a house for him nearby. When completed in 1895, The Breakers was the last word in opulent *summer* resort homes. These sons of Cornelius "Commodore" Vanderbilt, who had amassed millions in railroad enterprise, reaped the benefits of their father's shrewd dealings and deposited tons of marble on the Rhode Island shores.

It remained for another railroad magnate and wealthy heir, whose father, Jay Gould, was one of the great competitors of the "Commodore," to initiate his own spending spree in the *winter* resort of Lakewood, New Jersey. In 1896 this fortunate son, George Jay Gould, set out to surpass the other rich newcomers and to amaze the citizens of the town. Fine marbles not only from the United States, but from Italy, Ireland, and even Africa became the materials for his splendid estate on the sandy shores of Lake Carasaljo.

Part I

The George Jay
Gould Family

Background

Not only was George Jay Gould immensely rich, but he could trace his ancestry back through a lineage of Colonial aristocrats and Puritans. Long before the American Revolution the Goulds began to distinguish themselves in the life of the Colonies. In 1647 Major Nathan Gold, a native of St. Edmundsbury, England, came to Fairfield, Connecticut, with Governor John Winthrop. His surname, signifying worker in gold, was in 1806 changed to Gould. As a leading man in the community and assistant to the governor, Gould was among the signers of the petition to Charles II for a charter for the colony. According to Margherita Hamm, in 1607 he was rated as "the richest man" in the area, and "when he died in 1694, he was spoken of in the town register of Fairfield as 'the worshipful Major Nathan Gould, Esq.' "[1]

His son Nathan Gould, Jr., who began his career as town clerk of Fairfield, eventually became both deputy governor of the colony of Connecticut and chief justice of its Supreme Court. Three of his grandsons, Colonel Abraham Gould, Daniel Gould, and Abel Gould, fought in the American Revolution. The oldest, Abraham, married Elizabeth Burr, a descendant of John Burr, one of the founders of Springfield, Massachusetts, who came to America in 1630. In 1780 their son, Captain Abraham Gould, settled in Roxbury, in Delaware County, New York. His son, John Burr Gould, became the father of the famous Jay Gould, who amassed the fortune associated with the family name.

On 27 May 1836 Jason Gould, his given name shortened to Jay, was born at West Settlement, a small farming community near Roxbury. His mother, Mary More, a God-fearing woman of Scottish descent, died when Jay was five. Life for him on the 150-acre dairy farm with its big old white saltbox house, its barns, sheds, and cider mills was pleasant enough, with five doting older sisters lavishing attention upon him. But frail of body, young Jay displayed no inclination for physical labor or the life of a country squire. Clever and keen of mind, he looked toward the world of business. Following short periods of schooling at the nearby Beechwood Seminary and at Hobart Academy eleven miles away, he found employment as a clerk in a general store. During his free hours he taught himself surveying and mathematics. After a brief apprenticeship with an engineer, he mapped counties and townships in New York, Ohio, and Michigan. He also found time to write a history of Delaware County, which he published in 1856.

By the age of twenty this enterprising young man, having cleverly secured financial backing from Zadoc Pratt of Prattsville, Eastern Pennsylvania, built large tanneries there, laying the foundation for the great fortune that he afterward accumulated. Pleased with his investment, Pratt insisted that the name of the town be changed to Gouldsboro. Dividing his time between Gouldsboro and New York, Jay increased his bank account by a series of shrewd and calculated monetary dealings that often contributed to the ruin of his unsuspecting backers. Always ready to move wherever opportunity offered, he was attracted to Wall Street, where he manipulated a partnership in a brokerage that became the firm of Smith, Gould

17

& Martin. Thereafter he became involved with great corporate relationships and security maneuvers.

Shortly before the Civil War, Gould turned his attention to railroad enterprises and obtained control of the Rutland and Washington Railroad Company. He became the president, treasurer, and superintendent of the road. Eventually his name and wealth were linked with the Erie, the Union Pacific, the Texas & Pacific, the Wabash and Missouri Pacific Railroads, the Atlantic & Pacific and the Western Union Telegraph Companies, and the Manhattan Elevated Railroad.

Having successfully launched his financial career, the clever, iron-willed Jay turned his attention to romance and marriage. He wooed and won the gentle Helen Day Miller, the daughter of Daniel B. Miller, a prominent wholesale merchant of New York, a descendant of an old English family that had settled in Easthampton, Long Island, in the early Colonial days. Their happy union was blessed with six children—George Jay, Edwin, Howard, Frank, Helen, and Anna. Jay, the most loving and devoted of fathers, spared no expense to make life comfortable and pleasant for his fam-

Helen Day Miller shortly before her marriage to Jay Gould. *Lyndhurst, a Property of the National Trust Historic Preservation*

The young entrepreneur Jay Gould. *Courtesy of Lyndhurst, a Property of the National Trust Historic Preservation*

ily. During the winter they lived in Victorian splendor at 579 Fifth Avenue, New York, and in summer either on the beautiful estate, Lyndhurst, located at Irvington-on-Hudson, or on his yacht, the *Atalanta.*

For the remainder of his life Gould dealt with the bulls and bears of Wall Street and carried off some of the shadiest deals in the history of American finance, the most notorious of which was his attempt in 1869 to corner the gold market. In collaboration with his Erie Railway partner Jim Fisk, he precipitated such a panic that the nation's economy was paralyzed from coast to coast. This unforgettable day of 24 September is historically referred to as Black Friday. But having emerged from the panic the richer by $11 million, Gould continued to rule and tour his railroad "empire," tend orchids at Lyndhurst, enjoy the diversions of the wealthy, and increase the fortune that his spoiled heirs later squandered.

The heir apparent, George Jay, was born in New York City on 6 February 1864. A thorough education under private tutors with the goal of succession to the management of the Gould properties was followed by a brief period of study at Columbia University. After an extended tour of Europe and of the Gould railroads in the United States, George assumed the duties of a clerk in the office of the Western Union Telegraph Company, where his aptitude for detail resulted in his becoming an assistant to his father. Jay, indeed, depended more and more on his son for the information he needed to carry out his vast plans. George worked eight to ten hours a day and often into the night as accoun-

tant, telegrapher, typist, and even stenographer. In 1885 he took his father's place in the brokerage firm of Washington E. Connor, where he became conversant with the working of the Wall Street Stock Exchange. That same year his father gave him the power of attorney over all his properties. As an extra vote of confidence in his eldest son, Jay gave George a present of $500,000 for investment. The experiences with the brokerage firm and at Western Union were excellent preparation for the greater responsibility he would later assume upon his father's death in 1892.

The Gould mansion on Fifth Avenue. *Moss Archives, Pach photo.*

George and Edith Kingdon

At twenty-one George cut a handsome figure—slender and erect, a little over five feet seven, with dark hair and short, curly mustache. The Gould family maintained a box at Augustin Daly's fashionable Empire Theatre on Broadway, which George often attended. On 26 November 1884 a new play was presented, Stobitzer's comedy *Love on Crutches,* starring John Drew and Ada Rehan. Another member of the cast was the beautiful young actress Edith Kingdon, who had made her professional debut in New York City the previous month as Mysia Jessamy in *The Wooden Spoon* and was appearing for the second time with Daly's company. Playing the part of a winsome widow, Mrs. Margery Gwynn, Edith Kingdon was a vision of delight with her hourglass figure, ivory-white skin, large lustrous eyes, and long dark hair. As she took her bow after the final curtain, a bouquet of violets bearing a card inscribed with the name of George J. Gould fell at her feet. For young Gould it was interest at first sight, with love developing soon after. Night after night he sat in the front row of the theater watching the lovely ingénue, hanging on every line she spoke. Backstage, her dressing room was a horticultural bower as the romantic millionaire raided the town's best flower shops for posies to send to the surprised and bewildered young lady. For more than a year he pursued her with telegrams, dinner dates, and gifts.

The heir apparent. George Jay Gould at age twenty-one.
Museum of the City of New York

As the romance moved swiftly toward the point where the Gould heir asked her to become his wife, family life at the Jay Gould mansion on Fifth Avenue was far from dull. For Jay Gould was vociferously against his son's alliance with an actress—even one as charming as Edith Kingdon. There were frequent clashes between father and son before the former realized that nothing he could say or threaten would make George change his intention to take Edith for his bride. In the end the loving father had to admit defeat. He placed a large sum to George's credit in the latter's bank and instructed his son to buy for Edith the most beautiful engagement ring in all New York. Helen Gould, however, was inconsolable. She could not reconcile herself to the probability of her son's marriage to a young woman beneath his class, and hoped his infatuation would soon cool.

Edith, however, did not fit the nineteenth-century stereotype of an actress. A proper and gracious young lady, she had been raised in an upper-middle-class home in Brooklyn and had found

Edith Kingdon, the lovely ingénue, shortly after she won the heart of George Jay Gould. *Theatre and Music Collection, Museum of the City of New York*

enjoyment in amateur theatricals. Only the death of her father and the necessity to help the family finances had prompted her to accept employment on the public stage. In the early 1880s, seeing her in an amateur performance in a Brooklyn theater, a business manager of the Boston Theatre thought that he recognized promising material for his stock company. Edith consented to try out for the cast of a new play on the road. She opened as Eva Malvoise in *Youth* in the Academy of Music in Baltimore on 30 January 1882, and for the next two years continued on the road. She played Mabel Hungerford in *The World*, Daphne in *The White Slave*, and Ada Summers in *A Free Pardon*.

In March 1883 she played the part of Ellen Maitland in *£50,000, A Story of Pluck* at the Boston Theatre, and from that time until she was engaged by Augustin Daly she acted leading roles in Boston successes. As Princess Meta she starred two hundred and fifty nights in *Jaima*. She appeared also in *Love and Money* and *Kit*. That same year she made her New Jersey debut in Newark's Old Park Theatre in the play *Across the Continent*. One success led to another, culminating in 1884 in a European tour with the Augustin Daly Company and subsequent roles on the New York stage.

Edith's lineage can be traced back to the twelfth century and to John Kingdon of Coleridge in Devonshire, England. A cadet of the House of Kingdon of Trehunsey, Quethiock, Cornwall, he was a member of a distinguished and scholarly family. Her father, Charles D. Kingdon, was born in Torrington, Devonshire, in 1834, and her mother, Mary Carter, at Benwell near Newcastle, England, in 1844.[2] After their marriage the couple first settled in Canada. Within a few years they came to Brooklyn, New York, where Edith was born in August of 1865.[3]

In spite of his mother's hopes, George's love for Edith did not cool; the violets he threw at her feet never faded in their true significance. In two years, on 14 September 1886, they were married in a quiet ceremony at seven in the evening in a flower-decked room in the Gould home, Lyndhurst, with every member of each family present. The Reverend Washington Choate of the Irvington-on-Hudson Presbyterian Church officiated. Edith was attended by her mother, Mary Carter Kingdon. After the ceremony the young couple and Mrs. Kingdon returned to New York City in an ordinary passenger car on the local express. At Grand Central Station a carriage awaited to whisk them away to the Gould mansion on Fifth Avenue.[4]

In an interview for the *New York Telegram* the playwright David Belasco recalls that Augustin Daly "was furious." Edith possessed abundant talent and was one of the most promising players of

Lyndhurst, the Gothic Revival castle designed by Alexander Jackson Davis. Purchased by Jay Gould in 1880, it was occupied by his family until 1961. *Lyndhurst, a Property of the National Trust Historic Preservation. Photo by Louis H. Frohman.*

his company. He snorted and fumed at Gould's taking her away from him.[5]

Shortly after their marriage George and Edith moved into a home of their own at 1 East Forty-seventh Street, not far from the family mansion on Fifth Avenue. Their possessions of all kinds—objects of art and gorgeous furnishings—soon demanded the larger and more sumptuous residence that they acquired at Fifth Avenue and Sixty-seventh Street. Because George enjoyed spending money as much as his father had enjoyed making it, Edith was surrounded with all the luxuries wealth could provide. She had fabulous jewels, fashionable clothes, and furs fit for a queen. Nearby, George kept a stable with six pairs of horses and eight carriages. Each morning, attired in riding dress and furs, his wife enjoyed a brisk drive in Central Park. Everywhere she went, every part of the day, she was a flawless example of exquisite costuming. George derived as much pleasure from his wife's public appearances as she did. Teasingly he taught the parrot to say whenever she appeared, "Oh, what an extravagant girl you are!"

For a time the socialites gossiped about her place in New York society. How would this comely girl, bred in less affluent circumstances, respond to the new order of gaiety and correctness into which her marriage thrust her? From the moment she became Mrs. George Gould, Edith discovered that the Gould family was not *persona grata*, for Jay Gould was hated and feared, and his wife, Helen, was a quiet homebody. Setting out to change the Gould social status, Edith furnished her own answers that silenced wagging tongues. David Belasco describes her as a hostess "so glorious, so dignified, breathing an air of such gentle culture to the manner born," that society opened its arms to her and became a slave to her charms.[6]

During the next few years the newspapers were full of colorful accounts of Edith's colorful parties attended by newly made millionaires or old friends

from the theater. George Gould's sister Helen disapproved of this lavish expenditure of Gould money on a purely social existence, and she clashed frequently with the young couple. But the thoroughly approving George was supremely happy. As a result of his wife's popularity, they regularly received invitations to the most important social events of the season. At first, members of New York's "Old Guard," jealous of Jay Gould's wealth, had placed obstacles in Edith's pathway. But eventually even Mrs. William Astor, the undisputed ruler of New York society in the 1880s and 1890s, came to admire the younger matron and gave her "seal of approval"—an invitation to the annual Astor Ball. This invitation spelled social success for Jay Gould's daughter-in-law. From that time onward her ascent up the social ladder was marked with one triumph after the other.

Edith's social aspirations in no way interfered with her desires for motherhood and family. On 15

The George Jay Gould residence at Fifth Avenue and Sixty-seventh Street, New York City, ca. 1899. *Museum of the City of New York*

Conspicuous wealth was to be found in the Gould Fifth Avenue mansion. *Moss Archives, Pach photo*

Everywhere she went Mrs. George J. Gould was a flawless example of exquisite costuming. *Courtesy of George A. Bishop, copy photo Vincent Hart*

into the social scene, Edith saw to it that Anna received her share of attention from eligible young men of her own class. One day, however, she learned to her dismay that her young sister-in-law was having a secret *affaire de coeur* with Frank Woodruff, a matinee idol. Having experienced the vicissitudes of the life of an actress, she wanted no part of the theater world for Anna. After Edith discussed the matter with George, Anna was shipped off to Paris under the chaperonage of Fanny Read.

According to the Paris newspapers, little dark-haired Anna Gould was the Doris Duke of her day. Paris gossipers credited her with the possession of untold millions. Among the eligible young bachelors flocking to her drawing room was the poor but good-looking Count Marie Ernest Paul Boniface de Castellane. His father, the marquis de Castellane, was a member of one of the best and oldest families of Provence, who in turn were related to the Talleyrands. Boni, as he was thereafter referred to, madly pursued Anna, for he desperately needed money. Anna's response was hesitant. As the youngest of the Jay Gould heiresses, she needed the approval of both George and her sister Helen. That summer, when the George

August 1887, their first child, Kingdon, was born. Within the next ten years, Jay, Marjorie, Vivien, and George, Jr., blessed the happy marriage.[7] The fortunate pair enjoyed their roles of parenthood and social climbing. In an address she delivered before a women's club, this gracious lady presents eloquent testimony to the success of society women as mothers:

> Despite assertions to the contrary, society women are just as good mothers and love children just as much as any other class of women. There is absolutely no reason why sharing in the pleasures of social life is incompatible with devotion in the domestic circle. After all, that comes first in every woman's heart. It ought to be, and in the great majority of cases it is the greatest pleasure that a woman can have.[8]

Edith Gould, indeed, lived her philosophy. She was first and foremost a devoted mother. In a series of newspaper articles, written four years after her death, one of the pleasing impressions given by her daughter Edith Gould Wainwright is the devotion of Mrs. Gould to her children.[9]

Although Helen Gould kept her distance, George's younger sister, Anna, was frequently in his wife's company. Planning to launch her fittingly

The young heiress Anna Gould captivated the fortune-seekers of Paris. *Lyndhurst, a Property of the National Trust Historic Preservation*

Count Paul Ernest Boniface de Castellane, whom Anna Gould married in 1895. *Lyndhurst, a Property of the National Trust Historic Preservation*

Goulds visited Anna in Paris, they were so impressed with Boni's credentials that they invited him to New York. They were quick to realize that a French count would make an ideal husband for Anna and thereby enhance their own social position.

A few months later Count Boni de Castellane arrived in New York with eight trunks and forty pieces of hand luggage, without the price of carriage fare in his pocket. George assumed the cost of the fare as well as the Waldorf-Astoria hotel bill. Disliking the young man, Helen Gould tried to discourage a liaison. But George and Edith showed him off to New York society in a round of parties and balls. They arranged a trip to Canada so that Anna and the Count could enjoy the winter sports. When Boni proposed to Anna in the Cathedral of Quebec, George and Edith rejoiced and began to plan for the wedding. The ceremony took place on 4 March 1895 at the Gould mansion on Fifth Avenue, with Archbishop Corrigan of Saint Patrick's as officiating clergyman. Afterward Boni and Anna went off to Paris, built a pink marble palace modeled after Marie Antoinette's Petit Trianon on the Avenue du Bois de Boulogne, and spent millions of the Gould fortune. Edith Gould had attained her heart's desire, had captured a title for her husband's sister, and would continue to dazzle the guests who flocked to her homes in the city and country.

Winter and Summer Sojourns

Early in the 1890s George began to consider a country place where his children could romp and play in the fresh air. At the time everyone was talking about the little town of Lakewood in south central New Jersey, which was quickly becoming a winter playground, a "society-page resort." In February 1892 he took his family to Lakewood, where they stayed at the Laurel House. So impressed was he with the town that in 1893 he leased Gray Gables, a cottage that stood at the southeast corner of Lexington Avenue and First Street. The following season, on 5 April 1894, Kingdon, Jay, and Vivien were christened by the Reverend G. H. McClellan of the Presbyterian Church. Returning in 1895, the family leased the handsome Colonial House, located on the corner of Madison Avenue and First Street.

As George's interest in the affairs of the little community grew, he considered the purchase of property. Since he needed a home in the country within commuting distance of New York, Lakewood seemed perfect. Other factors, however, influenced his final decision. He realized that this community with its fresh country air was an ideal place to rear his growing family. He foresaw the tempting possibility of living in the manner of an English country gentleman with spacious grounds for field sports and the hunt, and he preferred to be taxed as a resident of New Jersey rather than New York. On 14 January 1896 George went to the office of Captain Bradshaw on Seventh Street and purchased from the Land and Im-provement Company a tract of land bordering Lake Carasaljo. Additional purchases during the next two years increased the extent of his land to almost two hundred acres. On 24 May 1899 the property was deeded and recorded in the Ocean County Clerk's Office in Toms River.

In a variety of ways the young millionaire entered into the life of the town. In 1895 he was active in the Ocean County Hunt and Country Club as one of its founders and first president. He also served at times as a volunteer fireman. He and his family became members of All Saints Protestant Episcopal Church, his generous benefactions to which were mentioned in the local newspaper.[10] An item in the *New Jersey Courier* in 1898 casually reported that his Easter donation of one thousand dollars equaled that of the previous year.[11] Moreover, according to his daughter Edith, he made up any deficit in the annual budget. The family attended eleven o'clock services each Sunday when they were in town, and always occupied the third pew.[12] As an active member of the parish, his wife, Edith, participated in all manner of fund raising activities. Furthermore, her reputation as a charming Lakewood hostess was quickly established. Everyone looked forward to Gould hospitality at the outset of each social season.

As duly noted in the New York and local newspapers, the Goulds's summer vacations were often spent on one of their yachts. George was a member of the New York Yacht Club and an expert yachtsman. Among his vessels was the large schooner *Hildegarde*, once the property of the Prince of Wales. In 1894 he and his brother Howard purchased an 85-foot racing sloop, the *Vigilant*, the celebrated American Cup defender of 1893. That year, in a series of international races in European waters, he had defeated the yacht *Brittania* owned by the Prince of Wales. Having inherited his father's fabulous vessel, the *Atalanta*, he used it regularly for family cruises to the Caribbean, European waters, or Japan and the Orient.

The *Atalanta*, which had cost Jay Gould a quarter of a million dollars, was one of the most modern yachts in America. A "floating palace" having a length of 225 feet and a width of 26 feet, it carried four other boats as large as some other yachts: a six-oared cutter, a whale boat used for landing, a steam launch, and a dinghy or crew's work boat. Built for strength and power, it was a safe and sound ship. It even boasted the newly patented Edison electric lights. The parquet floors on the passenger decks and in the cabins were made from squares of maple, butternut, cedar, California laurel, and sycamore. The furnishings and fittings of its Victorian interior included draperies of gold-and-silver silk tapestry cloth, sumptuously upholstered chairs and sofas, oriental rugs, and rare pieces of china. The main saloon at its huge dining table accommodated thirty-two people. In addition to the owner's suite were eight staterooms for family and guests, with the very latest in bathroom facilities. Every imaginable comfort and luxury were provided. The children found special delight in the music room, where there was a player piano and a phonograph. The crew of fifty-two, including Captain John Shackford, a steward, three cooks, and six waiters, helped to make the trips comfortable and pleasant.

Sometimes the family cruised southward to their rustic lodge near Hyde Point, a little town in North Carolina, where they all enjoyed the sport of

Furlough Lodge, the Gould summer home in the Catskills near Fleischmann's, New York. *Moss Archives, Pach photo*

shooting. There, too, George kept large kennels where he bred some of the finest dogs in the country—pointers, setters, and spaniels—trophy winners not only in America but in England.

The month of August always meant grouse shooting in Scotland, another popular family sport. George usually rented a castle for his family and several friends. One of their favorite places was Farleyer House near Aberfeldy in Perthshire. A typical day would begin early in the morning with a sumptuous buffet breakfast. Then the family would travel to the moors on horseback or in automobiles, depending upon the distance. Hours of shooting were interrupted only by time out for lunch, brought along in hampers. Returning to the house about five, they rested and dressed for dinner. The evenings were spent playing bridge or dancing to the skirls of Scottish bagpipers from the neighborhood. A month's shooting would supply the Goulds with enough game to last through the winter. The birds were kept in cold storage both on the boat and in New York after their return.

Sometimes when George and Edith went off on a summer sojourn, their children were taken to Furlough Lodge, a large picturesque log cabin in the Catskills near Fleischmanns, New York, not far from where their grandfather, Jay, was born. Governesses, nurses, and maids accompanied the children in a private railroad car. The faithful staff took good care of the children and joined in the outdoor sports. On the Gould property were over nine miles of trout stream and a large lake, which were kept stocked with trout. In addition to the delights of angling for trout, canoeing, swimming, and long walks in the fresh mountain air filled the happy days. In the autumn, when the trees were a symphony of color, George and Edith would join their children for a stay of several weeks before they all returned to town by mid-October.

The *Atalanta,* the luxurious pleasure yacht of the Gould family. *Courtesy of George A. Bishop*

The Building of the Estate at Lakewood

Anticipating a repetition of these country pleasures on his newly purchased property on the edge of Lake Carasaljo, George in 1896 engaged the famous New York architect Bruce Price to transform this tract of land into a lavish country estate. He had in mind something on the order of the great estates in England or Scotland, the comforts of which he had often enjoyed. Faced with Gould's challenge, Price drew upon his wide experience in designing country homes. The two men soon agreed upon the style of an English estate of the Georgian period, which would substitute a gracious order for the wild virgin terrain. Consequently, the name "Georgian Court" seemed appropriate for the estate.

They then contracted with the firm of J. H. L'Hommedieu's Son & Company, prominently identified with the construction of elegant country dwellings in New York, New Jersey, and Connecticut. Their work included not only the erection of the buildings but also the grading of the grounds, laying out of roads and paths, seeding of lawns, and planting of shrubs. Such a notable meeting of minds existed between the owner, the architect, and the contractor that their ideas were put into material form with high standards of excellence in construction and with great fidelity to their plans. By autumn of 1896 George's dream was on the way to becoming a reality. A small army of local workmen laid road beds and made clearings for the proposed buildings: a gatekeeper's lodge, a mansion, and the stables.

The small gatekeeper's lodge, the first building completed, gave the interested townsfolk a clue to the proposed Georgian style. This little gem of a cottage, with gray stucco walls, trim in white wood and marble, decorative balustrades, and classical motifs, was situated to the right of the main entrance to the estate. Eventually it became the home of George P. Langford, the English butler and general overseer of supplies for the several Gould mansions. The five-room cottage seems scarcely large enough to accommodate Langford's family of five sons, whose rompings must have taxed its limited space. Returning to Georgian Court in 1979 for a brief visit, one of these sons, G. Frank Langford, reminisced about those boyhood days, particularly about the fun the boys had in acting as unofficial tour guides of the estate whenever the Goulds were on vacation.

In designing the mansion, Price was faced with a fascinating and difficult problem. For George Gould, a gentleman of considerable means, he had to create in the midst of a pine forest a house that was to be commodious and attractive without undue grandeur or display. Gould's original intention had been to spend approximately $70,000. But as work on the plans progressed, the architect's attempt to keep within this budget met with obstacles. A revision of the plans delayed the groundbreaking. Apparently realizing that none of the features usually typical of a large country residence could be sacrificed, Gould directed Price to incorporate them. However, he must have been

An early view of the gatekeeper's lodge, situated near the Seventh Street entrance to the estate. *Moss Archives, Pach photo*

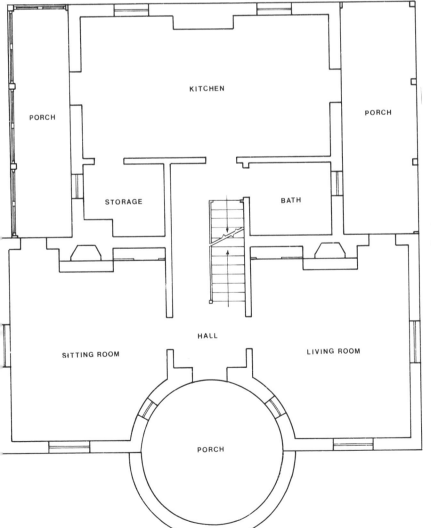

PORCH

KITCHEN

PORCH

STORAGE

BATH

SITTING ROOM

HALL

LIVING ROOM

PORCH

The first-floor plan of the small gatekeeper's lodge. *Plan drawn by Joseph J. Geis*

overwhelmed by the projected expense, for the mansion as finally constructed differs somewhat from the presentation blueprints now in the college archives.[13] Two huge rooms, a ballroom and dining room, originally to be symmetrically placed at right angles to the main axis of the house, were omitted. Consequently, the number of rooms on the floors above were fewer. Two hundred feet in length, with an average width of fifty feet, the fifty-room house provided comfortable accommodation for George and Edith, their seven children, and at least half a dozen servants.

For Price, the proper relationship of building to site was an important consideration. In an interview with Barr Ferree he states:

> The architect should make himself perfectly and personally familiar with all the surroundings of the proposed building and with all the conditions that, in any way, enter into its erection and designing. Personally, I like to design on the spot; it is the only way to obtain satisfactory results.[14]

When questioned about his primary concern in designing a country house, he replied that "a house is but part of a scene, and the more complete the scene, the more naturally the house is adapted to its surroundings, the better it fits into the landscape, the better the result."[15]

Thus it can be safely assumed that, while enjoying the fabled Gould hospitality in their leased home in the town of Lakewood, Price journeyed back and forth to the site to study its possibilities. Within a few months his architectural rendering showed a charming fusion of Georgian dignity and Norman grace, an English Georgian house with a French château roof. While suggesting the influence of Price's Canadian work of the same decade, the high French roof with its pedimented dormers and tall red brick chimneys made the practical allowance for a roomy third floor and a smaller floor above—a necessary consideration for George Gould's growing family. The house was set in such a way that its simple gray stucco walls, as the architect described it, would "take on an endless succession of changing shadows from the trees that almost touch it."[16]

In January 1897 the groundbreaking for the mansion took place. The foundation of the house rests on a bed of brown building sand, which was found at a depth of eight feet below the natural surface of the ground. Above this was a conglomeration of white sand, loam, clay, and marl in strata, veins, layers, and mixtures. Aside from solid rock, the sand on which the building rests is the best bottom on which to start foundations and has the advan-

The Gould mansion was originally surrounded by tall pines.
Photo by Richard Steele, courtesy of Mary Hurlburt

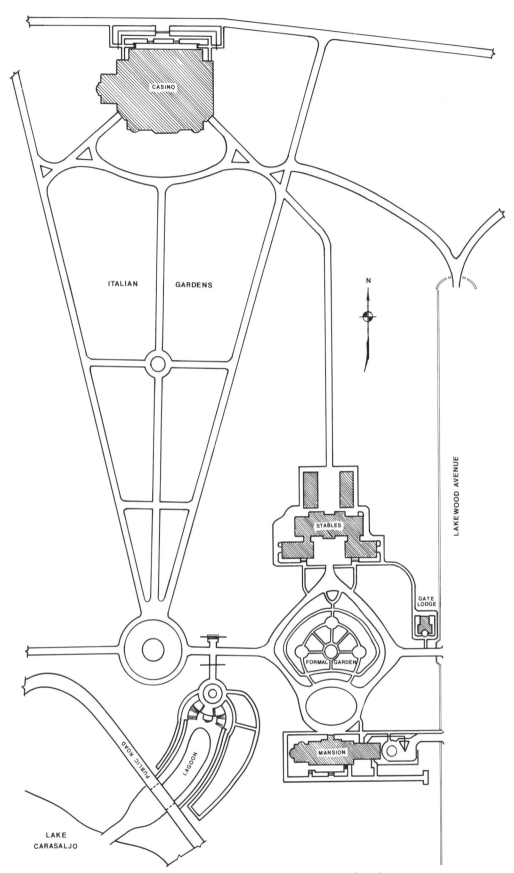

Bruce Price's plan of the George Jay Gould estate, showing roadways and paths, gardens, and the location of the four original buildings. *Plan drawn by Joseph J. Geis*

tage that rock has not, namely, that it will absorb all surface drainage and therefore insure a dry cellar. The completely excavated cellar, with its furnace rooms, more than a dozen large storerooms, and wine cellar, was designed with almost as much care as the floors above.

The foundation walls and piers are of hard New Jersey brick set in mortar, with internal steel rods reinforcing the greater spans. A house constructed in this manner possesses a substantial solidity and a resultant comfort not found in buildings of the skeleton type. As the *Architectural Record* of June 1899 stated, "When a man spends an ordinary fortune upon such a house as Georgian Court he wants a structure that will endure. To fill many houses with the magnificent furnishings, decorations and art treasures used at Lakewood would be like setting the Kohinoor in brass."[17]

Since, as Price maintains, the cost of the house was restricted, the walls of the exterior are finished in gray stucco. Characteristic of Georgian style, the soft gray walls are accented by white wood and marble trim around windows and doorways, as well as by fruit-garland swags, urns, and decorative balustrades. Handsome creamy terra-cotta quoins adorn and emphasize the exterior corners. From designs and models approved by the architect, the terra-cotta was made by the Perth Amboy Terra-Cotta Company, famous for the quality of its terra-cotta, which approaches the excellence of the product of the Renaissance Della Robbia family. Like his great contemporary Louis Sullivan, Price was fascinated with the decorative possibility inherent in terra-cotta and used it with great taste on the Georgian Court structures. Consequently, despite his limited budget, Price's use of decoration created an overall effect far more elegant than that of any of the other mansions or hotels in the town.

On the north side of the mansion a handsome porte-cochère supported by marble columns protects the large entrance doorway made of heavy glass and wrought-iron grill work. At the east end of the building a high stucco wall ornamented with

By 1909 a thick layer of ivy covered the gray, stucco walls of the mansion. *Moss Archives, Pach photo*

Detail of the north facade of the mansion, ca. 1950. *Photo by A. Aubrey Bodine*

marble and terra-cotta, which encloses the service area and kitchen garden, serves to extend the length of the house. A somewhat similar effect is achieved at the west end by the one-story, glass-roofed conservatory wing. The architectural treatment of the south side of the house facing Lake Carasaljo results in the most lavish expression of late Georgian style. This facade is emphasized by elaborate broken pediments, exquisite wrought-iron balconies, and rich terra-cotta ornamentation. A veranda with a floor of red terra-cotta stretches the length of the house and gives access to two entrances. Marble-bordered, brick-paved paths lead to its broad marble stairways. Flanking the central stairway are two large equestrian bronzes called "The Falconers," the work of the Russian sculptor Eugène A. Lansère (1848–86). The pieces are dated 1876 and 1878 respectively.

During the residency of the Goulds, flower-filled urns surmounted the posts of the elegant balustrade. This pleasant sunny spot overlooking the lake was often used as an outdoor classroom for the children as well as a favorite lounging area for family and guests. The Goulds, enthusiastic believ-ers in fresh air, sought to take advantage of all the health-giving features of the locality.

By the summer of 1897 rapid progress had been made in the construction of the mansion, and ground was broken for the stables nearby. From the outset George Gould saw to it that all his build-ings boasted the latest in modern conveniences with a good measure of self-sufficiency. Early in October an artesian well was sunk to a depth of six hundred feet by Kissner and Bennett of Belmar, New Jersey. When connected to the water tower incorporated in the stables' design, this well sup-plied water for the buildings and gardens on the south half of the estate. In the superintendent's building located across the street from the gatekeeper's lodge, a private electric plant was in-stalled by Westinghouse, Church, Kerr and Com-pany, Engineers. Consisting of a 30 HP and 90 HP gasoline engine and generator, it supplied direct current to the estate buildings. Although huge chimneys provided adequate drafts for fireplaces in all the principal rooms, coal-fueled steam-heating furnaces at all times kept the buildings cozy and dry.

Architect Price tastefully incorporated these creature comforts into the interior construction of

Bronze "Falconers," the work of Eugène A. Lansère (1848–86), flank the marble stairway leading to the veranda on the south side of the mansion. *Photo by Vincent Hart*

the mansion and other buildings. Water flowed abundantly into well-appointed baronial bathrooms, service areas, and laundry facilities, the latter located in the east wing of the stables. For the convenience of the occupants of the house, near the doorway of each room were installed toggle switches to control the lighting fixtures and electric buttons to summon the servants. In all of the rooms of the main floor of the mansion, decorative gratings of marble or iron concealed the radiators, which were recessed into the foot-thick walls. The sturdy iron radiators used for the rooms of the upper floors were manufactured by the well-known H. B. Smith Company of Smithville, New Jersey.

The interior workmanship of the house is of the finest, and the materials are of the very best quality. Found among the marbles are Green Vermont, Pavanazza, Royal Irish Green, Black Egyptian, and Gray Billear Roman. The woods used are quartered white oak, Zambesi, East Indian mahogany, San Domingo mahogany, white pine, and poplar. The ornamental plasterwork rivals that done by the Italian *stuccatori* in the finest English Georgian mansions of the eighteenth century. The upper lights of the large double-hung sash windows throughout the house are lead-glazed panels of lancet shape; over the principal doorways are elliptical lead-glazed fanlights. Parquet floors are laid in the elegant rooms of the first floor.

Describing the interior plan of the mansion, Bruce Price makes the following comprehensive statement indicating his familiarity with the Beaux-Arts planning popular with American architects in the last decades of the nineteenth century:

> The proper way to plan a house is to treat it on architectural principles, and that, of course, means the employment of axial lines. . . . you enter a large hall, from each end of which, to the right and left, runs a corridor that connects every part of the building. This corridor could have been continued indefinitely, but naturally stops just where it was wanted to stop. Now the merit of this plan to my mind is that the moment you enter the hall, the moment you come into the house, you have the whole of it before you. You not only know where you are, but you see the entire house as soon as you have come into it. This seems to me an immense advantage. Not only is it a perfectly logical, utilitarian plan, but you are at home the moment you are inside the door. There is no need to find your way around.[18]

This type of open plan was enhanced by his method of color selection. According to Prentice Treadwell, an associate and collaborator, "The color study of the interior of Georgian Court was made first as a whole, each room being a chord in the general harmony, and considered in its relation

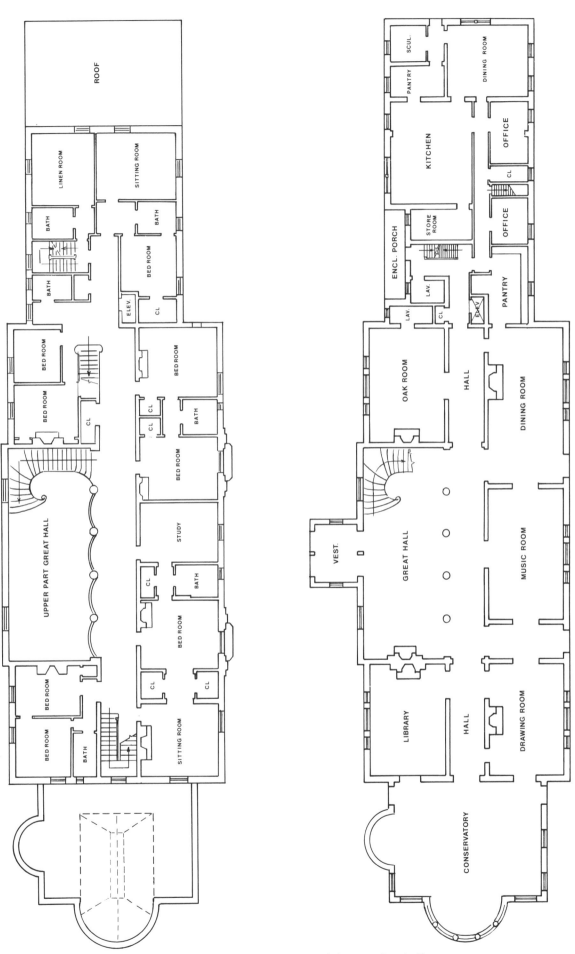

The plans of the first and second floors of the mansion indicate Price's preference for open planning and the employment of axial lines. *Plan drawn by Joseph J. Geis*

to all the others, while each room is a complete harmony in itself in every detail."[19]

Following the tradition of English Georgian architects, Price paid special attention to the entrance hall. An exquisite little marble vestibule, illuminated by small windows with Art Nouveau glass, leads into the great hall where the visitor is struck by its warm, inviting look. The deep crimson wall coverings and the gold and ocher tones of the elaborate plasterwork complement the colors of the beautiful frieze that decorates the upper part of the west, north, and east walls. This huge canvas, painted by the muralist Robert Van Vorst Sewell, represents scenes from the Prologue to Chaucer's *Canterbury Tales.* (A complete description of this art treasure is given in Part III.) The window draperies of red Tuscan silk velour match the dark shade of red in the painting. Deep red rugs and the figured velour of Italian Florentine armchairs conform to

Detail of the entrance vestibule showing the iron grillwork of the outer door and a wrought-iron lantern. *Photo by Vincent Hart*

Elaborate gilded stuccowork and Art Nouveau glass ornament the north entrance to the great hall. *Photo by Vincent Hart*

The balcony sections of gilded bronze curve outward between the Ionic columns. *Photo by Vincent Hart*

the general color scheme. The comfortable plush setting was designed to lend itself to the most fashionable parties and balls as well as to intimate family gatherings.

The great hall, forty-eight feet in length and eighteen feet wide, runs through two stories with a gallery and balcony on the south side. Recalling baroque magnificence, four enormous columns of the Roman Ionic order support a marble architrave and the balcony balustrade. The balcony sections curve outward between the columns, resembling the boxes in a theàter. Supported on genuine marble bases, the shafts of the columns, built around cores of iron almost a foot in diameter, are made of imitation marble by the process known as "scagliola," in which a base of finely ground gypsum is mixed with glue, soft chips of marble, spar, or granite dust, and, when dry, brought to a high polish.

The curvilinear balustrade railing is made of cast bronze and continues as a handrail to a gracious curving staircase that forms an integral part of the design of the hall. From Price's designs the railing was modeled and cast by the John Williams, Inc.,

Bronze Foundry, New York, a company noted for artistic metalwork in all the finer homes. At that time the work, which was finished with a heavy plating of gold, attracted considerable attention for its design and magnificence. Although gilt metal railings then were not uncommon, this is the first instance where the entire work was coated with this costly metal. A story is told about the craftsman who was applying the pure gold on the balcony railing. Realizing how fast it was being consumed and how very expensive it was, he is reputed to have warned Gould, "This is eating up money. Do you have to have this?" Gould replied, "It will last forever, will it not?" The workman agreed, "Yes, forever."[20] Nevertheless the owner must have been to some extent influenced by the kindly admonition, for a less costly gilding was continued on the staircase rail.

Dominating the west end of the hall is a huge fireplace enframed in free-standing marble columns of a modified Doric order and topped with a grand Italian baroque-style pediment. Filling the space within its curved lines are two young boys carved in high relief, winged and clothed in armor. Reputedly they symbolize the Gould children, and they support the George Gould monogram—two interlocking Gs, the second in reverse. Again to the

The gracious curving staircase of the great hall. *Photo by Vincent Hart*

Under the huge curves of the marble pediment, sculptured youths, winged and clothed in armor, symbolize the Gould children. *Photo by Vincent Hart*

doorways that give access to the rooms are flanked by fluted pilasters with Ionic capitals and crowned by broken pediments with gilded urn motifs centered. Classic decorative detail is picked out in gold and deep red. Gilded sunburst designs and plasterwork borders of bound sheaves and fretwork ornament the flat ceiling. The lighting fixtures—double wall brackets with ball-shaped glass globes and Chippendale-style pendant lanterns with glass panels strikingly illumine the woodwork and plasterwork.

The walls of the corridor of the floor above that overlooks the great hall are decorated in the same deep crimson, white, and gold tones. Above a gilded cornice the coved ceiling is ornamented with white stucco filigree. During the residency of the Gould family the wall space served as an exhibition area for the master's collection of paintings and prints.

Price's design for three rooms on the sunny south side was intended to delight the lady of the house. These rooms, rectangular in shape, eigh-

north, above the heavily ornamented entrance doorway, gilt cupids flank the monogram prominently centered. In fact, the interlocking Gs occur no less than fifty times in the elaborate plasterwork of the hall. Undoubtedly George Gould was pleased and flattered.

Suspended from the center of the coved, coffered ceiling is a ten-foot electric chandelier composed of 150,000 crystalline beads draped in four graduated tiers. Concealed within, electric bulbs rise from five circular frames, which vary in diameter. The style is Louis XIV with classic decorative detail—beaded swags, acanthus leaves, and pendants, all of crystal. From this fixture soft light passing through the myriad of small prisms of glass diffuses a pleasant glow enhancing the warm color tones of the lavish decoration.

Extending from the great hall and parallel to it is the spacious corridor connecting the first-floor rooms. Along its length the lower half is wood wainscoting painted gray and gold; deep crimson wall coverings adorn the upper half. The nine

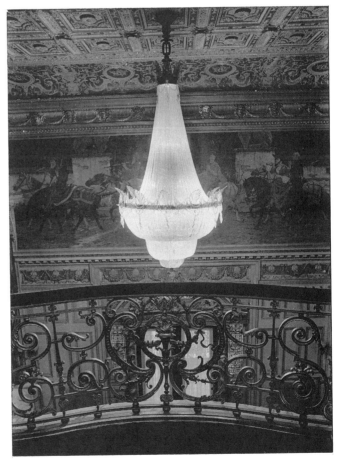

The great hall rises twenty-five feet to an elaborate plasterwork ceiling. Pendant from its center is a ten-foot Louis XIV-style chandelier. *Photo by Vincent Hart*

Deep crimson carpeting and upholstery fabrics offer rich contrast with the light-gray and gold tones of the spacious corridor. *Photo by Vincent Hart*

teen feet in width but varying in length, have a ceiling rise of twelve feet. In each room three windows symmetrically grouped in the south wall, the central one arched and larger, allow glimpses of the tall white pines and of Lake Carasaljo. Wide, rectangular doorways provide access from one room to another in accordance with Price's preference for open planning.

Centrally placed among these three rooms is the elegant music room directly across from the main entrance. Its smaller scale is a counterpoint to the palatial scale of the great hall. Thirty feet in length, it is decorated in dainty French rococo style, with gilded woodwork and plasterwork and with panels painted in pinks, blues, and other pastel colors. At considerable expense to Gould these panels, thirty in all, were painted by the celebrated decorators Charles M. Shean, George W. Maynard, Harper Pennington, and Irving R. Wiles.[21] Those on the walls depict goddesses in flowing garb surrounded by intricate floral borders. On the flat part of the ceiling are grouped symbols of music, art, and learning; in the coves are lords and ladies in garden settings in the Fragonard mode. Gilt brass sconces of elaborate leaf-scroll design, reproductions of Louis XV appliqués in the Palace of Fontainebleau, cast soft light on the painted goddesses. Each piece of furniture in this room, richly carved and gilded

Detail of the woodwork and stuccowork over the doorways that give access to the first floor rooms. *Photo by Vincent Hart*

TheThree Graces in low relief adorn the slanted ceiling under the grand stairway. *Photo by Vincent Hart*

The second-floor corridor overlooks the great hall. The lighting fixtures are special designs by Bruce Price. *Photo by Vincent Hart*

Detail of cornice and plasterwork of the curved corridor ceiling. *Photo by Vincent Hart*

with powdered gold, bears the owner's monogram. In two gilt, French Vernis Martin curio cabinets are arranged delicate porcelains and bisque figurines. The soft blues of damask upholstery fabrics, draperies, and Oriental rug harmonize perfectly with the colors of the panels.

To the right of this room, separated by a small corridor leading to the veranda, is the drawing room, twenty-six feet in length. Its décor echoes the same mood of rococo charm and intimacy. On the coved ceiling the ornamental gilt plasterwork of fanciful curved and lattice-pattern designs incorporates seven painted panels of idyllic landscapes. Over the four door lintels small friezes painted in grisaille depict cupids in classic poses. Above the friezes broken pediments and garlands of gilded stucco add to the decorative effect. A fireplace flanked by ornate pilasters and overmantel dominates one wall. As in the music room nearby, the

Detail of the painted and gilded boiserie in the music room. *Photo by Vincent Hart*

Enframed with gilded plasterwork, painted symbols of musical instruments adorn the music room ceiling. *Photo by Vincent Hart*

Detail of the rococo-style panels in the coves of the music room ceiling. *Photo by Vincent Hart*

Each piece of the carved and gilded furniture in the music room bears the George Gould monogram. *Photo by Vincent Hart*

Fanciful curves and lattice-pattern plasterwork adorn the drawing-room ceiling. *Photo by Vincent Hart*

leaf-scroll sconces are derived from those at Fontainebleau. Comfortable reproductions of Sheraton furniture make the room pleasantly inviting. Originally flowered wall fabrics blended with the soft rose tones of upholstery, draperies, and rug. It was in this room, in the English tradition often called the "morning room," that Edith Gould received her callers.

On the other side of the music room is the dining room, thirty-six feet in length, where chaste, classic simplicity prevails. The warm, light-gray tones of the painted wall panels, relieved by white woodwork and a sparing use of gold, contrast beautifully with the rich tones of the mahogany furniture. Sixteen fluted, Ionic pilasters, which alternate with the panels and door and window openings, give the room its architectural character. The capitals of the pilasters are ornamented with gilded edges and stucco fruit garlands also gilded.

Monotony is avoided in the design of the wall surface by a carved molding employing the rinceau motif placed horizontally slightly below the center. Above it, plain panels are framed with a simple white wood molding; in the dado dainty gilded plaster moldings enframe narrower panels. Just below the ceiling, simply ornamented by a double row of bound sheaves, the cornice with dentils rests upon a stucco fruit frieze in relief. The window and door surrounds are exquisitely carved with the egg-and-dart motif. In harmony with the predominating color of the room, six wall sconces of a graceful classic design are finished in white and gold. A notable feature of the room is a fireplace of Royal Irish Green marble said to have been quarried under the sea off the coast of Connemara. The face of the mantelpiece is ornamented with swags, lions, and classic urns carved in relief. At the present time, the pale yellows in drapery and rug tones increase the light and airy effect. Originally the room décor included soft apple

greens in draperies, wall coverings, and carpet—reputedly to match the green of Edith's eyes. In accordance with the taste of the era, ornately framed oil paintings crowded the wall panels; the serving tables were loaded with sterling silver and cut glass.

On the north side of the house George's two favorite rooms reflect the masculine taste. Likewise rectangular in shape, they are eighteen feet in width and twenty-six feet in length. The windows, similar in treatment to those of the south side, reveal a view of the elliptical lawn and formal garden beyond. The first of these rooms, the library, with its dark mahogany paneling and bookshelves, suggests the Renaissance period. Above the shelves that line the lower half of each wall, burnt wood panels especially designed by J. William Fosdick highlight the names of great literary figures and statesmen. The ceiling, beamed and hand-painted, recalls sixteenth-century French château style. On it the names of illustrious artists, musicians, writers, philosophers, and characters from mythology are lettered and incorporated into elaborate

Leaf-scroll sconces flank the overmantel of the fireplace in the drawing-room. *Photo by Vincent Hart*

The atmosphere of the dining-room is light and airy. The dark tones of the polished mahogany furniture offer a striking contrast. *Photo by Vincent Hart*

Dainty classic motifs decorate the cornice, door surrounds, and pilasters of the dining room. *Photo by Vincent Hart*

The delicately carved fireplace in the dining room is Royal Irish Green marble. *Photo by Vincent Hart*

In the library a fireplace of black African marble is complemented by the rich colors of the carpet, painting, and vases. *Photo by Vincent Hart*

The beamed and hand-painted library ceiling recalls sixteenth-century French château style. *Photo by Vincent Hart*

A corner of the library during the residency of the Goulds. *Georgian Court College Archives, copy photo Vincent Hart*

figured and foliated designs. Dominating the east wall, a black African marble fireplace is flanked by imposing mahogany columns of Tuscan style surmounted by ornate capitals and gilded balls. Six brass sconces of Elizabethan design provide soft illumination. Window and doorway draperies of cut blue mohair bordered with Aubusson tapestry harmonize with the blues, reds, and golds of the rug and the rich colors of the ceiling painting and the book bindings. During the residency of the Goulds, family photographs and Victorian bric-a-brac gave the room a cozy, cluttered feeling.

Down the corridor, across from the dining room, stood the billiard room, now a lounge. Gold draperies and green rug tones complement the warm brown of the oak-paneled walls. Along the walls above the paneling a two-foot-high tapestry frieze in shades of green and ocher leads the eye to the splendid beamed ceiling ornamented with plasterwork throughout. On either side of the

A feature of the billiard room is the handsome beamed ceiling ornamented with delicate plasterwork. *Photo by Vincent Hart*

fireplace of gray Billear Roman marble and along the opposite wall are oak and glass cabinets, which once housed the numerous trophies won by George and his sons. Missing now is the tripartite chandelier and the game table it once illuminated, but six triple wall brackets of Italian Renaissance style provide illumination for the comfortable interior.

At the west end of the house is a conservatory forty feet in width and thirty-six feet in length. It once provided a space varying from the twelve-foot height of the first-floor rooms to about sixteen feet for palms, ferns, and potted floral plants. The walls and floor are constructed of marble, with detail in classic temple style. On each side, where the ceiling is lower, two unfluted marble columns with Ionic capitals support a curved entablature decorated with a painted frieze in low relief. In the center of the room a curved leaded-glass roof permits soft sunlight to suffuse the interior. The conservatory is further illuminated by ten double casement windows and by two doors with transoms. Ten brass wall brackets of classic design were formerly finished in verd antique. At the right an alcove

lined with variform rocks held a little fountain and many ferns. Furnished with marble benches, comfortable wicker pieces, and draperies of specially woven linen and mohair, the room became a favorite spot of Edith Gould, where she often relaxed or delighted her children with stories. (This room is now a chapel. See Epilogue.)

In the service area at the east end, the large kitchen embodied the dream of every housewife, with its white-tiled walls, red and white terra-cotta tile floor, and shining copper kettles. There were caldrons, roasting pans, and kettles large enough to prepare a feast for a trainload of gourmandizing guests. In the elegant butler's pantry, storage cabinets for precious china and crystal were fitted with shelves of heavy glass and doors of silver-plated bronze and leaded glass. In nearby storage rooms and pantries were printed rules for the direction of the servants so that the management of the house would be carried out with the utmost care.

On the first sleeping floor the bedrooms are tasteful reproductions of historical models. The master suite reflects the Louis XVI period. There Edith and George slept in regal splendor in a bed ornamented with painted friezes and golden scrolls, its canopy an exact reproduction of that in

Massed greenery and potted plants filled the sunny conservatory. *Georgian Court College Archives, copy photo Vincent Hart*

Marie Antoinette's apartment at Versailles. The tall recessed panels of the upper walls of the bedroom and sitting room are covered respectively with rose and beige damask; the low dadoes are wood-paneled. Dainty classic motifs carved and finished in tones of ocher ornament the door and window surrounds. Marble fireplaces, elaborate stuccowork, mirrors, and gilded sconces increase the richness of effect. In George's study darker colors complement the wainscoting of Circassian walnut with exquisite carved detail brought out in gold and peacock blue.

In the other suites, kept in readiness for the visits of Edith's mother, Mary Kingdon, and of close friends, the paneling, mantelpieces, and lighting fixtures recall the "Adam" style. The fireplace openings are set with simple slabs of marble. Swags and foliated ornament in low relief decorate the wooden fireplace surrounds. The

suites were named according to the dominant color or décor—the Purple Room, the Cupid Room, the Green Room, and the like.

Simpler in design and furnishings, the second sleeping floor was planned especially for the children, with large, sunny bedrooms, nursery, classroom, and a great play hall. At the east end of this floor and on the one above are bedrooms originally intended for governesses and servants. The general effect of all these rooms is homey and immensely livable.

On 30 December 1897, although the interior decoration was not completed, the Goulds moved into their Lakewood home.[22] For almost another year artists and craftsmen continued the embellishment under the watchful eyes of the owners. In order to complement the period style of each room, fabrics and furnishings were carefully selected. Every piece of furniture, fashioned from special designs, conformed with the color and ornamentation of the room for which it was planned. No expense was spared in the choice of fine woods, carvings, fabrics, and mountings.

Large mirrors add scale to the master suite sitting room.
Photo by Vincent Hart

Objets d'art were everywhere in evidence— marble statuary, gilt and polychromed bronzes, and Japanese lacquer pieces. There were Sèvres porcelain urns, Chinese porcelain vases, Minton porcelain garnitures and Dresden figurines, carved ivories and jades, as well as paintings and prints too numerous to mention.

George and Edith requested appointments that to each seemed indispensable. For example, in the Louis XVI master suite, large mirrors were installed so that, as she stood in front of one of them, Edith could see herself in her lovely gowns from four angles. Nearby, in George's study, wire connected him with his ticker tape on Wall Street. Later, when the Casino was built, a similar connection in the best guest suite accommodated his close friends, who could thus be informed of the latest news of the stock market. As the estate neared completion, George, immensely pleased with what he saw, is reputed to have said to an associate, "Take a good look, for what you see before you will never again be duplicated in my day or in the future."

The Gould mansion was clearly a dwelling of a man of wealth. Yet, although adorned with a magnificence appropriate to its owner, it was also comfortably adapted for everyday use. The rich decoration and furnishings, characteristic of an era when wealthy owners sought to recapture the splendor of an earlier age, were all within the bounds of good taste. Edith Gould added touches that made it a home, not a palace, where precious periods of family privacy were enjoyed. Writing in *Munsey's Magazine*, Katherine Hoffman describes the delicacy and domesticity that characterized the house:

> There are cushions, there are window seats, lounging nooks and corners. There are green potted things, sweet and simple, and away to the right through the glass doors, there is the massed greenery of the conservatory . . . . Take the matter of photographs, for instance. Here on one mantle shelf is the master of the house in the habiliments he most affects of late— the high top boots, the baggy trousers, the hunting coat and stock of the cross country rider .. . . Mrs. Gould herself is everywhere—standing, sitting, smiling, severe, with one baby or a group of her children or alone.[24]

In every season, under the direction of Peter Gascoyne, superintendent of gardens, a crew of more than fifty men kept the great estate grounds in perfect condition. Both George and Edith Gould supervised the men in the care of the grounds as well as the extensive greenhouses, which occupied an area of three acres. There they raised prize orchids and other blooms that were exhibited in the

There were antique Italian walnut armchairs with embroidered and appliquéd seats and panels, Louis XIV wing-back chairs upholstered in rose satin damask, mahogany tables with vert marble inlay, carved and gilt armchairs of Venetian design, Louis XV gilt tables and chairs with mother-of-pearl inlay, French marquetry tables and chests, Sheraton tables of inlaid mahogany, beds of satin-wood with hand-painted medallions, and a grand piano with gilt case and painted panels in Louis XV style.[23]

Flanking the polished mahogany doors, red-plush portieres faced with satin or damask afforded privacy. Tapestries, silk brocades, and velours, all specially woven after the designs of the decorators, complemented the period style of each room. There were blue velour draperies with Aubusson tapestry borders and valances, others of rose satin damask or apple-green silk. On the first floor were Axminster rugs, Persian rugs, and Feraghan rugs as well as Kazaks, Hamadans, and Koulahs; and on the floor above, fine French carpeting.

During the residency of the Goulds, family photos and *objets d'art* were everywhere in evidence. *Georgian Court College Archives, copy photo Vincent Hart*

annual Flower Show in New York. Over more than one hundred acres of close-clipped lawns and hedges, flower-filled urns, and beds of flowers added to the charm of the estate, which between the years 1896 and 1902 had been completed in the face of both engineering and artistic difficulties. (A complete description of the gardens, statuary, and other artistic features is given in Part III.) Because the sandy soil of the property was considered inadequate for the cultivation of a variety of trees and shrubs, five thousand carloads of fine loam were brought from Monmouth County to provide a rich top layer. The lush greenery of the forest was preserved wherever possible and other trees were imported: cypress, blue cedar, blue spruce, copper beech, weeping beech, ginkgo, larch, and Japanese and Lallan pine. Eventually magnolia trees, lilac bushes, roses, rhododendron, and azaleas grew up beside the native laurel. Bobwhites, woodpeckers, chickadees, mockingbirds, herring gulls, mourning doves, and countless starlings made the site their sanctuary.

To enclose the property Price designed a costly fence, twelve feet high. The black wrought-iron paling, set in a brick and marble base, was originally tipped in gold. The strong pier posts faced with creamy terra-cotta were topped with large marble balls. Near the northeast edge of the property a wrought-iron gate flanked by colossal marble and terra-cotta piers and archway was planned for the admittance of the sportsmen and their steeds. Near the gatekeeper's lodge an elegant gateway admitted the fancy carriages of family and guests. Its terra-cotta and marble flanking piers, surmounted by cast-bronze lions in verd antique, introduced the lion motif found here and there in sculptured form throughout the estate.

Even at this point in its development Georgian Court was distinctly a showplace. Guests at the local hotels usually made it one of their first sightseeing trips. Katherine Hoffman describes its popular appeal as follows:

A view of one of the extensive greenhouses about 1905. *Moss Archives, Pach photo*

On the first day of their sojourn, the guests at the ornate caravansaries of the town leave their palm-lined corridors, their sun parlors, their big fireplaces, their deep-cushioned chairs, to drive or to stroll out to Georgian Court. They date their first engagements with the sight of the Goulds' house as the fixing point. This one will take the new baths after she gets back from a walk out to the Goulds'. That one wished to go to the Goulds' before the doctor comes. The result is that the pine bordered road between the hotels and Georgian Court, on a clear forenoon or afternoon, is as full of flashing harnesses and shining carriages as Fifth Avenue just before the winter twilight.

Katherine Hoffman adds that "the place is worth the pious pilgrimage made to it."[25]

The months spent by the Goulds in their new mansion were enlivened by the presence of numerous guests. Soon after its completion in December 1898, the owners invited friends for a house party. From all accounts the rainy weather caused the party to drag. George then resolved to provide a place on the estate where his guests could enjoy themselves no matter what the weather. He commissioned Bruce Price to design an elaborate recreational complex. Within one year Bachelor's Court, or the Casino as it was later called, was ready. With its magnificent facilities and housing for a small army of guests, it was reputed to have cost $250,000.

This huge structure, two hundred eighty feet long, with an average width of one hundred seventy-six feet, is situated about a quarter of a mile northwest of the mansion. The foundation walls and piers are of hard New Jersey brick set in mortar with internal steel rods reinforcing the greater spans. In order to harmonize with the other buildings, the exterior design is English Georgian. Like the mansion, it is finished in gray stucco with trim in white terra-cotta brick, marble, and wood. The treatment throughout is unified by the repetition of the arch form in windows, recesses, and decorative brickwork. Balustrades of marble with white terra-cotta spindles and balconies of wrought-iron add a

Colossal piers flank the entrance near the intersection of Lakewood Avenue and Ninth Street. *Photo by Vincent Hart*

Seated left, George and Edith Gould pose with weekend guests on the mansion veranda. *Courtesy of George A. Bishop, copy photo Vincent Hart*

Detail of the south facade of the casino. *Photo by Darue Studios*

touch of elegance to the second-floor areas. Quoins of white terra-cotta brick adorn and emphasize the corners and the three major entrances.

Facing southeast, the main entrance doors of solid oak are set within a slightly recessed arch twenty feet at its keystone and fourteen feet in width. In the tympanum, separated from the doors by a large marble lintel with decorative consoles, is a sculptured decoration in high relief, a copy in marble of the painting *Automedon and the Horses of Achilles* by the French artist Henri Regnault (1843–71), now in the Museum of Fine Arts in Boston.[26] Similar in size and design, the southwest entrance is decorated with a sculptured relief of a charioteer driving four racing steeds. Since the building featured George Gould's dominant sport interest, polo, the choice of motifs was felicitous. A veranda overlooking the nearby sports field stretches almost the entire length of the north side of the building. At the west a purely decorative portico,

curved and balustraded, continues the Georgian spirit.

The allocation of the interior space offered a unique solution to the problem of boredom among weekend guests. Dominating the entire center of the structure, a tanbark ring the size of the old Madison Square Garden in New York provided an exercise run for horses and polo ponies. Rising on a slant from the twenty-five-foot-high walls and trussed by light iron girders and braces, the roof peaks at the center. The large central area, one hundred seventy-five feet in length and eighty-six feet in width, was constructed of glass. (This glassed span has since been replaced by a wooden and shingled roof.) The walls are faced with white terra-cotta brick. Between huge brick pilasters placed at twenty-foot intervals, a pattern of rectangles set in red brick provides a pleasing color contrast. The upper wall space is decorated here and there with lion heads and medallions of stone in high relief. Above the riding area are archways and balconies from which spectators could watch the ponies or whatever else George's ingenuity could

Above solid oak doors a sculptured decoration in high relief adorns the southeast entrance of the casino. *Photo by Darue Studios*

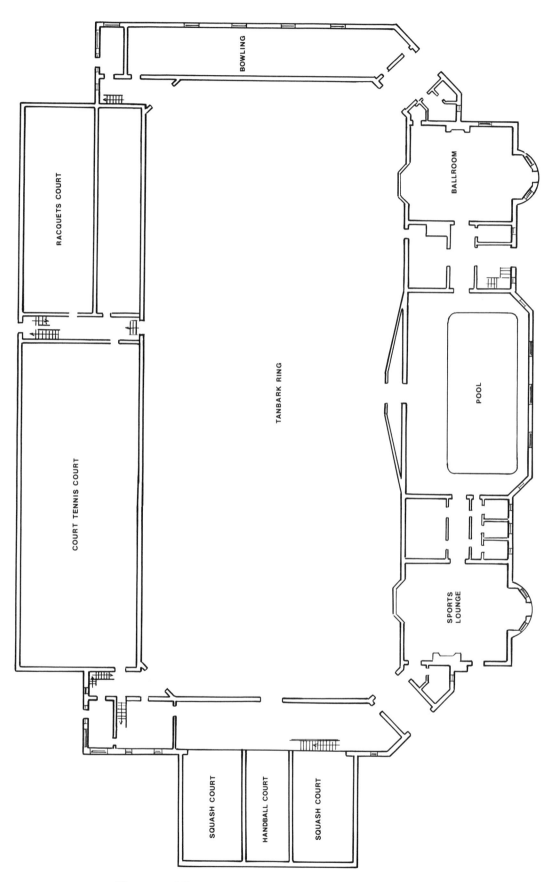

The ground-floor plan of the Casino shows the location of the
principal recreational areas. *Plan drawn by the author*

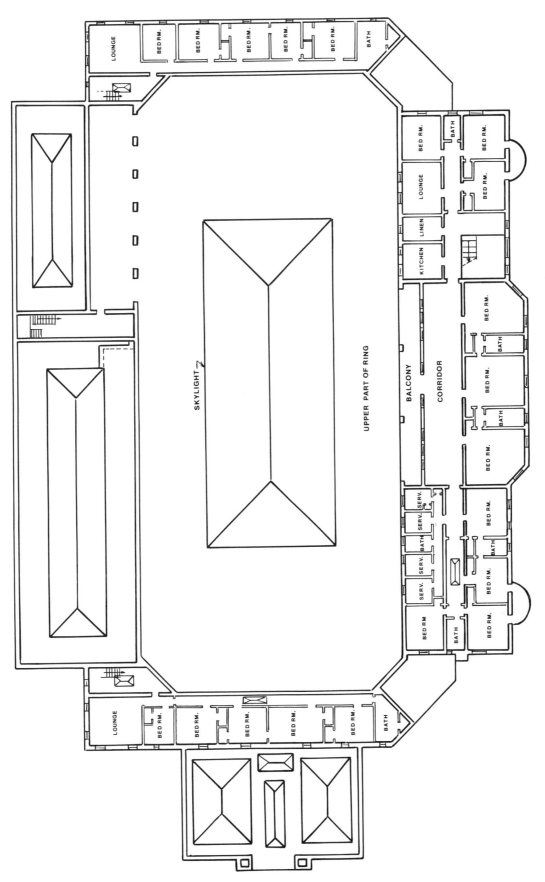

The second-floor plan of the Casino indicates the accommodations available to many guests. It also shows the skylights,
which provided illumination for the sports areas. *Plan drawn
by the author*

A decorative portico on the west side of the casino continues the Georgian spirit of the architecture. *Photo by Vincent Hart*

The tanbark ring in the casino. Potted trees along the sides were often kept there during cold weather. *Georgian Court College Archives, copy photo Vincent Hart*

devise. On one occasion, indeed, he was to bring a circus to the Court for the amusement of his friends. At another time he arranged for a chess game with live chessmen, who provided a delightful spectacle as human actors costumed like chess pieces made the various moves with medieval pomp. Edith Gould brought a motor-driven moving-picture machine to the Casino, where the latest and best picture plays were shown for Sunday evening entertainment.

Surrounding the huge tanbark ring, the latest in sports facilities were provided. To the right of the main entrance and extending the length of the east side, were bowling alleys—among the first of their kind, installed by the Brunswick Balke Collender Company. On the south side was a swimming pool constructed of porcelain-faced brick and holding 100,000 gallons of water. The marble walls, the marble pillars supporting the ceiling area around the pool, carved marble benches, and arched French windows spoke of classic elegance as well as modern comfort. An artesian well sunk that year near the Casino supplied water in abundance. An elaborate pump and piping system in the basement allowed for drainage toward the lake a quarter of a mile away. Adjacent to the pool a dressing-room area with showers and Turkish bath led to a commodious trophy room and lounge dominated by a fireplace of medieval capacity. The walls were covered with mounted game birds, and fish from sharks to rainbow trout, Indian weapons, elk and deer heads, and an array of sports trophies that George and his sons had won. A few steps away on the west side of the structure were squash courts, shooting galleries, and a billiard room. Occupying most of the north side were a huge glass-roofed racquets court and a "court tennis" court, one of six in the country at the time.

The huge ring readied for a gala event ca. 1905. *Moss Archives, Pach photo*

In marked contrast to these sports facilities was the elegant ballroom located to the left of the main entrance. Its charming Georgian interior, illuminated by day by large arched windows and by night by crystal chandeliers, was the setting for many a fashionable afternoon or evening gathering. Elegant, too, were the comfortable suites on the second floor that accommodated the weekend guests.

The formal opening of Bachelor's Court on 21 December 1899 was marked by a grand Christmas party. In mid-afternoon the guests began arriving by train from New York and Philadelphia. They were met by carriages from the estate and driven either to the mansion, Bachelor's Court, or Laurel-in-the-Pines, the resort hotel nearby. Among the privileged ones who stayed with the Goulds was the grand dame of old New York society, Mrs. Stuyvesant Fish. Other notables included the Herman Oelrichs, the Sidney Smiths, the Charles Snowdens, the marquis de Talleyrand, and the Philadelphia Drexels.

A tour of the Court facilities, afternoon cocktails, and a sumptuous dinner at the Laurel-in-the-Pines hotel preceded the evening theatrical performance. For the presentation Edith had converted the carriage house of the stables into a little theater, perfect in every detail of stage, scenery, electrical effects, and seating. Through an illuminated archway decorated with Christmas greens, flags, and ensigns, ushers—among them George Gould himself—clad in scarlet coats, conducted the guests to their places. The first two playlets, *A Pair of Lunatics* and *The Marble Arch*, were performed by both amateurs and professionals. Among the latter were Boyd Putnam and Bijou Fernandez of Broadway fame. But the third one, *The Twilight of the God* by Edith Wharton, seems to have been written expressly for Edith Gould. Her part, that of Elizabeth Warland, was really the entire play. With her graceful and dignified performance Edith renewed the histrionic triumphs that she had left behind when she deserted the stage to become the bride of the young millionaire. Her costume of purple velvet trimmed with semiprecious stones was trailed by a ten-foot train lined with real ermine. It was costly enough to make even George complain.

A chess game with live chessmen provided a delightful spectacle for guests of the Goulds. *Courtesy of Dr. Raymond A. Taylor, copy photo Vincent Hart*

Bowling alleys extend the length of the east side. *Photo by Vincent Hart*

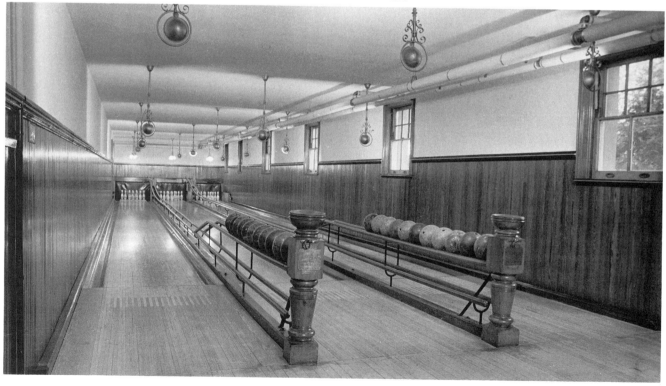

Marble walls and columns add elegance to the swimming-pool area. *Photo by Vincent Hart*

Later that evening, beneath the frieze of the Canterbury Pilgrims, the mansion's great hall rocked with the music of a Hungarian orchestra. Elisha Dyer and Mrs. Stuyvesant Fish led the cotillion. Again Edith was gorgeously attired, this time in a gown of white lace-trimmed satin. Her famous pearls hung around her neck, and a diadem of sparkling diamonds crowned her head. During the evening Santa Claus appeared, pushing before him a huge snowball out of which a beautiful tinsel-and-spangle-clad fairy emerged, bearing gifts of gold for all the guests: bonbon dishes for the women, and pins for the men fashioned in the shape of golf sticks or horseshoes. At midnight a supper catered by Delmonico's was served. Dancing continued till dawn.

Thereafter, each weekend during the "season" the Goulds entertained a stream of house guests in the Casino, who reputedly brought with them a retinue of personal servants and pet poodles. Under one roof, these fortunate ones could rise early, take a plunge in the pool, have access to a Turkish bath and steam room, breakfast daintily, choose from among at least a dozen sports, or simply lounge before a roaring fireplace.

Despite an active social life, Edith and George were devoted parents. In fact, Georgian Court, notwithstanding its many attractions, was built largely for the benefit of their children. As was the Gould custom while they were in residence in the Fifth Avenue home, the sunniest room of the mansion was reserved for the current baby and the next sunniest for the previous baby. The family usually held a happy little ceremony when the reigning monarch of the nursery had to move out and give way to the new little king or queen.

Although Edith already had all that most women crave—success and fame, love and marriage, wealth and high social position—motherhood brought her great joy. As she told Elizabeth Meriwether Gilmer, "My acquaintances have sometimes pitied me because I have had so many babies, but I have not one child too many."[27] Under her watchful care, all the Gould offspring lived healthy, simple, and unaffected childhoods. Although each child had a trained nurse in attendance until two-and-a-half years old, Edith herself tucked them in bed each evening and nursed them when they were ill. She always saw to it that they dressed simply and ate plain, nourishing food with a minimum of sweets.

Under tutors and governesses they studied every imaginable subject. The general supervisor of their education was Miss Caroline Cortis, whom the children affectionately called "Aunt Carrie." All of them spoke and wrote fluent French, Ger-

A broad veranda stretches along the south side of the mansion. *Photo by Vincent Hart*

During the Gould residency, flower-filled urns adorned the pleasant, sunny veranda. *Courtesy of Mary Hurlburt, photo by Richard Steele*

After attending one of the children, Dr. Paul Kimball, the family physician in Lakewood, takes a spin on the estate grounds. *Moss Archives, Pach photo*

man, and Italian taught them by, among others, their beloved Madame Emma Jourdain, Fräulein Helena Schacko, and Signorinas Annunciata Lucci and Clelia Fiorillo. At fifteen Kingdon, dubbed the

scholar of the family, could speak seven languages, including Arábic. At seventeen Vivien wrote Greek poetry, studied Latin with her brothers, and was fluent in five modern languages. All had a marked talent for drawing, possibly inherited from Edith, whose father was an artist for *Harper's Magazine*.

Whenever weather permitted, classes were held outdoors on the broad veranda of the mansion. Mrs. Gould's enthusiasm for fresh air was loyally seconded by Kate Williams, the trained nurse in charge of the nursery, and Dr. Paul Kimball, the Lakewood family physician. The school day began at nine and lasted until one o'clock when luncheon was served in the nursery dining room. Even this time of day was not all play, because each day the children found on the table a placard that read "Speak French" or "Speak German." They were never permitted to use English while eating this meal.

Having studied infant psychology, Mrs. Gould was quick to detect and encourage the slightest evidence of talent in her sons and daughters. When she noticed her five-month-old Georgie waving his arms rhythmically, she decided that boxing would be his future sport. Consequently, as soon as he was old enough to walk, a champion

Young Georgie poses for the camera before a recital. *Moss Archives, Pach photo*

A corner of the mansion conservatory becomes a backdrop for Vivien, the charming ballerina. *Moss Archives, Pach photo*

Little Edith and George, Sr., in a quadricycle. *Moss Archives, Pach photo*

boxer was brought from England to give him lessons. When Vivien started dancing to the tune of the nursery piano, Edith telegraphed to New York for the best available ballet instructor and arranged for her daughter to have a three-year course. Though George became an accomplished violinist rather than a boxer, Vivien learned to dance beautifully and made a charming ballerina with her tiny, slender figure and her dark curly hair.

George Gould was a loving and devoted father. Since his business trips and sportsman's holidays took him away from his family for extended periods of time, he wrote to the children or sent them gifts every few days. Each ordinary work day he hurried from his New York office in order to catch the four o'clock train for Lakewood so that he could spend time with his children before dinner. A sportsman himself, he saw to it that they spent many hours in outdoor exercise. All sorts of athletic diversions were provided—pony riding, tennis, bicycling, squash, swimming in their private pool, miniature golf for the little ones, and cross-country riding for the older children. Kingdon, Jay, and even Marjorie and Vivien became expert riders to the hunt and learned to take care of their own mounts. George, who often played polo with his sons, encouraged excellence in many sports. A famous tennis champion, Frank Forester of Knightsbridge, England, was brought to this country and provided with a home for his family so that he could coach the Gould children in tennis and other racquet games.

Edith impressed upon her children the importance of making the most of their good looks by dressing in the best of taste. She purchased all their clothing at a French dressmaking establishment in the Rue de la Paix, Paris, that specialized in children's clothes. Always appropriately garbed herself, she had them change their clothing in order to suit every occasion; she was a stickler for etiquette.

George Gould delighted in the knowledge that Edith's gowns and jewels were the envy of many other women. *Georgian Court College Archives, copy photo Vincent Hart*

With them she presided at one o'clock luncheon, elegantly served on the best silver service. But dinner at eight-thirty, either alone with George or with special guests, was to her the most important event of the day. Assisted by Margaret, her personal maid, and even by Madame Jourdain and Miss Cortis, she selected her gown and jewels with great care.

George took pleasure in providing costly gems for his wife's adornment—a diamond collar and tiara, a corsage of emeralds with each stone large enough for a solitaire ring, strings of pearls, one of which hung down below her knees, and bracelets and rings set with precious stones. He delighted in the knowlege that her gowns were the envy of many other women. They were made by a dressmaking establishment in New York, often according to her sketches. Each summer her wardrobe was supplemented by the latest in Paris fashions. In each of the Gould mansions a wardrobe of at least twenty evening gowns was always in readiness for her choice, their degree of formality determined by the social requirements of the location.

Mrs. Gould's beauty and charm were described by Nell Brinkley, the artist, as follows:

> I think the thing in her face that first strikes and holds you is the eyes of her; and after that the fine sweetness and tenderness and utterly womanly look in the whole of her face and motions. Her eyes are brown, with a clear gold in them when she holds her face to the light. They are quite wide and fill quickly with laughter in answer to the least smile of anyone around her. Her skin is smooth, with a faint tinge of color; her mouth rich and warmly colored and quick to laugh. She is a bit tall; and her body is finely shaped and straight as a dart.
>
> She walks swiftly, and in a busy way that makes you think instinctively of the children she has mothered—the many of them. Her hair is deep brown, and her hands are warm and silky when you grasp them.
>
> She is wonderful. My heart is gone out of me with the fineness of a woman who is a motherly woman. It is tenderness and sweetness, and big-heartedness and patience; and Edith Kingdon Gould is all that.[28]

This beautiful lady was indeed the heart of a happy home.

The family spent a good part of the year, usually from late October to May, at Georgian Court. Under the kindly but firm rule of Theresa Bently, the housekeeper, and William Bishop, the butler, a staff of about twenty kept the household running smoothly. Edith herself took an active interest in the affairs of the house. Each morning after a leisurely breakfast with George in her sitting room, she went over the day's menus with the butler. Afterward, she was chauffeured to the local markets where she selected the fresh foods for the carefully planned meals. Later, in the afternoon, she looked over the rooms of the mansion, straightening things here and there, so that everything would be in order for the arrival of the evening's guests.

In 1901 another mansion, Kingscote, was added to the Gould property. From its resemblance to the other buildings on the estate, it would appear that Bruce Price was the architect, although no actual record exists. Furthermore, in the *Ladies' Home*

Journal of 1900, Price published a rendering similar to it in general design, but of less expensive materials of construction. The first of a series of model suburban houses of moderate cost designed by foremost architects of the day, Price's design became noted for its low estimated cost of $7,000.[29]

The house was intended for George's eldest son, Kingdon. Consequently, when completed it was called King's Court, later Kingscote. Although Kingdon was only in his teens, George evidently anticipated his heir's future need for a palatial home of his own. As it happened, the house was not built at a cost of $7,000. The final figure was closer to $300,000. Perhaps the difference in cost between the *Journal*'s estimate and this completed building may best be explained by the use of more expensive materials, including marble.

The architect followed the Georgian style of the existing buildings and used the same materials for the exterior—red brick base, gray stucco walls, creamy terra-cotta quoins at the corners, and trim in marble and white wood. The elegant classic design is enhanced by three porticoes symmetrically placed, one at the main entrance on the west and the others flush with the front facade on the north and south sides. A piazza bordered with marble and paved with red tiles extends the entire length of the west side and continues under the side porticoes. Piers faced with terra-cotta and marble columns with Ionic capitals support the entablatures and the wrought-iron balustrades of the porticoes. Centered on either side of the main entrance in slightly recessed arches are French doors, which open on the piazza from the two front rooms. The spaces above the arches are adorned with terra-cotta fruit swags draped from voussoirs and decorative animal heads.

A marble stringcourse acts as a visual separation between the first floor and the second. Just above it and centered between the windows are two Della Robbia–style medallions in decorative oval frames enclosing draped infant figures. Classic motifs adorn the cornice, which overhangs the second floor. A dormered hip roof encloses the third floor area.

Like the mansion, the interior plan of Kingscote is a similarly open axial plan. The wide entrance hall has a handsome staircase at its rear that separates at the first landing and becomes double. The rooms that open off the hall are entered through wide polished-mahogany sliding doors. The focal point of each large room is a fireplace with an ele-

Kingscote ca. 1904. A fire in 1908 destroyed the roof and much of the interior. *Museum of the City of New York*

gant wood-carved mantelpiece in the "Adam" style. Except for the library, which is paneled in dark oak, the walls and paneling throughout the house are painted in the light colors of the early Georgian style.

As it happened, the adult Kingdon Gould did not choose to use this lovely mansion as his residence. For seven years Henry Lloyd Herbert, chairman of the Polo Association and a friend of the Goulds, lived there. In 1908 a fire, presumably caused by a defective fuse, destroyed all of the interior. Since Price had died in 1903, between 1909 and 1910 another famous architect, Horace Trumbauer, who had built for the Goulds elsewhere, restored the house.[30] After its restoration in 1910, George gave it to his daughter Marjorie, who was married that same year to Anthony Drexel, Jr. The couple resided there part of each year until the early 1920s.

During the summer of 1901 George and Edith anticipated the arrival of their sixth child. In order to make his wife comfortable that particularly hot summer, George and the family cruised around the Long Island area on their yacht, the *Sybarite*. In this way he could spend as much time as possible with Edith and the children, and yet be dropped off at the New York Yacht Club pier to take the train to his office in the city or to nearby sports events. On 3 August, while the yacht was lying at anchor in Cold Springs Harbor, Oyster Bay, Long Island, Dr. William B. Anderson, the family physician, announced the birth of a baby girl. Upon hearing the news, George was so overjoyed that he gave each crewman a gift of forty dollars and had the *Sybarite* bedecked with flags. The family and the physician remained on the yacht until October, with trained nurses attending Edith and the infant.

When the chill autumn winds began to blow, the family returned to Lakewood, where Edith happily planned for her child's baptism. Ten women worked on the white satin christening gown and the baby's layette decorated with fine Irish lace and delicate embroidery. The Goulds decided to make the christening a gala event. On 27 January 1902 three hundred guests were transported from New York on the Gould private train. The ceremony took place at twelve noon in the great hall of the mansion, which was transformed into a chapel for

In 1905 the family posed for this portrait in front of the mansion. *Left to right:* **(seated) Vivien, George, Sr., Edith and Little Edith, George, Jr., (standing) Jay, Marjorie, and Kingdon.** *Moss Archives, Pach photo*

the occasion. Placed in the center of the hall, the baptismal font was bowered with countless American Beauty roses. Edith's cousin, Bishop H. T. Kingdon of Canada, baptized the infant with holy water brought specially from the River Jordan. The baby was named Edith Catherine after her mother and after her mother's sister, who had died as a child. Two devoted friends of the family, the noted sportsman Henry Lloyd Herbert and the society leader Mrs. Stuyvesant Fish, acted as godparents. Afterward everyone enjoyed a lavish spread prepared and served by the delighted Gould staff. Edith Gould Wainwright remembers her most cherished baptismal gift, a jewel-studded gold-bound prayer book inscribed, "Edith Catherine Gould from her godmother Marian J. Fish, January 27, 1902."[31]

She also recalls the happiness of her childhood days, the homey atmosphere of the well-ordered household, and the love that bound the family together. She remembers that "Mamma and Papa were the most congenial couple. They read the same books, discussed them together, and often read aloud to each other." She never saw anything but perfect harmony between her parents.[32]

When the seventh and last of the Gould children was born on 3 March 1906, she was named Gloria.

Edith takes little sister Gloria for a ride around the mansion.
Moss Archives, Pach photo

Before the birth Edith had been reading Hall Cain's *The Christian*. So impressed was she with the author's characterization of Glory Quayle that she chose the Latin form of that name for her little girl. Gloria was baptized in the conservatory of the mansion—the sunlit room at the west end that was always banked with plants and seasonal flowers.

Georgian Court: Mecca for Sportsmen

George Gould's expensive stables indicated his keen interest in riding and polo. They were an essential part of the total concept of the country estates and clubs that he had seen in England and endeavored to re-create in Lakewood. He had enjoyed the games at the picturesque Hurlingham Club on the banks of the Thames at Fulham, famous for the origin and development of modern polo. Its delightful house, stables, and gardens became a prototype for other fashionable clubs—Ranelagh, with its pavilions and tea rooms; Barns Elms, with its Old World character; Roehampton and Eden Park, to name just a few. Built in 1897–98, Gould's stable complex with its Georgian simplicity and central tower had an architectural character like that of the pavilion at Ranelagh.

The stables were located to the north of the mansion, separated from it by a roadway and a formal garden. The exterior, finished in gray stucco with trim in light brick and wood, echoed the style of the family residence. The central part of the structure was dominated by a tall octagonal tower, which functioned as the water tower for the estate. Its steeple was crowned by a twelve-foot bronze statue of Mercury—a delicately balanced weathervane especially designed by Bruce Price. Recessed in the wall over the south entrance was a large clock with Westminster chimes, which sounded every fifteen minutes and could be heard all over town.

The complex consisted of six wings: four huge wings connected by a center arcade were parallel to the mansion and two smaller ones were located at right angles to the mansion. Most of the interior

space of these wings was allotted to open stalls and box stalls of solid mahogany, with appropriate fittings by Mark W. Cross and Company of New York. Close to one hundred and fifty horses and polo ponies were comfortably accommodated and cared for by more than fifty grooms. The stables

Stable detail ca. 1899, showing workmen erecting the statue of Mercury on the steeple of the tower. *Moss Archives, Pach photo*

69

The stable complex as it appeared ca. 1928, after it became known as Raymond Hall. *Photo by Irving Chidnoff*

were a marvel of good order and sumptuousness, as befitted the residence of blooded horses, for Gould traveled far and wide to purchase the most perfect breeds. Each immaculately clean stall had the name of its occupant inscribed on a brass plate—Scrambled Eggs, Countess, Prince, the Spotted Speeder, among others—while the steeds' robes and halters hung nearby. (A watercolor painting of the handsome interior of one of the wings hangs in Raymond Hall, the former stables converted to college use.)

Under competent riding masters the Gould children learned not only to ride, but to saddle and unsaddle their mounts, and to see that they were properly stabled and fed. No child of George could ever ride into the stable, dismount, fling down the reins, and say to a groom, "Take care of it." Their father's concern and care for the animals were shared by all the children.

On the second floor of the complex, above the center arcade, was a spacious area used as a carriage room. The Goulds's many vehicles included a buckboard surrey, an opera bus, a road break, a Victoria, a buggy cart, a basket phaeton, a breaking cart, broughams of various styles, and eventually, the latest in automobiles. An electrically powered cable elevator located in the center of the arcade lifted the vehicles up and down as needed. When their number of autos increased beyond the capacity of the carriage room, a space was provided for them at one end of a first-floor wing.

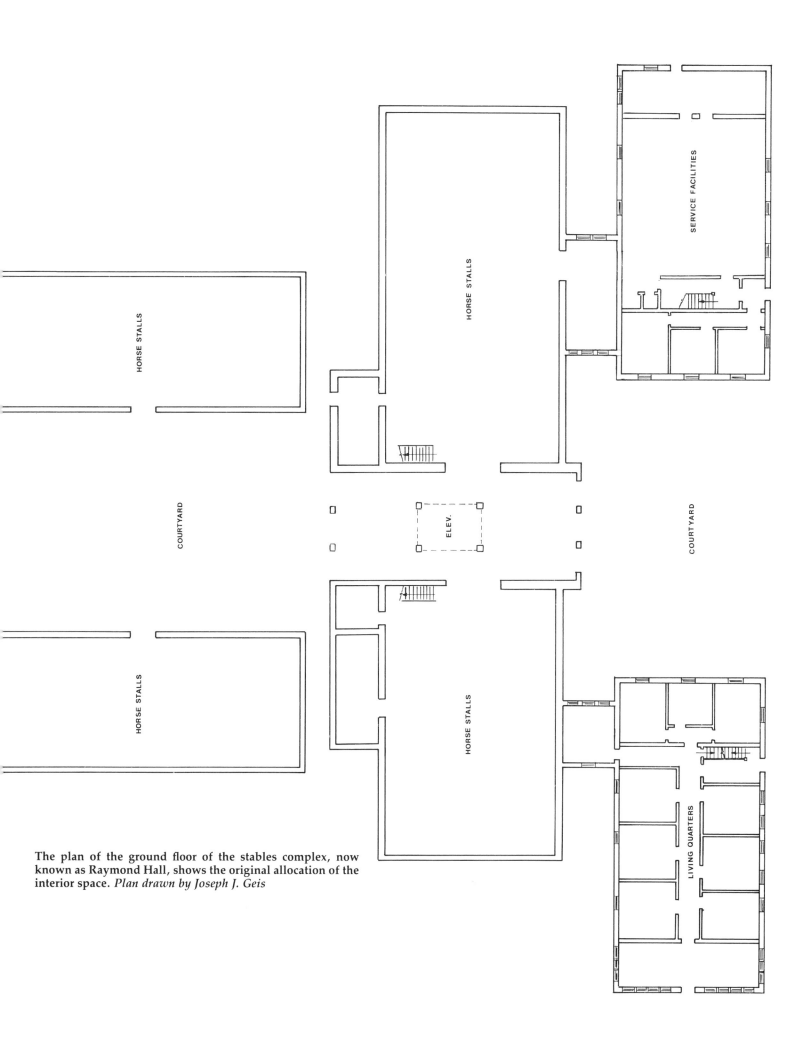

HORSE STALLS

HORSE STALLS

SERVICE FACILITIES

COURTYARD

COURTYARD

ELEV.

HORSE STALLS

HORSE STALLS

LIVING QUARTERS

The plan of the ground floor of the stables complex, now known as Raymond Hall, shows the original allocation of the interior space. *Plan drawn by Joseph J. Geis*

Solid mahogany stalls accommodated George Gould's horses.

George Gould owned a Panhard, one of the first automobiles in Lakewood. Once when he was driving it, he knocked over a farmer's wagonload of wood. He promptly gave the dismayed man ten dollars. When other farmers heard about it, they went out of their way to encounter him. George's gift to Edith of a shiny black roadster prompted her to master the challenge of a motor-powered vehicle. She became known all over town as a skillful and careful driver. Miniature electric automobiles made specially for each of the children enabled them to "speed" along the roads of the estate.

The Casino, or Court as it was often called, became one of the greatest attractions in the town. Its size and appointments were the talk of the sports world, and prominent sportsmen flocked to its doors. The huge central amphitheater, built for the owner's dominant interest, polo, was an ideal place to exercise the steeds, especially in cold or inclement weather. By 1899 George Gould was known as "the patron of Lakewood polo."[33] Having organized the Lakewood Polo Club, built three polo fields on his property, and equipped about forty polo ponies, he had the most complete outfit of any man in the country.

Interest in polo, which continued each season, attracted a constant stream of participating players from all parts of the country and from Canada. From about 1909 Georgian Court became the training ground of the American Polo Association, where the selection was made of America's Cup and World Championship teams prior to the international matches in June at the Meadow Brook Club in Westbury, Long Island. At Lakewood the sandy soil and the sunnier climate gave a good, firm, playable footing, while the Long Island field was still soggy and slippery after the winter thaw and the spring rains. Over three hundred ponies were brought to town for the tryouts, and the Gould stable alone housed over $200,000 worth of polo ponies.

The practice matches were covered by the major newspapers on the eastern seaboard. Sports writers extolled the generosity of George Gould for making polo possible even in midwinter. Among the famous players cited were the "Big Four" of polo—Devereux Milburn, Larry and Monte Waterbury, and Harry Payne Whitney. Also noted were the hard-riding players—L. E. Stoddard, Rudolph L. Agassiz, René La Montagne, Foxhall Keene, and Malcolm Stevenson.

The "cottage colony" turned out in force for all the matches, their solid line of traps and auto-

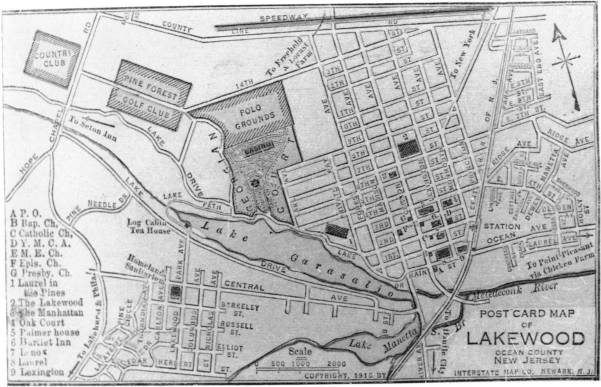

A map drawn in the early 1900s indicates the location of the Gould polo grounds. *Courtesy of Gene Hendrickson, copy photo Vincent Hart*

Workmen preparing the polo fields for the practice matches. *Moss Archives, Pach photo*

Testimonial given to Mrs. George J. Gould in 1900. *Courtesy of George A. Bishop, copy Vincent Hart*

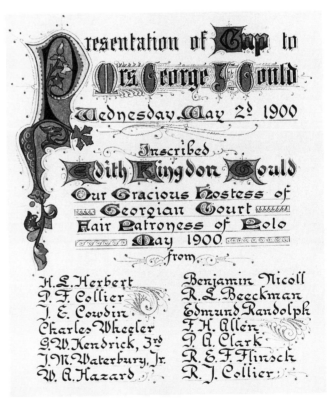

mobiles banking the edge of the field each afternoon of the practice. As many as two thousand spectators cheered the colorfully garbed riders as they dashed over the turf. Between matches they sipped refreshments under the black and yellow tents erected here and there. The popularity of the events also attracted George Wesley Bellows, famous American artist, who in 1910 came to the estate and painted his notable oil painting *Polo at Lakewood.*

In 1911 the members of the Hurlingham Polo Club of England came to compete in the practice matches in preparation for the international games. In honor of the Britons, numerous teas,

The Lakewood "cottage colony" gathers for the practice matches of the American Polo Association. *Moss Archives, Pach photo*

luncheons, and dinner parties were given by the Goulds and other prominent families of Lakewood. The governors of the Country Club marked the occasion by a gala Polo Ball—the highlight of the polo season.

Indeed, during the spring months, polo took first place in the social life of Lakewood. Its popularity was reported in the *New York World*, 6 April 1913:

> Everybody talks polo, thinks polo and goes to polo. The coming of America's leading fourteen experts has served to make the spring season here one of the liveliest in years, and the bookings at the hotels continue as at the height of the season.

The Goulds wined and dined the poloists vying for spots on the international team. In May 1913, at a special dinner marking the selection of the players who would represent the United States, Henry Lloyd Herbert, president of the American Polo Association, praised George for his efforts to advance the interests of polo and for his hospitality and true sportsmanship. Edith was cited as "the most consistently charming hostess in the world," who made all her guests "so collectively and individually happy."[34]

In an article entitled "Polo and the Business Man" appearing in *The Independent*, George expressed his keen personal interest in the sport, saying:

> Polo is a boon to the man of business. . . . The effect of the game upon the tired body is tonic. Also it stimulates the mind and leaves it tranquil. After a well-played match a man is at peace with the whole world. He can take up business problems with renewed vigor and mental clearness.[35]

Kingdon and Jay Gould shared their father's interest in polo. Their outdoor exercise from early childhood had made them sturdy athletes. Careful instruction in riding and in polo both on their indoor ring and their outdoor fields was followed by spirited performances for the Gould guests and at the annual horse show of the Lakewood Country Club. By the time the eldest, Kingdon, was sixteen, and Jay one year younger, the boys were classed among the best players in the country. With their father and the fine player Benjamin Nicholl, they appeared on the polo field and held their own with the veterans of the game. A huge oil painting of these two sons mounted on their ponies hangs on the east wall of the Casino amphitheater. Painted by Richard Newton in 1903, the handsome work is a continual reminder of the early days at Georgian Court.

But however much he excelled at polo, young Jay Gould's first love was court tennis. The Casino at Georgian Court housed a court for this favorite sport of kings and courtiers, which is thought to have originated in France during the twelfth century and was referred to as "tennis royal." Court tennis is considered the forerunner of all racquet games, and its intricacy requires great skill in performance. In courts designed for the game are areas called penthouses—projecting sheds with slanted roofs—found on the left side wall and both end walls. A contender plays the surfaces of the walls, ceiling, and floor, and strives to put the ball of tightly wound cloth out of reach of the sixteen-ounce racquet of his opponent. Scoring is complicated, with additional points being made when the ball is hit into a number of netted openings called galleries in the left-wall penthouse. Spectators sit in a screened-off gallery on one end wall, called the dedans. Between them and the net is the service side of the court; beyond the net, the hazard side.

Lakewood's Champion Polo Team. *Left to right:*Kingdon Gould, Jay Gould, Benjamin Nicoll, George J. Gould. *Courtesy of Mary Hurlburt*

The skylighted Gould court, the second private court to be built in America, is one of the finest ever constructed. The walls are faced with the famous mineral black cement invented by Joseph Bickley. The composition floor laid in large slabs gives a lively and true bounce to the ball. The court is of regulation size—one hundred ten feet long, thirty-eight feet wide, and almost thirty feet high. Along the slate walls are crowns painted as markers. In the spectators gallery, where the guests of the Goulds cheered on the players, a sign still serves notice: "Silence is requested when the ball is in play."

In this court Jay Gould mastered the demanding sport under the tutelage of Frank Forester, the English professional whom Gould had hired to train his son. The first lessons began in the spring of 1901. In an incredibly short time Jay grasped the intricacies of the game. He spent many hours in practice and was soon able to offer fairly strong opposition to his mentor. His first match was played in 1902 against James Henry Smith of the New York Racquet and Tennis Club, who was his father's guest. Jay won easily, 2 sets to 0, without a handicap.

In 1903 Ernest A. Thompson, one of the famous New York players, came to Lakewood and taught the young prodigy the play known as the railroad service. In delivering this service the racquet meets

Coach Frank Forester, the French champion Ferdinand Garcin, and Jay Gould pose on the Gould court. *Moss Archives, Pach photo*

the ball over the head of the player, who stands along the side-wall penthouse. When it leaves the racquet it speeds along the penthouse like the train along its tracks. Jay learned to deliver this play with deadly effectiveness and was soon devising variations of it. Jay gave the play a lasting vogue and won it recognition as an essential part of the game. But it was not only this play that made him famous. As noted in *The Pageant of America*, "In Gould the followers of court tennis found their ideal champion. Covering the court with almost incredible speed he never erred in his judgment of distance and direction."[36]

From about 1904 the Gould court became a mecca for court tennis players. Although leading professionals found George Gould's legendary hospitality attractive, they came chiefly to play against young Jay. Among them were Punch Fairs, Tom Pettitt, Fred Tompkins, Jack White, and Alfred White. Eustace M. Miles, the British court tennis champion, spent many days imparting his technical knowledge and experience. Ferdinand Garcin, the French master, shared his expertise. When in 1905 the world court tennis champion, Peter Latham of London, visited the States, George arranged for a special tournament in Lakewood, where Jay met the British player. The outcome was a big surprise. Gould carried the professional to 9-7, 6-2. Then in another match, paired with George Standing, he defeated Latham and Charles E. Sands, the American amateur champion. On that occasion Latham predicted a great future for Jay, which was realized when he won the American and English championships.

The young athlete decided to try for the national championship the next year. Under Coach Forester he made rapid progress and startled the athletic world in March 1906 by first winning the Gold Racquet award at Tuxedo Park, where he defeated

The skylighted court tennis court in the Casino as it appears today. *Photo by Vincent Hart*

Pierre Lorillard, Jr. Since nearly all national entries competed at Tuxedo, the Tuxedo Gold Racquet not only decided the championship of the club but was the preliminary tournament for the United States championship.

In the national amateur tournament three weeks later Jay met the best players in the country, J. J. Cairns and Joshua Crane of Boston and Charles E. Sands of the New York Racquet and Tennis Club. Young Gould fought against overwhelming odds, but defeated each in turn. Not yet eighteen years old, Jay was the youngest American amateur champion in the history of athletic sports. That same month he sailed for England, where he challenged the British champion. Although he lost that year in the final match against Eustace M. Miles, he returned in 1907 to become the victor—the first American to win the title. He repeated the victory the following year and captured the Olympic championship as well. Moreover, he thoroughly embarrassed the aristocracy of Tuxedo by winning their cherished Gold Racquet for the third year in a row. In order to save themselves further embarrassment, the board of the club voted to abandon the tournament.

Repeatedly winning the national championship, Jay challenged George F. Covey, professional at Crabbet Park, England, on 16 March 1914 for the world's court tennis championship. Young Gould emerged victorious from this match played at the Philadelphia Racquet Club. A return match was planned but never held because, with the outbreak of World War I, his family did not want him to risk a trip to Europe. In 1916 he wrote a letter to the Philadelphia Club indicating his desire to retire from the championship. As a result Covey took the world title by default. Jay continued to engage in the sport and retained the American championship for nineteen years and the English title for most of that time as well.

He was acclaimed by court tennis authorities as the greatest court tennis amateur of all times. In *The Racquet Game* Allison Danzig states that "when he went on the court the tennis world saw the most finished style developed in America, one of the most perfectly executed and absolutely deadly strokes that ever cut down a ball."[37] In summing up Gould's genius Danzig states:

Not only did he lay down hopelessly unbeatable chases, but his certainty on the volley, his accuracy and force in playing for the winning openings and his ability to kill the ball even when coming off the tambour made it practically impossible for any amateur to "live" in the same court with him. So annihilating was his floor game that it was seldom that he had to resort to an attack on the openings, and as a rule he did it only for the sake of variety.

One can use only superlatives in attempting to do justice to the play of Jay Gould and after doing so one is left with a sense of their futility.[38]

Delight and amazement followed upon his every play, to the delight and satisfaction of George and Edith.

In addition to its reputation as a center for polo and court tennis, Lakewood was a focal point for golf enthusiasts. Tournaments would start there in the spring, travel to other prominent golf sites, and then return to the town around Thanksgiving for the final rounds. The sport had begun in Lakewood about 1895 with a nine-hole course and clubhouse on the land that later became the John D. Rockefeller estate. With George Gould as one of the founders and first president, the Ocean County Hunt and Country Club introduced and popularized golf. Two years later the Golf Club of Lakewood was constructed at the end of the Gould estate on property owned by Nathan Strauss. The sport not only attracted the experts but was popular with the transient guests conveniently accommodated by horse-drawn stages back and forth from the hotels. In 1898 the first professional golf tournament ever held in the United States was played in Lakewood. Ten pros played thirty-six holes for a purse of $150.

In 1902, when Strauss refused to renew the lease, the golfers looked for another tract of land. Soon afterward the Hyer Farm of one hundred acres was purchased. Following the merger of the two earlier clubs, this site became the Lakewood Country Club, with George Gould as president. A beautiful clubhouse was erected and the courses laid out. On 11 February 1903 George hosted the formal opening. During the gala evening of dancing and cheer, Edith Gould, resplendent in steel-gray silk with shimmering spangles, a diamond tiara on her head, and the famous pearls around her neck, was on the dance floor almost constantly.

About 1912 the Goulds constructed their own private course on the northwest end of their estate—a nine-hole course designed and executed by "Willie" Norton, the famous professional. It was laid out especially for Edith so that she could have her exercise. She played frequently with George or with her lady friends in an effort to keep down her increasing weight. Unfortunately, as she grew older, Edith became addicted to sweets. Try as she might to conquer it in public, her addiction continued in secret with bags of bonbons hidden here and there in the house. Nonetheless, in her continual attempt to retain her legendary figure, she exercised regularly in a variety of ways, particularly at her favorite sport. She was on the links each morning while at Georgian Court, until the snows of winter prevented her.

Gould Railroad Interests

When Jay Gould died on 2 December 1892 after a long, silent bout with tuberculosis, George assumed the management of the Gould enterprises. Having been indoctrinated from the age of twenty in the complexities of the businesses that his father had shrewdly engineered, he gave promise of being a worthy successor. According to his father's will he received an extra $5 million in addition to his share of the estate of $75 million. The money had been given to him in recognition of his "remarkable business ability" displayed in the management of his father's affairs, especially during the last three years of the latter's life. The will further stipulated that if the other members of the family were unable to agree upon the administration policies of the leading corporations controlled by the Gould interests, namely, the Missouri Pacific, the Wabash, the Manhattan Elevated, and the Western Union, George was to have full authority to vote the stock of these companies.

The general public wondered how this young heir of twenty-eight and family "dictator" would ever be able to wear the mantle of his father—one of the cleverest financiers New York had ever known. As reported by the journalists, shortly after George took over the vast interests entrusted to his care he had a serious disagreement with J. Pierpont Morgan, owner of the New York Central and its allied railroads, over the proposed purchase of the New York and Northern Railroad by the Manhattan Elevated Railroad. Much angered, the young magnate left Morgan, vowing never to set foot in his office again. According to Robert N. Burnett in an article published in *Cosmopolitan*

Magazine, one of Jay Gould's closest friends, hearing of the altercation, volunteered a bit of advice to Gould in about these words: "George, as an admirer of your father, and as one interested in your highest welfare, I seriously hope you will not commit the blunder at the beginning of your career, of antagonizing the leading interests in the business world."[39]

Evidently the advice did not fall on deaf ears, for within a short period of time Jay's heir began to display a remarkable astuteness in making alliances with the great powers in the world of business. By gaining the friendship and financial backing of John D. Rockefeller, Andrew Carnegie, and other capitalists, he placed himself in a position where he could proceed with a comprehensive plan for the expansion of the Gould railroad "empire." Jay Gould had left a system of about six thousand miles extending from Toledo and Chicago to Denver and El Paso. George sought to realize the unfulfilled ambition of his father—to extend the lines eastward and westward to the Atlantic and to the Pacific. He planned to double the mileage, making it one of the great transcontinental systems of America. To his present holdings—the Wabash, the Missouri Pacific, the Texas Pacific, the St. Louis, Iron Mountain & Southern, the St. Louis Southwestern, the International & Great Northern—he added through syndicate purchase the Denver & Rio Grande, the Central Branch Railroad, and the Wheeling & Lake Erie, to make a total mileage of over sixteen thousand miles.

He became recognized as one of the seven men who "dominated the financial and railroad policies of three-fourths of the railroad territory of the United States," the others being J. P. Morgan, William K. Vanderbilt, Alexander J. Cassatt, James H. Hill, Edward H. Harriman, and William H. Moore. These men exerted a controlling interest in each railroad line, even though, in some instances, they owned less than half the stock.[40]

Eventually, however, George's dream of a system extending from San Francisco to the North River was hampered for three main reasons. First of all, unlike his father, whose constant dedication to work surpassed personal interests, George allowed "Society" to lay heavy claims upon him. The numerous sporting activities, the parties and balls at home, and the yachting trips abroad consumed large amounts of his time. Being rich, he could choose between work and play. And his choice was too often the latter. Extended trips took him far from his office at 195 Broadway. Since he disliked delegating authority to his subordinates, no one was left in charge with authority to make important business moves. If one of them assumed authority, he was usually overruled by George. On one occasion he testily remarked to the president of the Wabash, who had expressed a protest against one of his decisions, "Ramsey, can't I own my own property as I want to?"[41] Sometimes he transacted important business by cable or telegraph. This mode of operation irked his executives, encouraged bickering among them, and sowed the seeds of disloyalty.

Second, the other heirs, George's three brothers

Jay Gould, founder of the Gould railroad "empire," posed for this portrait in the late 1880s, when he was in his fifties. *Moss Archives, Falk photo*

and two sisters, were of limited help in running the "empire." Each of his three brothers—Howard, Edwin, and Frank—had elected themselves presidents of the railroads under their control. But the pressures of their domestic troubles, or their involvement in other investments, contributed to a gradual slackening of interest. George had the last word in all the disagreements among them; thus the responsibility of the business fell upon him. Had Helen Gould been chief executor of the Jay Gould estate and manager of the railroads, affairs might have been vastly different. In her interest in touring the Gould lines, she resembled her father and frequently clashed with George over policy and management. Finally, during the first few years of her stormy marriage to Boni de Castellane, Anna, the youngest, managed to diminish the family fortune by $10 million. While the Gould heirs appropriated the dividends of the railroads and failed to oversee proper maintenance, the Gould lines deteriorated.

But the most serious threat to George's goal came from another sector, a new railroad and financial power that was ultimately to weaken the control of the Gould holdings. In 1897 Edward H. Harriman, with the backing of the powerful banking firm of Kuhn, Loeb & Company, began to expend huge sums in the development of the Union Pacific Railroad—a line that paralleled the Missouri Pacific toward the north. Remaining confident of his monopoly and of his own powers, George Gould did not in time correctly assess the capabilities of his dangerous competitor or realize his intentions. Again, unlike his father, George did not fully understand the complexities of corporate operation. The ensuing amazing prosperity of the Harriman line was achieved largely at the expense of the Gould system.

Both the Gould and Harriman lines from Chicago—the Missouri Pacific and the Union Pacific—ended abruptly at Ogden, Utah. The Southern Pacific line, managed by Collis P. Huntington, was the gateway to the Pacific. Huntington impartially divided his freight traffic from the coast between Gould and Harriman, who in turn supplied him with the western flow. By playing the cards correctly, either magnate could have bought out Huntington and gained the monopoly to California and the Pacific. Since he was also a member of the Union Pacific board, Gould was disinclined to do this, whereas Harriman, with no scruples, succeeded in making the last days of Huntington miserable with his importunities. Just when the tension was becoming most acute, Huntington died. Within a two-month period, Harriman, Otto Kahn, and Jacob Schiff, the astute president of Kuhn, Loeb & Company, purchased a majority in-

Helen Gould, *right,* and her friend tour the Gould railroad "empire" in a comfortable parlor car. *Lyndhurst, a Property of the National Trust Historic Preservation*

terest in the Southern Pacific stock from Huntington's widow. Then Gould really became aware of Harriman's true intentions and approached him about purchasing a half interest in the stock. The latter's refusal sparked George into action. He went ahead with plans for his own access to the coast, a new line—the Western Pacific Railroad, from Salt Lake City to San Francisco.

By 1901 a Harriman-Gould feud was in full progress. Gould was expelled from the Union Pacific board. As Gould proceeded with expansion, Harriman did his best to bottle up the Gould lines. Meanwhile, during these same years George, with great daring, made the decision to build eastward to the Atlantic. The practical difficulties for this eastward move were enormous. In addition to purchasing the Lake Erie Railroad and the controlling interest in the Western Maryland, he planned to take in a Pittsburgh station on the way to the coast. This eventual penetration of Pennsylvania Railroad territory alienated its president, Alexander J. Cas-

satt, so that Gould gained a powerful new enemy.

For many years the Western Union Telegraph Company, a Gould corporation, had built its poles and strung its wires along the Pennsylvania lines. Its contract with the Pennsylvania was about to expire in 1902. When Cassatt learned about Gould's purchase of the Western Maryland, he notified him that he would not renew his contract on any terms. As Gould vacillated and appealed to the courts for protection against the Pennsylvania, Cassatt acted swiftly and mercilessly. He sent men to destroy all the Western Union poles. Within a two-day period, 60,000 poles and 1500 miles of telegraph line were leveled—a destruction of $5 million worth of property. Cassatt gave the right-of-way instead to Western Union's rival, the Postal Telegraph Company.

Gould's projected move into Pennsylvania territory had also alienated his own Missouri Pacific bankers, Kuhn, Loeb & Company. He found sympathetic allies, however, in the Equitable Life Assurance Society. Since during this era clever men took advantage of every opportunity for personal profit, it was no particular crime for life-insurance companies to participate in speculative railroad finance. Having formed a syndicate composed of himself, James Hazen Hyde, Louis Fitzgerald, and men closely identified with the insurance company, they raised $20 million for the Pittsburgh enterprise.

Between 1901 and 1905 the Gould company built sixty miles of track, requiring twenty tunnels and almost as many bridges, from the terminus of the Wheeling and Lake Erie at Jewett, Ohio, into Pittsburgh. Serious accidents and natural disasters plagued the operation. Against all these things Gould might have succeeded had it not been for other unfortunate circumstances. First of all, he shifted an additional $20 million in expenses upon his Wabash line—a burden that ultimately ruined it. Second, he blundered in failing to take into consideration that his new line was, in fact, primarily a freight road, whereas the station he built in Pittsburgh, approached by an elevated track, was designed for passengers, not for freight. Moreover, neither the Wabash Pittsburgh nor the Wheeling and Lake Erie terminal was double-tracked. Sympathetic to Gould's goals, the Carnegie Steel Company had tons of freight ready for transport, but the Gould line had no loading facilities. Third, the financial panic of 1907 seriously jeopardized the entire operation. Railroad stocks dropped drastically in value. By 1908 the move eastward seemed doomed and the entire Gould "empire" was in danger of dissolution.

The Wabash Pittsburgh line, with practically no business, passed into the hands of receivers. That same year the Wheeling and Lake Erie declared its insolvency. The International and Great Northern, the Wabash, and the Western Maryland went into receivership. The Denver and Rio Grande and the Missouri Pacific degenerated under mismanagement. Although the Gould lines badly needed money, no banking house was ready to provide it. The crisis was compounded by the fact that an issue of $8 million in notes on the Wheeling and Lake Erie Railroad was coming due. The holders of these notes dominated the Gould lines east of the Mississippi River. As a result of these misfortunes Gould lost the confidence and support of the men who had made his syndicates, as well as the services and allegiance of at least two of his strongest railroad men—Joseph Ramsey, Jr., and Russell Harding.

After this Pittsburgh debacle the newsmen referred to George Gould as the "sick man of the railroad powers." But writing in the magazine *World's Work* around that time, C. M. Keys makes a sympathetic assessment of Gould's situation, saying:

> To every man who attempts great things there comes a moment of fearful crisis, of nervebreaking strain, of terrible pregnant decision. To Mr. Gould it came in the midst of the "rich man's panic," in what looked like a long period of collapse. He failed at that moment to rise to the occasion. It was a fearful occasion, and there may not be in the United States a man who could have met it under those circumstances.[42]

Certainly George Gould did not lack ability. He at times displayed great energy and courage. But his indecisiveness and his vacillation resulted in moves that were of dubious value to the railroads and inimical to his banking connections. Had he been, on the whole, a more aggressive and masterful person, a more astute and careful organizer, he might, in spite of these misfortunes, have realized his goals.

Ironically, at that point Gould's bitterest enemy, Edward H. Harriman, came forward to "bail him out"—on his own terms, of course. Having formed a syndicate with Kuhn, Loeb & Company, he paid off the notes on the Wheeling and Lake Erie. Meanwhile John D. Rockefeller had been buying heavily in the stock of the Western Maryland. A committee financed by Harriman's banking company took over the bankrupt Wabash. Thus a Harriman-Kuhn-Loeb-Rockefeller financial power assumed a position of vantage in the reorganization of the eastern Gould lines.

Between 1905 and 1908, while Gould was losing his railroads in the east, construction work continued on his Western Pacific road, despite delays incident to the San Francisco earthquake of 1906, the panic of 1907, and recurring hostilities with Harriman's Union Pacific–Southern Pacific lines. But his hold on the Missouri Pacific was being seriously threatened. Gould was no match for the clever Harriman, who had become a tactless, overbearing tyrant. When Harriman died on 9 September 1909, he could count one less enemy. However, Kuhn, Loeb & Company had purchased heavily at 1907–8 panic prices in the stock of this railroad. Rockefeller had acquired a large interest in the Missouri Pacific, of which the Deutsche Bank of Berlin, representing substantial German investment, was a minority stockholder. In 1911 they pooled their resources in an advertised attempt to eliminate the Goulds and gain control of this line. Moreover, since Gould's disgruntled stockholders had had no dividends in four years, they were more than willing to vote for new management. By the spring of 1911 Gould recognized the hopelessness of the situation and agreed to retire as president of the Missouri Pacific and to relinquish the directorate to representatives of Kuhn, Loeb &

Company, John D. Rockefeller, and the Deutsche Bank.

However, when the time came to retire, Gould refused. Making one last attempt to hold on to the railroad, he turned to the powerful banking firm of James Speyer & Company, currently hostile to Kuhn, Loeb & Company, and sought funds for the rehabilitation of the Missouri Pacific. This firm agreed to provide an initial $23 million in return for his surrender of the presidency. A new president, under the supervision of the bankers, was to control the money.

And so, remaining in nominal control, George Gould apparently turned the tables upon his enemies. He elected a new Gould board of directors. James Speyer was given the place occupied by a representative of Kuhn, Loeb & Company. B. F. Bush was named the new president of the Missouri Pacific. Gould himself, a member of the board of directors, remained the largest stockholder and bondholder of this line as well as of the Denver and Rio Grande, the line that connected it with his new Western Pacific.

By 1 July 1911 the Western Pacific was completed at a total cost of $77,797,797 and opened to full operation. Adhering to exacting standards of construction, Gould's company had created one of the most spectacular examples of railroad engineering of its day. Tracks were laid with heavy rails. Forty bridges were constructed of cement and steel. Forty-three tunnels, which had been cut through the Sierras, resulted in the lowest road grades of any transcontinental line. This road was to revolutionize the carrying of freight from Salt Lake City to San Francisco.

During the last few years of the construction of this line, a situation developed that was to work for awhile in Gould's favor. Between 1908 and 1911 the United States government prosecuted its suit for the dissolution of the competing line—the Union Pacific–Southern Pacific merger—as a combination in restraint of trade under the Federal Anti-Trust Law. Finally, after a lengthy legal battle, on 2 December 1912 the Supreme Court ordered the Union Pacific to dispose of its Southern Pacific stock. This decision was a victory for George Gould and a blow against the men who were continuing the Harriman schemes of railroad combination and conquest, namely, Jacob Schiff, Otto H. Kahn, and Robert S. Lovett. With his own access to the coast, Gould had established a powerful rival to the Union Pacific. Given sufficient time he could have succeeded in diverting more business toward his own line. His competitors, however, had no intention of relinquishing the battle for control of traffic to San Francisco.

By 1914, although the Western Pacific was experiencing traffic growth, it fell far short of earning the interest on the First Mortgage debt. Pressures to sell out were forthcoming from the Union Pacific directors. To make matters worse, the directors of Gould's Missouri Pacific needed help with notes of $25 million that were coming due on 1 June 1914. Once again James Speyer & Company came to the rescue to insure solvency for this line. Meanwhile Gould feared that the Missouri Pacific was headed for receivership. Accordingly, while openly defying his enemies, he quietly effected an entire surrender. A private letter of 14 May 1914, addressed to his sister Anna, the duchesse de Talleyrand, was made public in 1919 when she and her brother Frank brought an action in the New York State courts for the removal of George as executor of Jay Gould's estate. The letter reads:

> Some weeks ago the railroad situation was looking so uncertain that Ed. and I, in consultation, decided to sell the Missouri Pacific stock held by the estate and have let all go except one share. It looks as if we might drift into a receivership and, if the road does, there is no telling where the stock might go to. I was induced to recommend the above policy to the boys partly on account of notes coming due June 1 and because of this impossibility of getting banking houses to underwrite their extensions or to buy the Iron Mountain bonds under the notes. I knew, as we had a big block of stock, every one would lay down on us and expect us to do the extending or paying the $25,000,000 notes. As we stand now we are the biggest creditors and can afford to take chances with the rest. Helen I don't think approved, and I know she did not like the way the sale was made.[43]

With this move, even before the Kuhn, Loeb bankers or Wall Street knew about it, George Gould severed once and for all the control of this railroad, which for more than thirty years had been identified with the Gould name.

As Gould moved out of the Missouri Pacific directorship, Kuhn, Loeb & Company moved in in order to readjust the finances. Since the notes had been paid with the help of Speyer & Company, there was no immediate danger of bankruptcy. By 1 July 1914 these "Readjustment Managers" assumed possession of the Missouri Pacific and set out to manipulate the boards of this road, of the Denver & Rio Grande, and of the Western Pacific. Their efforts were directed toward a complete elimination of Gould interests in the railroads.

On 6 July 1914 the members of the Kuhn, Loeb firm and the directors of the Missouri Pacific met and adopted an extraordinary resolution, which was not made public until several years later when Western Pacific litigation forced it into the light:

Resolved, That this Board requests the directors who are also directors of the Denver and Rio Grande Railroad Company to express to the Board of said Denver Company that in the opinion of this Board it would be unwise to pay the September 1st coupon of the Western Pacific First Mortgage unless prior to that date the Boards of the Denver Company and the Western Pacific Company have reached an agreement respecting the rearranging of the financial relations of the two companies and until a plan based upon such agreement shall have been promulgated by the companies' bankers.[44]

Since eight of the twelve members of the Missouri Pacific board were also on the board of the Denver & Rio Grande, a conflict of interest resulted.

For the Missouri Pacific directors, this resolution of threatened repudiation and breach of contract had no rational or honest purpose. The Missouri Pacific was the Denver's principal stockholder and had an investment of its own money in excess of $10 million. The investment would almost certainly be lost by following the course of action involved in the resolution. In *Wall Street Fifty Years after Erie,* Ernest Howard assesses the situation in these words:

That resolution could not possibly have motivated anything but hostility to those interests in all their relations to the new transcontinental line in competition with the Union Pacific in which the "Readjustment Managers" had a predominating interest. They had tried to destroy that competition from without and had been foiled by the United States Department of Justice and under George W. Wickersham and by the United States Supreme Court. They were now at work from within to destroy that competing line, whether principally to their purpose in readjusting Missouri Pacific's finances or only incidentally—it does not matter which.[45]

When the directors of the Denver & Rio Grande met on 6 August 1914 to consider the resolution that came from the Missouri Pacific meeting of July 6, they registered surprise and shock. Those members who had presumably been involved in writing this resolution disavowed any connection in the matter. The question before the meeting was whether the First Mortgage bonds on the Western Pacific should be paid or should be defaulted in accordance with the resolution. Their discussions reflected no intention of giving up the Western Pacific, which had been in operation only three years and in which $40 million of the Denver's money had been placed. The large attendance of the directors, among them George Gould and his son Kingdon, reflected the importance of the deliberations. Edgar L. Marston, one of the interlocking directors, made a resolution in favor of payment. The majority of the directors adopted this resolution. The Western Pacific First Mortgage coupon was paid on 1 September.

But before this meeting adjourned, according to Ernest Howard, there was apparent "some tendency to yield to the whispered and tempting suggestions coming by way of the Missouri Pacific's repudiation resolution that the Denver's burdens might be lightened in respect to the Western Pacific with a coerced if not a voluntary consent of the latter's bondholders."[46] A statement was prepared to this effect but not expressly ordered for publication. When it leaked to the press, it belied the attitude of the board taken in the Marston decision in favor of the Missouri Pacific resolution of 6 July. Thus, at this meeting the Denver directors had declared the value of the Western Pacific and at the same time regarded it as a burden.

As a member of the board, Gould was finding his position more and more precarious. His enemies on both boards, stalling for time, became involved in confusing and tumultuous meetings, in excessive wrangling with the bondholders, and in extensive and costly litigation. Their diversities of interests, loyalties, and purposes resulted in a deadlock. When the next quarter payment on the Mortgage coupon came due on 1 March 1915 and no money had been turned over to the Trustee of the Western Pacific bonds, default ensued. Obviously, the Denver was unwilling to bear the burden. On 3 March 1915 the Western Pacific went into receivership.

George Jay Gould had already lost his railroads east of the Mississippi. Furthermore, he had been driven out of the Missouri Pacific. The Western Pacific had now been cleverly detached from the Denver & Rio Grande. His position on the Denver board had been made hopeless. Consequently, his transcontinental system must have become no more than a bitter memory.

No one at the time, not even his closest associates, could understand him or surmise what was going on in his mind. No one knows for certain just what part Gould played in all of these dealings. For many years he had fought against the removal of the Gould name from the railroad map. Despite all of the intricate machinations against him, he somehow managed to look after his personal financial interests. When he fell, he did nothing on behalf of the minority stockholders who had lost their investment. Several years later, on 17 April 1922, a case was brought up in Justice Delehanty's court in New York City where, speaking as guardian for the children of Anna Gould in an estate battle with her brother, the lawyer William

Nelson Cromwell sums up this handling of the railroads in these words:

> I knew the late Jay Gould as a great railroad man, though we may differ as to the extent of his greatness. The son had the egotism to believe that he had inherited his father's greatness. This great railroad magnate ruined a dozen railroads in the Gould system. The roads went into his hands prosperous and came out wrecked. He showed the most idiotic hypocrisy. The roads were rehabilitated and refinanced until his pockets bulged. It is one of the the most remarkable instances of finance of which the world has ever heard. He started with a bombastic flourish and ended with a wreckage colossal.[47]

He had failed as a railroad developer, but through his keen speculative instincts and by means of his market operations he could still be numbered among America's multimillionaires.

However, it must be conceded that because of his indomitable ego and will to succeed, and despite his uncertain judgments and nearsighted calculations, George Gould had played a significant role in the development of the cross-continent railroad system of the United States. For many years he had maintained supremacy over a vast and fruitful territory.

Heirs and Heiresses

In the midst of all these business vicissitudes, life was as delightful as ever at the Gould mansions in Lakewood and New York. The weekends were spent at Georgian Court where George and Edith usually entertained four or five parlor carfuls of city guests. Colorful tallyhos met them at the railroad station and transported them to the estate in picturesque procession. Some were lodged in the mansion, others at the Casino, or at nearby Laurel-in-the-Pines. Away from the tribulations of the railroad disputes, George was the solicitous and genial sportsman-host. Edith, the ever-charming hostess, arranged these weekend gaieties with consummate artistry. Balls said to rival those at Buckingham Palace attracted a steady stream of pleasure seekers. Masquerade parties turned the great hall of the mansion into a place of lively revelry.

In the relaxed setting of this country paradise, international poloists and court tennis players as well as the great ones of the theater world mingled with the "aristocracy" of New York and Lakewood: Harry Lehr, "King Lehr" of the social set and inveterate opportunist, following on the heels of Edith's dear friend Mrs. Stuyvesant Fish, found Gould hospitality entirely to his liking. In his sparkling illustrations the artist Howard Chandler Christy captured the regal splendor of the mansion décor and the glitter of the fashionable crowds.[48]

During the week the family usually went to New York to be on hand for the opera and other social events. On opening nights at the Metropolitan Opera House, Edith was one of the most resplendent women in the Diamond Horseshoe. On these special nights it was not unusual for her to wear her celebrated pearls and jeweled tiara. Of course, a detective always sat close by to guard the precious stones. Yet display of the jewels was not her reason for attending. A real music lover, she had a keep appreciation of opera. The famous tenor Enrico Caruso once said that he sang better when Mrs. Gould was in the audience, for he felt that he was singing to a critic as well as a patron. Years later, after Edith's death, a gentleman sitting next to her daughter Edith at the Metropolitan said, "The opera does not seem the same to me any more since I cannot look up and see Mrs. George Gould."[49] Undoubtedly the Goulds had a personal interest in the opera house, for Jay Gould had contributed a considerable sum toward its construction.

As the children reached their mid-teens, Mr. and Mrs. Gould planned for their entrance into the social world. The care that they had always lavished upon their children was in no way diminished. For example, when Marjorie was old enough to go out with young men, she was always accompanied by a chaperone. When young men called at the Gould home, one of the governesses would remain in the drawing room. She would sew or knit and from time to time try to draw her young charges into conversation about studious topics.

On 7 January 1909 Marjorie made her debut into New York society. She had been named Marjorie Gwynne after the character Edith had portrayed in the play *Love on Crutches* on the night when she first met George. Beautiful, charming, and poised, she was one of the most popular girls that year.

The Goulds host a masquerade party. George is seated in the center of the fourth step; Edith is standing to his left costumed in a dark gown and large white hat. *Courtesy of George A. Bishop, copy photo Vincent Hart*

The occasion was marked by a brilliant dinner dance at the Plaza, an affair of the utmost grandeur. According to newspaper accounts, the entire first floor, a suite of twenty rooms, was reserved for the function. These rooms were transformed into bowers and pergolas, with Southern smilax intertwined with hundreds of American Beauty roses. In great abundance, too, were choice orchids from England and Kentia palms from the South Seas. In the drawing room Mrs. Gould and Marjorie received the guests, the mother in pale blue satin and her wonderful ropes of pearls, daughter Marjorie radiant in satin charmeuse, the color of American Beauty roses, a single American Beauty rose in her dark hair. Following the cotillion led by Phoenix Ingraham and Miss Gould, fabulous golden favors were distributed to the guests. There were jeweled pins, rings, and charms for the women, and jeweled scarf pins for the men.

Afterward the guests dined sumptuously, drank choice wines from France, and danced till dawn.

The splendid affair was eclipsed only by Marjorie's wedding the following year to Anthony J. Drexel, Jr., scion of the famous banking family. For months before the wedding all events connected with it were duly reported in the newspapers, including a description of the wedding cake, which cost $2,600. At the bakery on West Sixty-eighth Street this concoction and eight hundred heart-shaped white satin boxes for the slices were guarded by policemen the night before the wedding. The next day, 19 April 1910, a crowd larger than had ever been assembled for a New York wedding braved the pouring rain as they waited near Saint Bartholomew's Church on Madison and Forth-fourth Street for a glimpse of the bride and groom. The interior of the church was a bower of spring flowers—calla lillies, pink roses, apple blossoms, and daisies. Bridesmaids and flower girls were dressed in blue satin and pink chiffon; the bride was arrayed in white satin charmeuse. These

The great hall is crowded with costumed guests and "butlers-in-waiting." *Courtesy of George A. Bishop, copy photo Vincent Hart*

Edith's mother, Mary Carter Kingdon, poses before the masquerade with George, Jr. and her namesake, Kingdon. *Moss Archives, Pach photo*

lovely spring colors were echoed by the costly gowns of the hundreds of socialites who had been favored with an invitation. Later, following a lavish reception at the Gould mansion on Fifth Avenue, the couple left for Furlough Lodge in the Catskills. As a wedding gift George gave them a mansion of their own, a completely furnished house at 1015 Fifth Avenue.

Special family events were occasions for added splendor at Georgian Court. On Vivien Gould's eighteenth birthday a Colonial Ball made the date, 7 May 1910, a memorable one. The fête also honored Marjorie and Anthony Drexel, who had just returned from their honeymoon. The grounds of the estate were elaborately decorated. Many of the townspeople flocked to its wrought-iron fence to catch a glimpse of the enchanted region with its illuminated water fountains and thousands of electric lanterns hung throughout the gardens.

Masked and clad in full Colonial attire, the guests assembled at the Casino, where each gentleman selected his partner. Then, with George and Martha Washington at the head of the procession, they made their way to the mansion for dancing. Lavishly decorated with spring blossoms, the entire first floor was used for the ball and for the tableaux planned as entertainment by the younger Gould children and their friends, likewise costumed in Colonial garb. The orchestra from New York, stationed in the hallway and concealed by screens and huge palms, played till dawn. The silk and satin costumes and powdered wigs effectively disguised the dancers until midnight, when the signal for unmasking was given.

During that spring eighteen-year-old Vivien met a dashing officer named Jack Beresford, who had come to Lakewood with the British polo team for the international competition matches. When they encountered each other at the edge of the Georgian

In April 1910 Marjorie Gould married Anthony J. Drexel, Jr. *Courtesy of George A. Bishop, copy photo Vincent Hart*

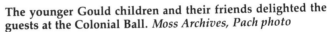

The younger Gould children and their friends delighted the guests at the Colonial Ball. *Moss Archives, Pach photo*

Court field, it was love at first sight. When her parents became aware of the infatuation, they were not pleased. Although from a good family, Beresford was in his forties and currently quite penniless. Then one day a few months later, Jack's older brother suddenly died and plain Major Jack Beresford fell heir to a title. Overnight he was transformed into a thoroughly acceptable suitor for Vivien's hand.

On 10 January 1911 the Goulds happily announced their daughter's engagement to John Graham Hope Horsley Beresford, fifth Baron Decies, lieutenant colonel of the Seventh Hussars and a member of the Distinguished Service Order. Preparations began for another splendid wedding only a month away. Edith hired two hundred and twenty-five dressmakers to make every piece of the trousseau; George ordered a diamond coronet for the new Lady Decies. This time reporters noted that the wedding cake was bedecked with electric lights and cupids emblazoned with the Decies coat of arms.

On 8 February Vivien and her lord were married at Saint Bartholomew's Church in New York City. Outside, mounted police tried to keep the thousands of onlookers in check; inside, the invited guests pushed and shoved one another for a glimpse of the celebrated wedding gown. Not only the beautiful gowns of the bride and her attendants but also the magnificent military uniforms of the groom and his ushers dazzled the excited crowds. After an elaborate reception at the Gould mansion on Fifth Avenue, the happy couple sailed for England and a manor house purchased with Vivien's dowry.

Several months later, on 29 April Jay, the Goulds' second son, married the lovely Anne Douglass Graham, member of an excellent family, in a beautiful ceremony at Saint Thomas's Church on Fifth Avenue, New York. Once again the crowd was so large that police had to clear the entrance for the bridal party. Anne's cousin the Princess Kawansnakoa of Hawaii attracted a large share of attention, too, both at the church and at the reception. As was their usual custom, all the Goulds gave precious jewels to the bride. Jay's gift to his bride was a town house on Fifth Avenue, not far from his parents' mansion.

The happiness of these first months of 1911 gave way to sorrow in June when Edith's mother, Mary Carter Kingdon, died. Ever since her daughter's marriage to George, Mrs. Kingdon had enjoyed comfortable suites in the Gould mansions and shared in the life of the family. Not only were Edith and her mother very close, but George also simply adored his mother-in-law. They spent many hours together. Although he loathed the game of crib-bage, he played it with her evening after evening. When her sight began to fail, he often read the newspapers to her. Having had no sons of her own, she found a son entirely to her liking in George. She also squandered her affection upon the children, especially Kingdon, her namesake.

The happiest years of her life were spent at Lakewood. Popular in the town, she was a leader in all kinds of charitable enterprises. Like Edith, this gracious lady dearly loved All Saints Episcopal Church, and gave time and contributions to its parish activities. They are also both remembered for three beautiful stained-glass windows placed in the church in memory of Edith's sister, Catherine Mary Kingdon, who had died at the age of four. Executed in Art Nouveau style, their jewellike colors complement the dark-timbered interior of the little church.

An active and energetic woman, she made light of the infirmities of advancing years. That May, when the family sailed for Europe on the *Kronprinzessin Cecilie*, Mrs. Kingdon accompanied them with the intention of spending the summer at Divonne-les-Bains on the Franco-Swiss border, a place noted for its curative treatments. The sea voyage, however, proved too much for her. Taken seriously ill, she died suddenly in Edith's arms at the Ritz Hotel in Paris shortly after their arrival. The funeral was held at the American Church in Paris.

Edith was grief-stricken. But the summer visits with relatives in France and England helped to alleviate her sorrow. They stayed first with George's sister Anna, who was now the duchesse de Talleyrand. For her life with Boni de Castellane in the pink palace on the Avenue de Bois de Boulogne had proved to be a marital and financial disaster. Consequently, in 1906 she divorced him, and two years later married his cousin, the prince de Sagan, who later became the duc de Talleyrand. The family then went on to London to spend some time with Vivien, the new Lady Decies, before the annual grouse shooting in August at Perthshire, Scotland.

Whenever the Goulds returned from their summer sojourns, the newspapers duly noted that their arrival back in town would mark the opening of another brilliant social season, climaxing as always in the Christmas round of festivities. Not only the affairs for society folk were newsworthy, but also the intimate family gatherings. At Christmas time a huge tree lighted with colored bulbs stood in the great hall of the mansion. Poinsettias from the greenhouse were placed here and there, and laurel and holly greens adorned the staircase and walls. Piled under the tree were mounds of gifts for the family, relatives, guests, and servants.

Every member of the family hung a stocking from the mantelpiece. Appropriately, George, Sr., used a long golf stocking.

On Christmas Eve Edith always played Santa Claus as George watched and reveled in his bounty. And bounty it was, for in addition to all kinds of toys—wonderful dolls, doll trunks lined with clothes, musical chairs, toy tea sets, and many games—the Gould children would often receive silver milk mugs, or jewelry, or little fur muffs. Sometimes their gifts could not be wrapped: electric automobiles that they could drive around the estate, or Shetland ponies, or even a set of electric trains large enough to seat a little engineer. These gifts, of course, hidden in the carriage house, were noted by special ownership papers. Edith Gould Wainwright describes a favorite toy that she received when she was seven—a tiny theater that had a curtain that rolled up and down, fifty changes of scenery, and electric lights that illuminated the fairy-tale characters.

The children, instructed in the art of giving by their beloved governesses, delighted their elders with presents that they had labored over for several months. There were pin cushions for all the family, embroidered bureau scarves and table covers for their mother, embroidered slippers or a waistcoat for their father, and all sorts of useful gifts. Even Archer, the French poodle, and Swifty, the fox terrier, received new collars.

After luncheon on Christmas Day, there was an annual custom known as "the Christmas Tree." The employees brought their children to romp with the Gould children. During the afternoon all

the little guests received toys and candy from the branches of the magnificent tree. Gold pieces were distributed to the household servants in proportion to the length of time each had been in the Gould service. In addition, as was his annual custom, George Gould also brought Christmas joy and gladness to many a Lakewood home as hampers of food and toys were taken to the needy families in the village.

At the annual Christmas Bazaar at All Saints, Edith Gould always took care of one of the booths. One local resident relates that she was so beautiful that little girls would willingly pay the admission fee just to gaze at her in awe. Along with other gracious ladies of the parish, Edith often raised several thousand dollars within a few hours.

The Goulds were well liked in the town. In addition to the fabled parties for the grown-ups, the children often entertained their little friends, formally or informally. As the Lakewood historian Mary Hurlburt relates, she and others often played with Gloria Gould. Under the watchful eye of the servants, the children played "hide-and-seek" in and out the lovely bedrooms, and "London Bridge" in the great hall. In the winter they went ice skating on the lake with an instructor in charge. During the warmer months rowing was a special treat, with the estate lagoon as the point of departure and return. The older children who were away at colleges or finishing schools often brought back friends for the weekends or vacation periods. When referring to these times when she attended the Charlton School in New York, Edith Wainwright remembers: "I always looked forward to Fridays when I could go back to my beloved Georgian Court."[50]

During the World War I years Edith Gould and other society women did whatever they could to

Under the watchful eye of the chauffeur, the Gould children enjoy their own autos. *Left to right:* **Kingdon, Marjorie, George, Jr., Jay, and Vivien.** *Georgian Court College, Pach photo*

help the war effort. On one occasion they sponsored an illustrated lecture, "France: Its Romance, Beauty, and Art" by Arthur Stanley Riggs, which netted $1500 for the aid of the French soldiers disabled in battle as well as the destitute women of France. During this afternoon affair her daughter-in-law Anne Gould sold medals specially designed by the French sculptor Lalique for the benefit of French war orphans. Edith also assisted Mrs. William Randolph Hearst, who had organized an Officers' Canteen at the New York Public Library. As chairman of the Mayor's Committee of Women on National Defense, Edith directed entertainments given at the Brooklyn Navy Yard and at various hospitals in the city. As might be expected, she took an active part in the work of the Red Cross. It is said that every phase of human concern attracted her interest and cooperation.

In 1918 she celebrated her birthday in Lakewood in a very special way. At that time the Lakewood Hotel was set aside by the government as General Hospital No. 9 for the returning wounded veterans. In the early afternoon of 18 August sixty soldiers from the hospital were transported to the Georgian Court party. Tables and chairs were arranged on the lawn in front of the mansion and seven butlers waited to serve. As the soldiers enjoyed a sumptuous repast, Edith greeted them individually and charmed them all with her beauty and gracious warmth.

Little Gloria Gould, aged ten, made her own special contribution to the war effort. Having written a play entitled The Lost Child, she produced a benefit performance in the rose garden of the estate with her little friends as the audience. The net proceeds of $38.50 accompanied a letter to the Red Cross in which she stipulated that the sum was to be used for the soldiers stationed near the Mexican border. A childhood playmate recalls that Gloria, who delighted in staging little theatricals, had trunks of costumes available for her use. Evidently Edith Gould was proud of her daughter's talents and provided necessary props. These playlets were often presented on the semicircular portico at the west end of the Casino, with the Gould house guests as the audience.

Thus far the Gould children were a constant delight to their parents. The care lavished on their upbringing seemed amply rewarded. Marjorie, Jay, and Vivien, who had married well, were firmly established in society. But in the spring of 1917 Edith became aware that her eldest son, Kingdon, was having a flirtation with their Italian governess, Signorina Annunciata Camilla Maria Lucci. From a fine but impoverished family, she had come to America eight years before to study art. Lacking sufficient means, she sought employment

with the Goulds. One day, while having tea with her friend Elizabeth Drexel Lehr, Edith confided her knowledge of the affair and her resolve to terminate it at once. As recounted by Mrs. Lehr in "King Lehr" and the Gilded Age, Edith sent for the lovely governess and tried to reason with her. Signorina Lucci listened in silence and then firmly insisted that Kingdon loved her and planned to marry her. The governess was promptly dismissed and left Lakewood that very day. A musician as well as a talented artist, she took an apartment in New York and set up a studio.

At twenty-nine Kingdon Gould was not to be thwarted. On 2 July 1917 he married Annunciata, a Catholic, in the rectory of Saint Patrick's Cathedral. The couple took an apartment on Sixty-sixth Street and Park Avenue. Kingdon saw his father frequently at the office, but Edith was inconsolable and refused to speak to him. However, when he enlisted in the army a few months later, her motherly heart was so softened by his courageous act that a reconciliation of sorts was effected. Edith could not yet bring herself to accept his wife. Nevertheless, she hastened to visit her son, stationed at Camp Dix, New Jersey. Bringing a party for all the men of the seventy-eighth Division, she urged him to visit Georgian Court whenever possible. At camp Kingdon was always careful to be just "one of the boys." When he was ready to leave, however, the chauffeur would be waiting just outside the gate. As local residents relate, generous Kingdon usually brought with him an automobile full of Lakewood boys. In 1918 he went overseas where his efficient handling of work at the Intelligence Office won him a promotion to the rank of lieutenant.

In the meantime, just five days after Kingdon's wedding, Edith suffered another shock when George, Jr., married Laura Carter of Ardena, New Jersey, in the home of Philadelphia's "marrying parson." This pretty young lady and talented dancer had been a recent graduate of Freehold High School, an orphan under the charge of Mr. and Mrs. D. P. Callahan, formerly of New York. Although they were snubbed by George and Edith, brother-in-law Tony Drexel came to their rescue and gave George, Jr., a job in his brokerage firm of Ligett, Drexel, and Company at 61 Broadway and the couple settled down in a New York apartment.

Daughter Edith was now attending Miss Spence's School in New York. During the summer of 1919, while visiting with a school friend at Easthampton, Long Island, she met and fell in love with Carroll L. Wainwright. He was a young man of good family—tenth in descent from Peter Stuyvesant on his father's side; his mother was a Philadelphia Snowden. But when Mrs. Gould became aware of the developing romance, her hopes were dashed for just the right match for her daughter, for Carroll was only nineteen and furthermore was aspiring to be a portrait painter. She confided to a close friend a plan to discourage the liaison, namely, to send young Edith abroad for several years. Hearing of this intended obstacle to their happiness Edith and Carroll planned to elope.

However, they did not act until after her graduation from Miss Spence's School on 25 May 1920. That night she placed some clothing and jewelry in a small handbag and hoped to find an opportunity to leave the house the next morning. Providence came to her aid when her father offered to drop her off at school in order to pick up some books she had forgotten. She telephoned Carroll to meet her a block below the school. Since his daughter was carrying only a small bag, presumably for the books, George suspected nothing. He left her at the school with word that the governess would call for her a little later.

A few minutes afterward Edith hurried from the building. Carroll was waiting for her a block away. They quickly boarded a train for Philadelphia, where they intended to be married. But because they were both below the legal age in Pennsylvania, the clerk at the marriage license office suggested that they go on to Elkton, Maryland, where the laws were more elastic. Having rented an automobile, they drove to Elkton. A sympathetic minister married them at three o'clock in the morning.

Aware that her parents were not at Georgian Court that week, Edith went back for her clothing and with her new husband departed for Atlantic City. Following a blissful honeymoon at the Marlborough-Blenheim, they took an apartment in Greenwich Village, New York, where with clandestine assistance from the Gould servants Edith learned to cook and manage a household. For several months Mrs. Gould stubbornly ignored the newlyweds. Eventually, however, all was forgiven at a family reunion on New Year's Day at Georgian Court.

The Goulds grew very fond of Carroll and of their new grandson Stuyvesant, born a year later. They leased an apartment for the young couple at Park Avenue and Eighty-first Street so that they could be closer to the family mansion. Now, to the delight of Edith and George, all of their married children, with the exception of Vivien in England, lived nearby, at least part of each year. Kingdon, Jay, Marjorie, George, Jr., and Edith gathered frequently with their offspring, numbering eleven, for happy family affairs. During the summer months as many as possible crossed the ocean to visit Lord and Lady Decies and their three children.

Gloria Gould was just fifteen at the time of her mother's death. *Georgia Court College Archives*

It seemed that events could not have shaped themselves more pleasantly for the Goulds until the great tragedy occurred that was to change their lives. Just fifteen, Gloria Gould, the last unmarried child and pampered darling of the entire family, went to New York on a beautiful weekend in mid-November 1921, to visit with her sister Edith and her husband and to attend a football game at New Haven. On Saturday the solicitous mother telephoned from Lakewood to remind her daughters to dress warmly for the game and to remember their rubbers. She announced her intention to come to New York the following day and to attend the opening of the opera season on Monday evening.

Late Sunday morning they were horrified when they received the call telling them that their mother was dead. They learned that after attending services at the parish church, their parents had gone out to play a round of golf on their private course. Their mother had just driven the ball off the fifth tee, not far from the large oak that is still standing, when she fell to the ground without uttering a cry.[51]

George's eye was upon the ball as it left the tee. When he turned after watching it drop to the earth, he saw his wife lying on the ground. He thought

The large oak on the Gould course, near the spot where Edith collapsed. *Courtesy of William Sandy*

that she had fainted. After trying to revive her, he carried her to the Casino nearby. A caddy was immediately sent to call a physician. When Dr. George W. Lawrence and Dr. Irwin H. Hance arrived about twenty minutes later, Edith Gould was dead. They said that she had had a heart attack. Upon examining her they learned that she was wearing a rubber suit that encased her from collarbone to ankles. Also contributing to Edith's death may have been her attempts at dieting, one of which was the consumption of large quantities of thyroid pills, which many women were finding helpful to reduce weight. Along with constant exercise Edith had used these means in an attempt to retain her legendary figure.

Having been quickly summoned, all of the Gould children, with the exception of Vivien in England, arrived that very day. Stunned and broken-hearted, they found it hard to believe that their beautiful mother, who was always full of life and enthusiasm, was no more.

A simple funeral service was held from the mansion in Lakewood and at Saint Bartholomew's Church in New York City. The officiating minister was the Reverend Ernest E. Matthew, rector of the Church of Heavenly Rest in New York, who had been for many years pastor of All Saints Episcopal Church in Lakewood and a good friend and adviser to Edith. A crowd of at least a thousand stood in respectful silence outside the Gould mansion in New York and at the church when the pallbearers carried the coffin to the hearse. Interment was in Woodlawn Cemetery in the Gould mausoleum, near which stands a beautiful weeping beech tree.

With Edith's death the curtain went down on the idyllic years at Georgian Court. Her daughter Edith recalls that "mother's sudden death made the Gould family seem like a ship without a captain." Edith continues: "She had dominated our lives and we literally did not know what to do without her; we could not adjust ourselves to her going."[52] The

sizable estate that this gracious lady left her children—dozens of pieces of jewelry worth almost a million dollars, the Fifth Avenue mansion, furs, wraps, and gowns—could in no way compensate them for her absence. They never forgot her constant attempts to make certain that life would deal gently with them. Poor little Gloria went to live with her brother Kingdon.

Heartbroken over Edith's death, and the constant target of accusation by his brothers and sisters for his mismanagement of the Gould fortune, George turned more and more to Guinevere Sinclair, who had been his secret love for almost eight years. It happened that on the evening of 30 December 1913 he had attended a musical farce, George Edwardes's London gaiety production *The Girl in the Film*, at the Forty-fourth Street Theater. That evening Guinevere, a tall, slender blonde beauty from Dublin, acted as understudy for Emmy Mehlen. Middle-aged George was again smitten by an actress. Although the play was unsuccessful and the company returned to London, Guinevere remained in New York in a comfortable apartment at West Seventy-fourth Street near Riverside Drive. In the country she became mistress of a large estate on Manursing Island just off Rye, New York, known as the old Cromwell place.

The blonde beauty Guinevere Sinclair, whom George Gould married in 1922. *Moss Archives, Pach photo*

Edith and George in an earlier, happier moment. *Museum of the City of New York*

George Gould obviously frequented this gray stone house of many gables, for his yacht was often sighted off the private pier of the estate. Guinevere also had a farm of two hundred seventy acres at Doansberg, six miles north of Brewster and just off the main highway to the Berkshires, which she and George sometimes visited. By 1922 there were three more little heirs to George's dwindling fortune—George Sinclair, Jane, and Guinevere.

When his wife, Edith, had become aware of the affair, she had tried bravely to cope with it. She was torn between her continuing love for her husband and the deep hurt caused by his no longer finding in her the full satisfaction he had experienced for many happy years. Of course, she had found some distraction and comfort in the devotion of her children and the birth of each new grandchild.

On 1 May 1922 George married Guinevere Jeanne Sinclair in a private ceremony.[53] The occasion was kept such a secret that speculation on the part of journalists went on for several months before the facts were known. The wedding ceremony was performed by Judge Harry E. Newman at his home on River Avenue in Lakewood, with no relatives of either party present. According to the judge, when Gould at the simple ring service tried to slip the circlet upon the finger of his bride, it proved to be too small. He managed, however, to work it up to the middle joint. Afterward the tearful bride kissed the nervous groom and received the congratulations of the witnesses. A waiting automobile drove them in the direction of Georgian Court.

The next month the couple and their three children sailed to Europe. Stopping first in France,

Marjorie Gould Drexel's children—Anthony, Edith, and Marjorie. *Moss Archives, Pach photo*

they visited daughter Marjorie and her husband, Tony Drexel, and then went on to England and Scotland. George had leased the old Castle Grant at Inverness-shire in the Scottish Highland, which he intended to be their permanent home. This lovely place offered many of the sporting pleasures that he had always enjoyed—rolling lawns for golf, an abundance of grouse for the shooting, and streams full of salmon.

Nevertheless, their happiness was to be short-lived. During the winter George's health began to fail. In early spring, in search of better weather, he leased the Villa Zoralde at Cap Martin, Mentone, France. From there he and Guinevere went on to Egypt to show the children the famous ruins. They no sooner had arrived there than George contracted pneumonia. He hastily returned to his villa in France, where his daughter Marjorie Drexel nursed him tenderly and, as her sister Edith recalls, was a pillar of strength for the family. At three-thirty in the morning on 16 May 1923 George Gould died. After the funeral service on 19 May, his body was brought back to America and buried next to that of Edith.[54]

Likeable, sociable George, devoted father and genial sportsman, had enjoyed his millions. Having spent lavishly, he and his family had lacked nothing that money could provide. Had he been content to live and play at Georgian Court and to manage the Gould enterprises carefully, he might also have been called a successful corporate financier. At some times too trusting, at others overconfident, he lacked his father's shrewdness and drive for making money. His decision to expand his railroad holdings with not more than coverage to lean on caused his eventual loss of much of the Gould fortune. When he died he left behind him an estate confused in part by the stipulations of his father's legacy. Before Jay Gould had died in 1892, he had arranged his estate-in-trust of approximately $75 million in such a way as to keep his family together. According to the will, each one of his six children would receive exactly one-sixth of the fortune. If one of them should die, that sixth would be divided equally among the others or their heirs, who must be blood children, born in wedlock. The four eldest, George, Edwin, Howard, and Helen were named executors of the estate. With the help of Helen, George was to manage the affairs of Anna and Frank, the two youngest children.

By 1923, at the time of George's death, Jay Gould's estate-in-trust was valued at $60 million one-sixth of which belonged to George. This share plus his own wealth acquired through investment brought George's estate to about $30 million. In his will he provided for all ten of his children and

Guinevere as well. Knowledge of this proposed settlement set up a storm within the family. His brother Frank, his sister Anna, and his seven children by his first marriage fought the disposition of the money. Litigation went on for four years, with everyone unhappy except the more than fifty busy lawyers. Several million dollars went to fees, taxes, and other expenses before a settlement far below the expectation of the heirs was finally reached.

Meanwhile Kingdon Gould, the executor of his father's estate, went ahead with the plans already initiated by his father before he died, namely, the sale of their beautiful home in Lakewood. Advised by diocesan authorities that it was on the market, the Sisters of Mercy of North Plainfield, New Jersey, bid for the estate. Since the enrollment of their College of Mount Saint Mary's, founded in 1908 in North Plainfield, was rapidly increasing, the Sisters felt the need for a larger campus. It seemed providential to them when the Gould estate went on the market. Equally providential was the fact that although many wealthy people, including the actress Mary Pickford, showed interest, none wrote out a check. The Sisters were able to obtain the property for about one-half the asking price of $800,000.

Kingdon, the eldest heir, knew that with them his beloved home would be in good hands. Furthermore, he probably was aware of his mother's latent interest in Roman Catholicism, as eloqently described by his sister Edith:

> Although Mamma was a devout Episcopalian, she had a great affection for the Roman Catholic faith. She frequently remarked: "If I had not been an Episcopalian I would have liked to become a Catholic."

Kingdon Gould, the eldest heir, negotiated the sale of the estate to the Sisters of Mercy of New Jersey *Moss Archives, Pach photo*

> She had a rosary and a priedieu in her room. I know she would be glad to know that the good Sisters of Mercy are now in possession of Georgian Court and are giving so much care to everything she loved so much.[55]

Kingdon's one request that they retain the name of the estate for the college was happily honored. In the spring of 1924 the Gould estate became Georgian Court College.[56]

Part II

Georgian Court's Architect—Bruce Price

Introduction

Selected by George Gould to transform the two-hundred-acre pine forest into a comfortable home site for himself and his family—to create Georgian Court—was the famous architect Bruce Price. That "elegant gentleman and erratic genius," as Vincent Scully describes him, was admirably suited by talent and temperament to alter the scrub pine terrain and create both architecture and garden design of enduring beauty.[1] In fact, he was one of America's most able and best-known architects during the last quarter of the nineteenth century.

Price began his career during the post–Civil War building boom sparked by the growth of industrialism in the United States. Within a few decades following the war, able businessmen had built industrial empires of iron and steel, wheat and beef, steamships and railroads, real estate and banking. Metropolitan areas had grown rapidly and the expansion of the Middle and Far West had created new economic frontiers. Accompanying this material prosperity, perhaps as a result of it, American architecture ventured into new and varied stylistic directions. The first was the result of the Romantic Revival in Europe, which encouraged the use of architectural revival styles of all periods in the design of homes, public buildings, and churches. One of these styles, the High Victorian Gothic, was a popular choice of the growing number of clients. House Pattern Books supplied architects and builders with a variety of medieval motifs reintroduced by the English revivalists. With construction in combinations of wood, rough stone, brick, and tile, there developed in America a picturesque eclectic

Bruce Price, architect of Georgian Court. *Architectural Record, 1899, frontispiece*

style reflected in the work of numerous architects, including Peter B. Wight, Russell Sturgis, and Henry Hobson Richardson. The adapted use of towers and turrets, high-pitched and gabled roofs, pinnacles and arches, pendants and brackets, moldings and panels resulted in the creation of rambling structures with restless surfaces, which seemed to reflect the individualism and energies of the enterprising owners. Another popular style, the French baroque revival manner termed the "Second Empire" style, which also came to the States by way of English publications, was particularly noted in the design of imposing structures topped by the high mansard roof. Introduced for public buildings by James Renwick in his design for the Main Hall for Vassar College at Arlington near Poughkeepsie, New York, the style became popular with American architects designing not only large civic structures but also homes in the country and the suburbs.

The second major direction was represented by the development of commercial-industrial buildings. The demand for increased office space, the invention of the passenger elevator, the use of cast iron and steel construction, the fabrication of plate glass, and the need for fireproof structures all contributed to the era of the tall building. After the Chicago fire of 1871 the need for rebuilding brought a flood of ambitious architects and engineers to that city who were eventually referred to as the Chicago School. Such men as Louis Henri Sullivan, Dankmar Adler, Daniel Hudson Burnham, and John Wellborn Root were among the acknowledged leaders of tall-building design in the States. The technical challenges of tall commercial buildings soon brought out the creative capacities of architects working in New York and other metropolitan areas.

Between 1880 and 1910 a third direction in American architecture followed the teaching of the École des Beaux-Arts, the prestigious Parisian school of art and architecture, and was labeled the "Beaux-Arts" style. Although such distinguished architects as Richard Morris Hunt, his disciple George Brown Post, Charles Follen McKim, William Rutherford Mead, and Stanford White had worked successfully in the earlier styles, they now sought a return to archaeological correctness and a more academic classical approach to architecture. Having studied the grand manner of Renaissance Italy, baroque France, and Georgian England, they made creative use of traditional elements with a composition governed by classical principles. Much of the vigor of the preceding decades gave way to a restrained propriety and elegance. Moreover, in 1893 this style set the tone of the World's Columbian Exposition held at Chicago.

Thereafter, many public buildings as well as private homes became opulent derivations of European palaces and villas.

Working within the revival current, Richardson emerged as one of the most influential American architects of the last half of the nineteenth century. During the 1860s and 1870s he and his followers, assimilating European and American influences, furthered the development of domestic architecture, including that which Vincent Scully has christened the "stick style."[2] This method of building, emphasizing a candid use of wood with its flat, vertical, exterior stickwork, suggests the underlying wooden-stud structure of balloon-frame construction. In this type of construction, which originated in the West, thin vertical two-by-four-inch studs held together by nails ran the entire height of the building and thus provided a light and sturdy frame that could be sheathed with wooden siding and other suitable material. A distinctive feature of this style was the use in the verandas of thin posts and railings usually termed stickwork. Precedents for the stick style were found in the earlier frame houses of Alexander Jackson Downing, John Notman, and Alexander Jackson Davis. Such popular architectural works as Downing's *Cottage Residences* of 1842 and his *Country Houses* of 1850 had exerted a marked influence on American domestic architecture. It remained for architects of the 1860s and 1870s to further develop these influences.

During those same decades a revival of the English Renaissance style usually referred to as "Queen Anne" was brought about by the work of Richard Norman Shaw and other English architects.[3] This semi-Tudor style with its half-timbering, leaded casements, use of slate, tiles, and shingles, and its new open handling of interior space was exhibited at the Centennial Exposition at Fairmount Park, Philadelphia, from May to November 1876. Also exhibited were examples of American neo-Colonial architecture. Although this style had been in vogue at seaside resorts from about 1872, Centennial enthusiasm reinforced interest in it. The Colonial house, with its wide halls, large fireplaces, low ceilings, and rough materials, seemed somewhat allied to the Queen Anne style with which, in the hands of Richardson and other American architects, it eventually emerged to produce a new and original domestic architecture, the shingle style.[4]

From about 1880 and for over a decade the shingle style was widely adopted in the States. As Henry-Russell Hitchcock describes it, "The characteristic use of shingles as an all-over wall-covering emphasized the continuity of the exterior surface as a skin stretched over the underlying wooden skeleton of studs, in contrast to the way the preceding stick style had echoed that skeleton in the external treatment."[5] This important domestic style was differentiated from preceding styles not only in its shingled exterior but also in its more open interior. The order and symmetry of the best of these buildings hinted at a growing interest in a return to classicism.

Richardson's influence also encompassed the design of civic and religious architecture, where he borrowed more directly from the Romanesque style rather than the High Victorian Gothic. His structures of the 1870s and 1880s, emphasizing rough masonry, strong rounded forms, and heavy arched entrances, exerted a sobering influence on American architectural design. The "Richardsonian Romanesque," as it is often called, was widely imitated during the 1880s and 1890s in all types of buildings.

In his disciplined control of architectural elements, his wide variety of commissions, and his successful handling of many styles, Henry Hobson Richardson provided a link between the emerging Chicago school and the Beaux-Arts group. Although he had been trained in Paris, he abandoned the more aristocratic modes in favor of the English revival styles. However, his brilliant assistant Charles Follen McKim, likewise Paris-trained, became the leader in the reaction against him in the mid-1880s, thereby furthering the return to academicism so characteristic of the last decades of the nineteenth century.[6]

The work of Bruce Price, truly an architect for his times, reflects these divergent and sometimes antithetical streams of influence. He designed structures in all of these styles or modifications thereof, and also made original and creative contributions of his own, notably that at Tuxedo Park, New York, in the mid 1880s. His Georgian Court commission recalls the style of Georgian England and the academic classical approach.

Early Life and Training

On 12 December 1845 Bruce Price was born in Cumberland, Maryland. His grandfather, Colonel Price, was an officer of Welsh ancestry in the American Revolution. When the colonel died he left four sons, among whom he divided his wealth in a most curious way. His real property he separated into two equal shares for two of his sons. The other two sons were to get an education. William, Bruce's father, was one of the two who chose to receive an education and he became a distinguished lawyer. Soon afterward, however, the two brothers who selected property died and left William and the remaining brother, Benjamin, with wealth as well as knowledge.[7]

William Price went to Dickinson College in Carlisle, Pennsylvania. Later he studied law and in 1825 was elected a member of the State Senate. He moved from his native Washington County to Cumberland, Maryland, where on 24 May 1842, at Emmanuel Episcopal Church, he married Marion Bruce, a descendant of the famous Bruce clan of Scotland. She was the granddaughter of Norman Bruce, the first president of the First National Bank of Cumberland. About 1800 Marion's father, Upton Bruce, had settled in Allegheny County. He was a first cousin of Francis Scott Key, who wrote "The Star-Spangled Banner."[8] In 1844 William and Marion were blessed with their first child, Marion. A year later Bruce was born and baptized by the Reverend Samuel Buel, rector of the church where the parents were married.

The Price home at 27 Washington Street, which is no longer standing, was built by Bruce's father in the 1840s from drawings by the architect John Notman. It had an enormous wide hallway that led from the central, front entrance through the entire house to the rear garden door. The original appearance was later somewhat modified by the exten-

sion of the attic, the peaked gable over the main entrance, and the dormers. These additions, including several wings that were added on the main floor, were designed by Price after the house had been acquired by his family's close friends the Lowndes family. The house stood across the street from a severe 1848 Greek Revival library. Perhaps these early classic influences had some effect upon the boy, who was later to make significant contributions in the field of house planning. Bruce retained a great fondness for this house and returned to it often during his maturity, to visit and to reminisce, as well as to complete several projects in the city of Cumberland.

In the early 1850s the Price family moved to Baltimore. In 1862 William Price was elected to the State Legislature from that city. He was later appointed by President Lincoln for a term as United States District Attorney. Young Bruce attended the public schools in Baltimore and then went on to the College of New Jersey (later Princeton). But his short stay of several months there was abruptly terminated by the death of his father. Returning to Baltimore in order to assume responsibility for the family, Bruce secured a job as a shipping clerk. In the evenings he studied architectural drafting with the established Baltimore firm of Niernsee and Neilson, whose work had played an important role in the architectural character of the city.[9] In 1864 Price entered the firm as a draftsman and remained four years.[10]

In 1868 Bruce went to Paris where he studied the architecture and enjoyed the city as it was in the last years of the Second Empire. With other students he frequented the ateliers and the cafés where the Impressionists Manet, Monet, Renoir, and the others were developing their artistic theories.

Career as an Architect in Baltimore and Wilkes-Barre

After his trip abroad, Price opened an office at the southwest corner of Lexington and Charles Streets with the more experienced architect Ephraim Francis Baldwin.[11] Their partnership was brief. In fact, the only known design by this firm is the Robert E. Lee Memorial Episcopal Church in Lexington, Virginia. Located on the campus of Washington and Lee University, it was originally designed in 1871 but not completed until 1883. The firm of Baldwin and Price submitted plans that were accepted, with some modification.[12] It replaced Grace Church, built in 1844, and was later named after its most celebrated vestryman, Robert E. Lee. The design betrays its early date of conception, especially in the tower, with its series of small gables that make the transition from base to steeple. A pleasant little stone building that resembles an English country church, it defies the red-brick and white-column style of the rest of the campus.

The young architect seemed to be cordially received by the citizens of Baltimore, many of whom knew the Prices of Western Maryland, where cousins of his mother and father were living. Consequently Price, a personable young man, was in frequent attendance at social gatherings. At one of these, a musical evening, he met his bride-to-be, the sixteen-year-old Josephine Lee, the daughter of Washington and Emily Lee of Wilkes-Barre, Pennsylvania, who was attending a young ladies' finishing school. Josephine was short, plump, not particularly pretty, but quite positive and sure in her judgments. She knew that Bruce was right for her and she quickly won his affection. In anticipation of his forthcoming marriage to Josephine, Bruce Price terminated his partnership with Baldwin and moved to Wilkes-Barre.[13]

In April 1871 Mr. Lee, a wealthy coal baron, gave them the finest wedding Wilkes-Barre had seen, as well as an extended honeymoon in Europe and the promise to set Bruce up in a firm of his own on their return. The only condition of the gift of the European sojourn was that Mrs. Lee and her eight-year-old son should accompany the newlyweds. Perhaps Mrs. Lee felt that her eighteen-year-old daughter needed her watchful eye and a more responsible guardian than Bruce. As it happened, soon after their arrival in Europe, they heard that the Kimberly gold mines had just been discovered in South Africa. This news so excited the dashing young Bruce that he took farewell of his bride and her family and informed them that he would return in two years. However, after several days he realized his foolishness and hurried back to the rather stunned family. The trip continued without further surprising events. While Bruce gathered valuable architectural experience, Mrs. Lee, who was very fond of jewels, purchased a great many of them. When the wedding party returned to Wilkes-Barre, Bruce designed a large cabinet of superb craftsmanship to house her collection of jewels.[14]

In 1872 the young couple settled in Wilkes-Barre, where Bruce opened his office. During the next five years he was to become an architect of some recognized national importance. Although he worked in semi-isolation from the sophisticated and avant-garde influences of the professional architectural world, his early work indicates some familiarity with post–Civil War architectural currents. He must have read the accepted books on the subject, especially those of Henry Hudson Holly and Edward Clarence Gardner. Moreover, he probably attended the Centennial Exposition at Philadelphia in 1876, which thereafter gave such impetus to American innovations in architecture and the allied arts. It took several years, however,

The rendering of the George S. Bennett House of 1876 is an excellent example of Price's early, picturesque bold line. *American Architect and Building News*

The design of the staircase hall of the Bennett House indicates Price's interest in the then popular Jacobean style. *American Architect and Building News*

before Price's designs received recognition in the periodicals concerned with building.

A fine known example of Price's early work is the Monument in Hollenback Cemetery, Wilkes-Barre, erected to the memory of the Honorable George W. Woodward, former chief justice of the Supreme Court of Pennsylvania. After Woodward's death in Rome in 1875, his heirs erected this monument of Meshoppen blue-stone. The simple mass, twelve feet long and eight feet high, has a rough stone base with a heavy cross on top, forming a cross-axis design. Pendant wreaths at the four ends of the cross are bold, full circles of abstract design, looking like the hard stones they are

Bruce Price designed this jewel cabinet, now in the Museum of the City of New York, to hold his mother-in-law's collection of jewels. *Museum of the City of New York*

rather than the leaves they represent. Although Price was to do other monuments later in his career, he never matched the impressive, somber quality of this early one.

From this point in his career Price worked almost without interruption for the wealthy. Undoubtedly his in-laws were responsible for his early important commissions in Wilkes-Barre. In later years, however, his clients and friends included the most socially and most financially prominent families of New York and the popular resorts. Having married well, he was able to thrive as an architect despite financial loss and difficult times. Young architects of the 1870s who lacked the means to employ large staffs were forced to do most of the work themselves. Consequently, the quality of the work was higher than in succeeding decades, when the increased volume of work made large office staffs necessary.

In 1876 Price designed the George S. Bennett House in Wilkes-Barre for relatives of Mrs. Price. The imposing residence, once conspicuously located on a corner lot in the city, is now replaced by the Y.M.C.A. The design shows a formal, symmetrically planned building dominated by a central tower with high-pitched roof. Although constructed of brick, it suggested the Queen Anne influence, with its projecting bays and dainty roof cresting. The raised platform of the side terrace, the stature of the enormous windows, and the monumentality of the composition created a fitting symbol for one of the centers of social activity in the city.

The earliest of Price's houses that still stand is the Paul Bedford House at 96 West South Street, Wilkes-Barre. Built in 1876, it was his first published work, as well as the first asymmetrical house plan to appear in his work. The stately brick house, although typical of the 1870s, has a simplicity of mass and roof line unusual in America at the time. The slate wall-covering used in the gables and the handsome ribbed chimneys reflect the work of Norman Shaw in England.[15]

Although apparently never built, a design for a house in Pittstown, Pennsylvania, published in 1877, is Price's most important work before he moved to New York City.[16] A characteristic wood house of the period in that the first floor has clapboard membranes nailed between the studs, it somewhat resembles the stick style, whereas the slate-covered upper stories anticipate the shingle style of the 1880s. This well-organized design indicates Price's search for order, clarity, and integration in house design, as well as a pleasing handling of solids and voids. With no one element dominating the design, each becomes part of an interlocking whole. Thus the dormers are not decorative

additions but elements cleverly incorporated into the general design. The eaves, with their exposed thrusting brackets, provide a rhythm of light and deep shadows balancing those of the ample veranda. The drawing for the plan of the house, the earliest extant Price drawing, is a typical plan of the time, showing less innovation than the exterior treatment. The cross-axial order in the fireplaces of the parlor and library only hints at his later interest in axial planning.

Another house of 1876, the Paine House, with its mansard roof treatment, tall windows, and absolute symmetry, indicates the Second Empire influence. The walls and floor of the vestibule were covered with terra-cotta tiles that Price had brought back from his European honeymoon trip. He was obviously aware of the current popularity of tile, as well as of the inferior quality of American-made tiles at that time.[17]

A revision of a design for a Fire Insurance Company Building, originally completed in 1875, was published in *American Architect and Building News* (22 December 1877) after Price had moved to New York. Although there is no record of the construction of the building, the illustration reveals the medieval influence often found in his early work. The proposed five-story structure topped with a belfry was to be of pressed and molded brick, with a basement trim of granite and free-stone. Exposed roofs were to be covered with terra-cotta tile, while the spandrels over the first-story windows were to be of ornamental tile with a symbolic figure of the Spirit of Fire Insurance spreading her wings over the city. Gargoyles and other medieval motifs were likewise planned in tile. The total composition of the design, which seems bold and heavy, is an early indication of Price's later geometry and almost harsh simplicity.[18]

Price designed two picturesque store-front buildings for Wilkes-Barre. One, Tuck's Drug Store, now destroyed, was built in 1877 of Baltimore pressed brick and Ohio stone. The small store of simple and direct design is hung between the two supporting side walls. On the first floor the large glass window, with changes in plane to provide protection from sun and rain, is flanked by two recessed doorways. Design contrast is provided by banded windows on the second floor. Romanesque machicolations near the top cornice and other medieval elements indicate Price's indebtedness to the designs of the European revivalists.[19]

The other storefront, the Wood's Building of 1878, completed after Price moved to New York, now considerably enlarged, became the Boston Store of Wilkes-Barre,[20] then Boscov's. The importance of the design lies primarily in the two great, swelling, bay windows two stories high, covered by eyelid roofs of tile that slide back into the building. For the rest of the century the eyebrow bay window was the main feature of many of the stores built in Wilkes-Barre. These bowed windows have unfortunately been replaced by large areas of glass, which lessen the quality of the building. The edifice is still quite impressive, even though the facade materials of pressed and molded brick trimmed with blue stone and terra cotta were subsequently lost under coats of paint.

The first few years in Wilkes-Barre were happy years for Bruce. His wife and his in-laws gave their continual support to the advancement of his career. In 1872 the couple's first child, William Lee Price, was born, and daughter Emily followed the next year. In later years Emily was to become the famous author of the celebrated book *Emily Post's Etiquette*, published in 1922 under her married name. But in 1875 tragedy struck the young Prices when their little son died. Perhaps the shock of this sorrow as well as the need for a more stimulating professional environment prompted Bruce in 1877 to move his practice to New York.

The New York Years, 1877–1885

In New York the Prices bought a four-story red brick house at 12 West Tenth Street between Fifth and Sixth Avenues, and Bruce immediately set about renovating it. The lower floors were reserved for his family and the two upper floors turned into flats for rent. At the time this was an original and daring idea. The word was just then coming into use: the word *flats* had not yet been replaced by *apartments*.

Here Emily spend a happy childhood. Sensing her keen interest in art, her father provided her with photographs to study and statuary to admire. He delighted in taking her to exhibitions as well as to inspect his buildings under construction, calling her attention to details of ornament and to the proportions of buildings. As a result Emily developed an appreciation of art and architecture that remained a lifelong delight. While father and daughter shared aesthetic interests, Josephine acted as financier of the family. She had what Bruce lacked, a shrewd business head and a genius for making money. She put his success in his career ahead of any other interest.[21]

Since New York then was the center of architectural development in this country, Price was quick to sense a milieu sympathetic to his tastes and powers. He opened an office on Lower Fifth Avenue, which he retained for the rest of his life. As an architect, he possessed tremendous vigor and capacity for hard work. His great personal charm and social graces won him many friends. Since everyone admired his taste, his practice grew rapidly.

His designs were frequently published in *American Architect and Building News*.

After the Chicago fire of 1871, many large cities, including New York, passed building laws that outlawed the construction of wooden buildings within city limits. This regulation obviously affected metropolitan architecture. While architects in the seashore and rural areas were assimilating the Queen Anne and Colonial styles and developing the shingle style, those in the cities were to create mountains of stone and brick with curious derivations from medieval and Renaissance forms.

Challenged by this demand, Bruce Price designed in 1878 the first fireproof apartment in New York, located on East Twenty-first Street. It was built for D. H. King, Jr., a contractor, for whom Price did a great deal of later housing. The six-story structure, described in *American Architect and Building News* as a "French flat," is an awkward building. Price seems to have been trying to fit his plan into a preconceived medieval facade, with less than complete success.[22] The projecting bays and their decoration on the second to fourth floors do not relate to the total design. The scattered floor plan was easily adapted to its later function as a hotel.

Two other houses of 1879 incorporating medieval borrowings indicate a better grouping of the architectural elements—use of arches, placement of doors and windows—and a more unified arrangement of interior space. In the planning of these houses Price was following the lead of other

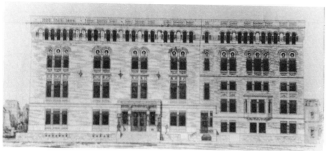

The design of 1879 for the Union League Club House in New York City illustrates Price's bold use of machicolations and a monumental arrangement of windows. *American Architect and Building News*

architects in attempting to relate knowledge of past styles with the housing needs and tastes of the present. Although these buildings were not particularly original in their conception, they were successful in a practical sense.

A third design of 1879, likewise medieval in character, was submitted for a competition sponsored by the Union League Club at Fifth Avenue and Thirty-ninth Street. The sheer size of the projected structure, with its monumental arrangement of the windows and of the machicolations supporting the cornice, proves Price's capability in handling large buildings. Richardson may have known of this design when he built the Marshall Field Warehouse in Chicago, from 1885 to 1887. Although the competition was won by Peabody and Stearns, Price had at least tested his skill in the design of large buildings and had introduced himself to his future kind of clientele—the people who were members of exclusive clubs.

In his search for prestige and professional recognition, Price had worked with commissions not totally sympathetic to his abilities. However, when he vacationed at Bar Harbor, Maine, one of the most friendly and informal of the fashionable resorts in this country, he found a type of commission more suited to his talent and temperament. Price seems to have responded to the social openness and freedom with a corresponding freedom in architectural design. He became well known for his seashore hotels for the vacationing city dwellers. In these buildings wood was still the preferred material. The carefree environment seemed just right for the informal stick and shingle architectural styles.

Price's Annex to the West End Hotel at Mount Desert, Bar Harbor, Maine, completed in 1879, is his early and important response to this development. The Annex, which adjoins a four-story hotel of clapboard with mansard roof, is covered with clapboard and crowned with a rather steep, shingled roof with an overhang supported by stick-like braces. The encircling shingled porches on the

two lower levels are supported by thin uprights, which give the effect of the stick style, although the rest of the building resembles the shingle style, with which it is more closely associated in spirit and chronology. Crowds of people flocked each summer to this great barn of a building, as Scully describes it, "boisterous and warm in its colors of Indian red, brown, and olive green."[23]

In another building of 1879 at Mount Desert, Bar Harbor, Price developed a much freer plan than in the Annex. The exterior of this large rambling cottage, called "The Craigs," is a picturesque amalgamation of elements derived from past styles. A large, turreted, projecting, circular bay at the center, echoing the round towers of the Loire Valley, is complemented by the use of half-timbering, Queen Anne plaster panels, sundials, and crudely carved barge boards. Before the ridge pole reaches the surface of the exterior wall, the roof breaks and forms a kind of protective, hovering mass over the building. As a result the gables are not tall and sharp. The eyelid dormers do the same thing.

The interior plan, organized on a multiple axis imposed by the irregular terrain, is developed in an imaginative way. Vari-shaped rooms opening out on several levels from the large central hall create an interesting directional flow of space. According to Scully, "the crudity of 'The Craigs' is the key to its vitality. Price's design at this period is without discipline, and it is hearty, violent and free. His sense of tumultous open space and his love of texture and variety represented in 1880 some of the vitality which marked the new summer hotel and cottage architecture."[24] A great fire of 1947 destroyed this house and many others.

Price received commissions for hotels and homes in other resort areas, notable among them being the hotel at Long Beach, Long Island, built in 1880. This immense structure, 875 feet long, was completed in sixty days. Of Queen Anne half-timbered style, its low roof, projecting gables, and curtain walls are covered with California redwood shingles. The timbering and the curtain walls are brought out in dark green and subdued gold tones. The hotel complex included eighteen cottages and 1275 bathhouses to accommodate the crowds from New York.[25]

A design for the Cathedral at Demerara, British Guiana, of 1880, fits into Price's work at this time. Although there is no record of the construction of the cathedral, the plan seems to indicate Price's attempt to apply the open-space construction of seashore homes to church design. His current preference for the round form, now logically applied to the apse, is bound to the rest of the chancel end by a low-lying, open veranda. On the transepts, which extend out from the center of the church, the use of a band of windows covered with a hooded roof, suggesting domestic architecture of the time, would have created dazzling interior light for this southern climate. The great mass of a tower incorporated into the facade seems heavy, but like the rest of the building is made of light timber covered with shingles—a clever attempt to use more glass and open space in a tropical climate, after initial testing at the seashore areas.

One of the most important marks in Price's early career was the First Methodist-Episcopal Church of Wilkes-Barre. Work had begun on the plans in 1876 before he left that city for New York. Several subsequent revisions resulted in a greater unification of design. Finally on 4 October 1885, after two years of construction, the church was completed and dedicated. Except for the facade, the building was of brick, as originally intended. The ends of the narthex and the facade are of yellow stone, the same warm yellow stone of the Price home in Cumberland, Maryland. Combining his own childhood impressions with those of later trips to Europe and the influence of Richardson, Price's final product was more Romanesque than his first one. The development from first design to final structure revealed the maturing personality of an architect who was now able to make a coherent synthesis of his knowledge and experience.

Behind the church a large Sunday school building designed by Price had been completed in 1877. It was placed beside the early brick church of 1849, which still stood. Built of brick, this great simple shape contains one large, two-story, semi-octagonal space, surrounded by radiating rooms on two different floors, which can be separated from the large room by sliding doors. This type of plan, accommodating the varying size of the audience, was invented by Lewis Miller and was first used in 1868 for the Sunday school for the First Methodist Episcopal Church of Akron, Ohio.[26]

Perhaps the least successful of Price's work during the early 1880s were the apartment and commercial buildings that showed his continued preference for the picturesque quality of medieval and French Renaissance features. His attempt to fuse these past influences with the standards and demands of city architecture resulted in structures that, although competently and sturdily constructed, seem out of place in an American city. These commissions included the following: an apartment house in Cincinnati, designed in 1881, where the various arrangements of the windows and the many sizes of dormers resulted in a confusing skyline; a building for the southeast corner of Broadway and Twenty-second Street in New York City, where Price used every type of the then current taste in domestic windows in this rather

large structure suggesting French Renaissance style; and in 1883, alterations on both the World Building on Park Row and the building at the southeast corner of Broadway and Twenty-third Streets in New York City.

Price's most successful work was domestic in nature. During the 1880s the development of an indigenous domestic architecture was steadily proceeding in the States. Although Richardson dominated the Boston area until his death in 1886, the gifted partnerships of Emerson and Little, Cabot and Chandler, and Peabody and Stearns were also much in demand. In the New York area no one architect took the lead. The noted firms of Potter and Robertson, of Lamb & Rich, of Rossiter & Wright, and of McKim, Mead and White all designed in variations of the shingle style, influenced, in turn, by past styles. Out of what seemed a chaotic amalgamation, the shingle style emerged as the most popular one and was rapidly brought into clarity and order.

According to Scully, Bruce Price was one of the most important figures in this development. Two houses of 1882 characteristic of Price's early shingle-style work along the eastern seaboard are the Roosevelt Cottage at North Oyster Bay, Long Island, and the Armisted Cottage at Newport, Rhode Island. Typical of the period, the houses were held together by a veranda along two sides. However, the interior plan of the former, with a hallway penetrating the entire house, indicates on Price's part a new sense of directional flow in interior planning, which he was later to develop more fully.

Another house built that same year, the J. M. Wayne Neff House in Cincinnati, Ohio, is of greater interest in that it was Price's first fully mature house design. No longer standing, it was located on the corner of Reading Road and Oak Street in what was then a very fashionable neighborhood. The general treatment, with its use of a large turreted bay and porches on three floors, exhibited his growing interest in the contrast of recessed cavities and projecting solids. The effect of shifting light on stone, plaster, shingle, and tile, gave the house a sculptural quality. On the first floor, rooms rotated around the entrance hall, which was the core of the plan. The irregularly shaped living room functioned as both anteroom and large gathering room. Sliding doors between library and dining room transformed space as needed. The extension of the main library window out into the veranda and the irregular, somewhat cantilevered extension of the dining room to accommodate the drop in site added to the interior space. This was a particularly good solution to the adaptation of structure to site. In this respect Price

The powerful forms of projecting solids and contrasting cavities make the J. M. Wayne Neff House one of Price's most significant early designs. *American Architect and Building News*

The east elevation of the Neff House. *American Architect and Building News*

became independent of the influence of Richardson, who had never made a similar use of site.

On the second floor the rooms opened from a large central hall. Despite its awkward shape for the arrangement of furniture, the partially curved room in the turret was to become a favorite with Price. It was presumably used as a sitting room for the adjoining bedroom and adjacent second-floor balcony porch—a desirable feature for the hot summer days and nights of Cincinnati. Insistence on a balcony, which was one of the prevailing creative elements in design in the 1880s, was an expression of a new informality of life and an interest in outdoor activity. The ultimate development of similar forms was to be expressed by Frank Lloyd Wright

in the early 1900s, in the low horizontal planes and overhanging roofs of his early Chicago houses.[27]

During 1883, after Price engaged in a partnership with George A. Freeman, their collaborative designs revealed eclectic details. Since Price had heretofore been relatively free from the academicism of the time, Graybill attributes this eclecticism to Freeman's influence.[28] Together they designed for George S. Scott a house called "Seacroft" near Sea Bright, New Jersey, the exterior of which is not particularly original or distinguished. The plan itself is a good example of the cross-axis arrangement favored by Price. A large central hall provides direct access to the other rooms and results in the free and relaxed atmosphere suited to a seashore home. The use of circular and polygonal forms extends the volume of the house visually as well as physically. Thus Price was becoming an able and noted practitioner in the control of open interior space.

In 1883 Price and Freeman designed both the Shepard House at Larchmont, New York, and the Hammersley House at Glen Cove, New York.[29] They also did ten cottages on the grounds of the Argyle Hotel in Babylon, New York. None of these designs exists, nor does that for a casino at Seabright, New Jersey of the same year. Their last effort at collaboration in 1883, the J. D. Platt House in Dayton, Ohio, is a more formalized and controlled example of Price's work. Costing an estimated $60,000, the handsome brick-and-stone residence has been destroyed to make way for the Greyhound Bus Terminal.

Later the same year Price turned his attention to a house in Wilkes-Barre for Priscilla Lee Bennett, a member of his wife's family. The second home that he designed for the Bennett family, it is considered his best work in that city. Price's professional popularity can be judged from the fact that this design was published almost immediately after its completion in the 1 December 1883 issue of *American Architect and Building News*. Although recalling the Queen Anne style, this mature work is to some extent a summation of his own work to date. The building materials of red brick on the first story, with brown stone quoins at the corners, contrast with the pink stucco and off-white half-timbering of the second story. The colorful scheme is completed by red slate shingles in the gables. A second-story overhang protects the cavernous front porch. The band of windows cantilevered over the void of the porch is a magnificent anticipation of later forms as well as a beautiful piece of design.[30]

The next year Price built "Seaverge" for George F. Baker. Located near Sea Bright, New Jersey, it was, according to Cleveland Amory, the "first really substantial cottage there."[31] The plan shows

Price combined brick, stone, stucco, and half-timbering in the Priscilla Lee Bennett House built in 1883 in Wilkes-Barre. *American Architect and Building News*

"Seaverge," with its shingled exterior and large porches, is typical of Price's seashore houses of the 1880s. *Stately Homes in America*

the curving carriage drive reiterated by the curve of the front porch. Inside the main entrance is the hall, serving as the primary living area. Like the second Bennett House, this house is elongated and thus eliminates the central hall. The plan also excludes the activities of new arrivals from the rest of the house. The library is the core of the design, entered from either side and projecting out toward the ocean. A large dining-room on the south balances the central hall on the north side of the library. Certainly the most important living space in the plan is the piazza along the ocean side. This continuous open area, with its spindly light-catching balustrade, is appropriate for a summer house at the shore. Instead of a traditional opening in the central wall of the house, with heavy structural members at the corners, Price created a deeply recessed entrance porch on the south bal-

anced by another porch on the north. The covered balconies of the second floor jut out over these porches. Originally the vast low-pitched Akron tile roof put a proper lid on the design. The tiles were later replaced by a varicolored absestos shingle roof which lacked the vigor of the tiles. With the brick on the first floor a bright orange-red color, the second-story tiles a different shade of orange-red, and a third shade of red for the Carlisle stone trim, the house was a pleasing riot of color. Unfortunately, the house has suffered the fate of destruction, as have so many lovely old homes. When Baker sold the Jersey Central Railroad to J. P. Morgan in 1901, he sold "Seaverge" and moved to Tuxedo, where he became known as the "Titan of Tuxedo."[32]

In the meantime Price was doing work in New York City, where his office was located. Aware of the requirements of the new fire laws, he was inclined to equate qualities of permanence with styles of the past. In 1884, using iron girders, brick, and stone, he designed at 600 Madison Avenue a house for Dr. Theodore G. Thomas that suggests the style of French sixteenth-century town houses.[33] Much of the five-story facade is glass, with varying arrangements of windows on each floor. Although this French style in which Price was working was widely adapted by other architects of the time, Talbot Hamlin, the architectural historian, singled him out for special commendation: "Bruce Price was an architect great enough to rise above the demands of the then fashionable forms and impose upon them unity, restraint, and even charm, despite the obvious eighteen-eighty character of much of the detail."[34]

By 1885 in the New York area, Price was a well-known architect whose reputation was established by publication throughout the architectural world. Financially solvent, as a result no doubt of his wife's careful management of their funds as well as of his own diligence, he was able to build a four-story extension on his own house on West Tenth Street.[35] According to Emily Post, her openhearted and openhanded father would help anyone who appealed to his generosity, to the point where Josephine felt it necessary to assume charge of his checkbook and his bank account.[36] Moving freely in New York Society, the family became acquainted with many wealthy persons who sooner or later would commission Price to design their city or country residences.

Tuxedo Park, 1885–1886

On 18 September 1885 Pierre Lorillard IV, tobacco magnate and sportsman, introduced Price to an area of wilderness in the Ramapo Mountains in Orange County, New York. This beautiful wooded area, dotted by three lakes—one almost two miles long, the others considerably smaller—had been acquired by Lorillard's father during the early years of the nineteenth century. Upon his death in 1843, along with his rich tobacco empire, he willed the land to his seven children. The rightful heir of part of it, his son Pierre, acquired the remainder of his 7,000-acre tract by buying out the other members of his family or by beating them at poker.

In 1880 Pierre Lorillard had become interested in Central American archaeology and along with the French government had cosponsored the first expeditions of M. Désiré Charnay under the auspices of the Peabody Museum.[37] Eventually, one of Charnay's discoveries was named La Ville Lorillard, and his illustrated report, later published in a book called *The Ancient Cities of the New World,* sparked a new interest for the millionaire. Charnay's drawings indicated that at La Ville Lorillard at Yaxchilan, Mexico, and at Palenque in the Yucatan, a podium of heavy rock usually isolates a building from the ground. Horizontal cornices with characteristic decoration emphasize the low masses of the temples and palaces. Centuries of overgrowth and accumulation add to the picturesque character of the structures. The rusticity and the simple geometry of the Mayan ruins must have so impressed the dominating and positive Lorillard that he sought to translate the architectural essence of this culture to the New York site. Evidently he saw in his property at Tuxedo the possibility of re-creating a primitive paradise where he and his chosen friends could live a kind of Mayan Renaissance removed from the materialism and distraction of New York City.

He commissioned, or one might say challenged, the architect to transform the area into an exclusive retreat for himself and his elite friends and to do it quickly. Price was to prove himself equal to Lorillard's challenge. Emily Post wrote a charming account of her father's first visit to Orange County with Lorillard. Arriving on the Buffalo express from New York City on a soggy, rainy day, patron and architect were both nevertheless charged with their respective enthusiasms. According to Emily Post's re-creation of her father's description of the trip, Mr. Lorillard was excitedly directing:

> I shall have the entrance there, with an important gateway and lodge. . . . Over there I shall have the station. There . . . I shall have a row of stores, and the village cottages beyond. I want half a dozen cottages. Perhaps I had better make it a dozen. Make some of them bigger—to hold two families. And the stables? Oh, yes, the stables—put them on the hill.[38]

After deciding upon the site for the clubhouse and for some of the cottages, the two very wet men hurried to catch the next train back to New York City.

The impetuous Lorillard expected the miracles that Bruce Price in a sense produced. The immi-

Emily Post in her study. On the wall behind her desk is a portrait of her father, Bruce Price. *Courtesy of William G. Post*

grant workers, housed in shanties on the periphery of the park, helped. The situation demanded and received incredible creative energy and spontaneity. By 1 October thirty miles of macadam and dirt roads were begun under the direction of James Smith Haring of New York, while Ernest Bowditch, an engineer from Boston, devised the construction of the water and sewage system. The labor of hauling pipes and lumber, of blasting rock, and of clearing sites for the buildings continued all through the bitter winter months as Price worked on his plans. As related by Emily Post:

Mr. Lorillard ordered houses in the same way that other people might order boots. He talked rapidly, and thought twice as fast as he talked, and he wished his orders carried out at a speed that equalled the sum of both. Once, just as he was leaving Mr. Price's office, he called back: "By the way, make it four cottages more, instead of two. Show me the plans tomorrow, and break ground for them next Monday."

If when he saw the plans, he did not like them, he insisted upon new sketches being made then and there, before his eyes, rejecting or accepting them from a few pencilled lines. He always knew what he wanted, never forgot a detail of a single one of the forty-odd buildings, and never changed his mind about them.[39]

Working in a fever of excitement, Bruce Price produced vigorous and original contributions to American domestic architecture. Overwhelmed with the power of the natural setting and trying to re-create cultural rhythms of the past, these two men complemented each other's abilities and tastes.

Affected by Lorillard's enthusiasm for primitive appearance, Price insisted that his buildings, which seemed to grow out of their rock bases, be stained the color of the woods and that the rock used in the construction retain its original moss and lichen. Wherever possible, trees and shrubbery were preserved. Thus the houses, set in the lush, rocky terrain of the woods, looked old the day Tuxedo Park was opened, and created the romantic setting envisioned by Lorillard. Within a nine-month period, with a work force of 1,800 Italian and Slav immigrants and at the cost of $1,500,000, the main layout of Tuxedo Park was completed. It included seven thousand fenced acres, roads, water, approximately forty buildings, and a variety of recreational facilities.

The small self-sufficient village of Tuxedo is located on Highway 17, forty miles northwest of New York City, outside the main gate lodge of the park. The office of the Tuxedo Park Association, originally a handsome little building suggesting the architectural style inside the gate, has undergone extensive alteration. The original office, extraordinarily simple in design, was contained under the high-pitched roof in the fashion of Bavarian and Swiss mountain houses. The large rough stones of the first floor rooted it to the ground, whereas the second floor of timber and stucco led to a still lighter shingled exterior of the top story. Window area increased with each level: a group of three on the first floor, four on the second; and on the third, the exterior wall replaced by an open balcony. The deep entrance porch created another void, thereby giving the design a plastic expression.

Next to the Association office was the Village Row, which included the Post Office, now in a separate, later building, and a group of approximately twelve small houses, with thirty others planned and included in the scheme. The villagers were the domestics and the gardeners of the park. Three basic house types were provided for their use. These were duplex or one-family houses, simple and compact masses covered with clapboard and shingles, their dominating gable roofs providing variations on the design for the office. These houses are generally grouped together in like de-

Large gable roofs dominate the cluster of houses that Price designed in the village of Tuxedo. *Photo by the author*

signs, along a curving street. Following the pattern of the park itself, the village is built on a series of circular lanes and has no through roads that might attract heavier and faster traffic.

The towerlike gate lodge at the entrance to the park, built of massive boulders in two sections, attests to Lorillard's insistence upon a forceful primitivism. At the right, the lodge, primarily a tower with an entrance porch, provides shelter for the gatekeeper. The keep, on the left, arches across a small stream to add to its picturesque character. At either side of the gate, a massive stone-boulder wall extends toward the twenty-four-mile-long encircling barbed-wire fence of the park.

Within the park itself the Clubhouse and Bachelor Annex, destroyed by fire in 1928, were the centers of social life at Tuxedo and accommodated weekend visitors. Set on stone platforms, these connected buildings were covered with wood shingles. Much of the first-floor area was surrounded by open piazzas, establishing a close relation between indoors and outdoors. The ballroom of the Clubhouse, a circular room seventy-five feet in diameter, had an inlaid floor of extraordinary workmanship. When used as a ballroom, the musicians occupied a platform at one side. When the room was converted into a theater, the platform became a large stage, with an area equal to the Madison Square Theatre in New York. The room was one of the most attractive auditoriums ever constructed. The ceiling was an immense dome, supported by large beams that curved to the apex, decorated in blue and gold. From every beam was suspended a chandelier of twenty-five candlestick gaslights.[40] Many and varied activities therein climaxed in the Club's Autumn Ball, at the first of which, in October 1886, as Cleveland Amory relates it, young Griswold Lorillard, son of Pierre IV, wore the tailless jacket to which the resort gave its name.[41] Consternation at this breach of Tuxedo formality soon gave way to acceptance there and elsewhere, and the "tuxedo" became accepted formal attire.

By June 1886 Tuxedo Park with its natural beauties and civilized amenities, was ready for inspection. Special trains brought seven hundred guests—the cream of New York Society—to see its wonders. The luxurious Clubhouse, overlooking a sparkling lake, was staffed by competent English servants. Out-of-doors, gamekeepers and boatmen garbed in the Club's colors, green and gold, awaited the guests' preferences. Facilities for many sports had already been completed or were under construction. Since Tuxedo was planned as a spring and autumn retreat, many of the cottages were rented for the shooting and fishing seasons. Soon these seasons grew to encompass the entire

Built of massive stone boulders, the gate lodge flanks the left side of the entrance to Tuxedo Park. *Photo by the author*

year, with its lovely changing vistas and seasonal attractions. Private year-round houses were planned for individuals who satisfied Lorillard's qualifications for membership in the select Tuxedo Club. Membership preceded home ownership and was not lightly conferred. Those of inherited wealth and impeccable social antecedents were considered first, and then, perhaps, those financiers who dealt with money. Within a year, so great was the pressure for membership that the initial ideal quota of two hundred gentlemen increased to four hundred. According to Cleveland Amory, membership was like "a guide to Who is especially Who in the Four Hundred."[42]

The early "small cottages" at Tuxedo, meaning "modest" structures containing from five to ten bedrooms plus accommodations for servants, were available to these favored few. These houses, expressive and powerful examples of American craftsmanship and the use of native materials, were Price's most significant contributions to architecture. While rooted in tradition and forming a continuity with basic concepts in the past, they were distinguished by great originality in the use of these concepts. Like Richardson and later

Wright, he expressed an architectural form that was uniquely American. In these houses Price brought the shingle style to a point of momentary perfection unequaled elsewhere and set the stage for the interesting domestic architecture of the first decade of the twentieth century.

Although different in overall design, the early houses share certain common stylistic elements. They are constructed of stone, timber, and sometimes brick, with large shingled areas. Set in ro-

This stone and shingled "cottage" of the early period is now painted white. *Photo by the author*

The long porch is an important feature of the overall mass of this early cottage. *Photo by the author*

mantic sites of dense vegetation, often on irregular terrain and mounted on stone podiums, they seem rooted to the earth and part of it. Their recessed entrances, hidden in the shadows and approached by wide stone stairways, reinforce the function of these houses as retreats from the rest of the world. The interior and exterior mingle in the spaces of the large verandas protected by the overhang of the second floor. Strong gable roofs and facades of simple geometric forms create a monumental dignity. Inside, open floor plans allow for an easy flow of space from room to room and from room to veranda. Native natural wood, used in exposed ceiling beams and wainscoting, usually constituted the interior finishes.

At Lorillard's insistence, four of these cottages at Tuxedo were built for Price's own use. The largest of the four became the Price summer home. Daughter Emily maintained that having lived there from her early teens, she and Tuxedo had literally grown up together. When she married Edwin N. Post, the banker, her father gave her one of the cottages, where the young couple lived until Emily

This cottage was once the Price summer home at Tuxedo Park. *Photo by the author*

was expecting her first child. Her desire to be closer to her New York doctor and that of Edwin to be closer to his office prompted their move to Dongan Hills, Staten Island.

Perhaps the most daring of Price's early houses at Tuxedo was the Henry J. Barbey House on Tower Hill, built for Mrs. Henry Barbey, a sister of

In springtime cerise azaleas line the approach to the mansion.
Photo by author

The main entrance to the Casino. *Photo by author*

The mighty Eagle is a focal point of the Italian Gardens.
Photo by Sister Mary Theresa McCarthy

A juxtaposition of the old and the new—a lion, symbol of
Gould financial power, and St. Joseph Hall in the distance.
Photo by Sister Mary Theresa McCarthy

e Barbey House on Tower Hill, no longer standing, was a
werful example of Price's early work at Tuxedo Park. *Cour-*
y of Samuel H. Graybill

Pierre Lorillard. Set on a rectangular base of rough stone on a slanting site, this house seems to grow out of the bedrock. Like many other houses by Price and his contemporaries, it depended a great deal on the effect of color. Although the house is no longer extant, Sheldon describes it as constructed of various types of pink stone, which contrasted with the pinkish green of the shingles above.[43] From illustrations, the house appears to be a simple contained mass, but the effect is deceiving. Although the first floor area is considerably smaller than the second, it contains a large hall as well as dining room and library, the space being taken up by two large covered verandas on the first floor. The second floor is extended to the edge of the veranda on these two sides. The corner tower pins it to the ground and incorporates the verandas in the general mass.

In the construction of the tower the use of different materials is particularly noteworthy. The heavy base of stone, resisting the perforations of three arched windows, is surmounted by the lighter covering of wood shingles. But at the corner, where at least the visual effect of structure must be stronger, the stone provides the necessary buttress a few feet higher. By contrast the shingles look paper-thin and seem to be just what they are, merely a covering. Price has made them curve around the corners and into the window recesses. Thus they contrib-

ute to a tremendous plasticity that is fully realized in the reverse curve of the capping roof. Right here is the epitome of the shingle style—the undulating surface covering. The main roof caps the rest of the house in a similar way. Four narrow slit windows recessed in the gable provide the necessary light and emphasize the enormous mass of the roof complex. The window arrangement is not symmetrical; indeed, Price seems to have let the windows fall where they may. On the side of the house where the ground is lower, he has made the roof slip lower down. Although an interesting corner effect is achieved, the design seems uncertain and not properly resolved.

The house, architecturally noteworthy in its originality, failed to satisfy the client. It is reputed that Mrs. Barbey, who had written her instructions from her main residence in Switzerland, had something far less imposing in mind—a small chalet where she could spend a month or two each year in her native land. Evidently her instructions were not too precise. The large house, with its great hall and fifteen-foot ceiling, impossible to heat in winter, was more than she had bargained for. According to legend, she took one look and never came back.[44]

A more successful early design at Tuxedo, and perhaps the best known, was that for the J. L. Breese House, later occupied by Pierre Lorillard himself.[45] Dominated by two large brick chimneys that flank the deeply recessed semicircular arch of the stone entrance, the monumental front facade is a symmetrical and well-ordered pattern of solid and void. Reminiscent of Richardson's work only in material and general form, this stone arch is handled with originality and power. In fact, Richardson had never used such a monumental arch in domestic architecture. Yet Price has succeeded in making it a focal point of the whole design. The red-brick chimneys that flank the arch, contrasting with the gray of the stone, become dominant elements in the facade composition. A second-floor balcony supported by thin columns creates a large void above the heavy mass of the entrance. The striking arch of the entrance is subtly reiterated in the curved form of the attic dormer on the third floor. The podium is built of a simple wooden frame with lattice coverings. Although actually a firm foundation, it suggests the screened qualities of Japanese work—an interest noted occasionally in Price's work and in that of his contemporaries originating in part from the exhibition of Japanese architecture at the Philadelphia Centennial in 1876. The rest of the exterior is covered with shingles.

The Breese House is symmetrical in plan. The entrance hall, entered from the recessed loggia, is a long central hallway that runs through the entire mass of the house. Across the middle of the hall an arch divides the space, thereby increasing its visual length. On either side of the front hall are the dining-room and parlor. The wide entrance to these rooms opened this entire cross-space into one large, flowing, interior volume. Price used sliding doors to close these rooms, avoiding too-large doors that would have swung through a large arc. Off the rear hall, the butler's pantry and study completed the scheme. As in most of these early houses, the kitchen was in the basement. Presumably, the second floor contained a similar division of space of a central hallway. Except for the stairway at the rear of the hall, this plan is not unlike that of the house in Cumberland, Maryland, in which Price was born. In this design Price may have been influenced by the symmetry of classic Colonial houses or was simply expressing his own preference for ordered unity, even in this informal setting.

One of the few early Price houses extant is an unnamed cottage of 1886 near the Clubhouse. The rendering by Frederick Wright shows a dark house, of timber and stone construction, partially hidden by the trees. Set on its rough stone podium, and topped by an overwhelming gable, the house, though an original form, recalls more primitive human habitats—perhaps the huts of New Guinea or of Central or South America, or the mountain lodges in Europe. However, it is safe to assume that Price was influenced by his study of the illustrations in Charnay's report and sought to recall their general character. A wide stone stairway leads to the veranda, which surrounds the front part of the house. After leaving the open front area of the veranda, the visitor is forced to follow the flow of space around one side or other before entering the house. In so doing, he enters one of the covered areas of veranda on either side of the main hall. Providing access to the stairway and other rooms, this hall is the center of activity of the house and a kind of informal parlor. It would seem that the word *hall* came to mean just that; in contrast to the more formal setting associated with the *parlor* of a city house.

The head of the "T" plan of the house widens out to include the separate dining and library spaces. This area has a more telling effect on the second floor, where it extends vertically as well as horizontally from the main mass. Apparently the second-floor plan is similar in the separation of rooms. No other solution would offer itself to the rather concise allocation of volumes. The front bedroom has a semi-protected balcony, which is formed by the combined concavity of the front wall surface and the convex extension of the front of the

balcony. This same projection gives protection from light and rain to the large hall windows below. The remarkably plastic effect of the total design of the cottage is augmented by the hollow spaces of the veranda and the strong triangular shape of the high-pitched roof.

Among the dozen or more early Tuxedo houses, features of several seem to have exerted a direct influence upon the work of Frank Lloyd Wright. According to Scully, the houses derive much of their historical importance from "their compactness of design. Like Wright's later houses, they exploited to the full the possibilities of shingle style open planning and of clear geometric order."[46] The William Kent House is similar in elevation and general appearance to the cottage just described. The plan is likewise T-shaped, but the arrangement of rooms differs. The parlor is located in the area that projects out onto the veranda, while a small entrance hall is in the subsidiary wing to the right. To the left of a central staircase and fireplace a dining room balances the hall; an extended rear wing includes a den and porch. Frank Lloyd Wright's Charles S. Ross House of 1902 on Delavan Lake, Wisconsin, is strikingly similar in plan. Using the same general arrangement, Wright reduced the size of his entrance hall but made the same area important as a covered exterior space.

The plan of the William Chandler House is quite different. A projecting porch surrounds two sides of the house. The almost square first-floor plan is interrupted by two large bays, which project on the two porch sides. These bays, while still under the extremities of the roof, which covers everything like a great lid, are powerful expressions of the dynamic movement of the interior volumes. The central chimney core is the only real separation of space between the halls, the parlor, and the dining room. The rest of the house revolves around this central pivot, suggesting again the later houses by

This rendering of the Chandler House indicates its original appearance. *Courtesy of Samuel H. Graybill*

The Chandler House has been moved from its original site and altered on the street side, but the porches and two of the bays remain unchanged. *Courtesy of Samuel H. Graybill*

Frank Lloyd Wright. There is a striking similarity between the street side of the Chandler House to that of Wright's own house of 1889 in Oak Park, Illinois. The publication of the design of the Chandler House in September 1886 in *Building* would have afforded Wright the opportunity of seeing this rendering three years before he built his own house. Wright's house is only two stories high, while that of Price is three. He enlarged Price's Palladian third-story window detail and made it the focus of his second-story design. The two bays in Wright's house cannot be sheer coincidence, but, unlike those of Price partially hidden by the veranda, they are more dominant in the design. However, departing from Price in this respect, Wright's facade is lower, thus indicating an effect of horizontality, which became part of the essence of his later work.[47]

In the Travis C. Van Buren House, built for the brother of President Van Buren, Price reversed the plan of the Kent House so that the main entrance is on the head of the T, with the veranda toward the rear. As in the Kent House, the effect of the huge veranda surrounding a room of the house almost literally brings the outside into the interior of the house. This interpenetration of space created here by Price becomes paramount in Wright's later designs.

The symmetrical exterior of the house was originally striking in its sheer simplicity, quite different from some of the more ornate architecture of the time. The entirely shingled exterior acts as a skin over the structure. The slightly inward-sloping pedimentlike gable in the center of the facade projected out from the wall, thereby emphasizing the strong geometry of its triangular shape. A row of four round-headed windows in the gable, a large Palladian window centered beneath it, and the other windows of the house constituted the decorative detail. George Sheldon in *Artistic Country Seats*, 1886, considered the Van Buren House to be Price's most original house and "perhaps the most original house in the United States." He notes the extremes of light and shade on the portal and the inward bending of the shingles in a great curve to the front door. "We find this effect wrought out for the first time," he said.[48] The manipulation of the shingles around the portal and around the end wall of the front steps is perhaps the supreme achievement of the use of this material. As Graybill notes, Price was a master at maintaining the sense of surface curving while achieving a quality of plasticity and monumentality. Evidently later owners have failed to appreciate Price's stark geometry of abstract forms. Stucco and half-timbering have replaced the shingled exterior. The Palladian window has been removed and the entrance brought forth and redesigned in a classical manner.

Price's early work at Tuxedo was a response not only to the current interest in Central American archaeology, but also to the dynamic personality of Lorillard. Later clients treated Price with the gentility his manner deserved, but from 1885 to 1886 this client exerted incredible pressure upon him and forced him to create first-rate work. As Lorillard's initial interest in his project decreased and his attention shifted back to horseracing, Price never again experienced such pressure or rose to such a level of forceful creativity.

Work at Tuxedo Park, 1886–1900

The construction of the early Tuxedo-style cottages continued all through the 1880s, the 1890s, and into the first decade of the twentieth century, until more than a hundred of these houses were scattered along the Park's winding roads. Following the original intent, they blended gracefully into the wooden landscape. But as the nature of Tuxedo Park changed from a seasonal playground to a year-round residential area, wealthy owners demanded more pretentious accommodations. These buildings were much larger, their plans less compact. Including other historical styles and the use of different materials, notably brick, stucco, and terra-cotta, Price's work gives evidence of being closer to the work of his contemporaries who were then beginning to design houses at Tuxedo. Probably the most startling example of a change of style is the house he designed in 1886 for Pierre Lorillard. Did Lorillard suddenly lose his enthusiasm for primitive appearance, or did another member of his family demand something more fashionable? Whatever the reason, Price may have been influenced by the work of his popular competitors McKim, Mead and White. The bent plan employed here could have been suggested by that for a house for the Misses Appleton, 1884, at Lenox, Massachusetts, designed by that firm, or he may have been recalling his own design of 1879 for "The Craigs" at Bar Harbor, Maine, where a central tower unites the two parts of a bent plan.[49] Whatever the motivation, Price's exterior is a curious amalgamation of such disparate elements as the "Queen Anne" tower and the Palladian window and detail. Unlike his early cottages, which seemed to grow out of the rock, this house, set serenely on a broad lawn, is an elegant pastiche of clapboard, stucco, shingles, and exaggerated decoration.

Another house of 1886, done in a Japanese style, is a notable example of the current interest in Japanese domestic architecture. Aside from the curved corners of the roof, which give the house an overly Japanese look, there are other subtle elements noted in an early photograph of the building. The whole design has become horizontal, with emphasis on the ridge pole and eaves. The lattice detail is, of course, Japanese in character, as well as the feeling of openness in the extreme right of the entrance facade. The lattice walls give the sense of open space and of the penetration of the outside into the building. This effect was unusual at the time, especially in a northern climate. There is no indication that the house still stands.

In 1890 Price built a large house for T. B. Burnham called "Boulder-Point." The designs created quite a stir when first exhibited in New York at the Third Annual Exhibition of the Architectural League.[50] Built around a huge boulder that is the focus of the design, it is a dramatic expression of his earlier "megalithical" style. The lower walls of the house are constructed mostly of large boulders, but more stable and solidly constructed than in his Gate Lodge, where they are placed vertically in an almost explosive pattern. Despite the precarious setting on a bluff immediately above Tuxedo Lake,

Price's design for "Boulder-Point," which was built in 1890, is a dramatic expression of his earlier "megalithical" style. *American Architect and Building News*

the house seems deeply rooted in the boulders of the Point. The large arches of stone of the porch and windows on the lake side are truly monumental. Parts of the second story are covered with wood shingles fitted into curving patterns at their lower edges. This whole shingle effect leaks down over the top of the stone construction. To increase the plastic effect, the shingled surfaces are seldom flat, but are curved—sometimes in several planes at once. The end gables, as in the Barbey and Van Buren Houses, slope gently inward as they approach their summit. The windows are sunken, creating deep voids into which the shingled surfaces bend. The eyebrow roofs over some of the windows emphasize this curvilinear mode of expression. The numerous window openings lighten the effect of this great stone skeleton as they allow the penetration of light and air. This creative work sparked European interest and was featured in a German magazine, *Kunst und Kunsthandwerk*, in 1911.[51] However, the impact of the rugged strength of Price's design has been lessened by changes by later architects: the addition of a large wing to the rear and the enclosure of the west-end porch.

Across a short stretch of water from "Boulder-Point" is another house of the same period called "Turtle-Point." Also built in 1890, the house is made of stones laid in horizontal layers, with a decided decrease in size of the individual stones on the higher layers. On the entrance side, the house fits around the curved driveway and is welcoming and warm with its play of similar colors in different materials. Near the top of the walls the stucco between the timbers is covered with small stones. Both stones and stucco in various shades of earth pinks reflect the general color of the boulder stones below. This native Tuxedo stone was easily acquired from rock slides in a form practically ready

for building. Three large archways give access to the recessed entrance porch. On the lake side the house fairly bulges out toward the water with several cone-topped towers.[52] Great arches enclosing the porches and arched windows and doorways skeletonize the whole structure and make it full of space and activity. Inside, the living-room is two full stories in height, with its extreme end filling the large tower facing the lake. The great window area in this tower floods the room with light and allows a beautiful view. On the entrance end an open stairway rises to a second-floor balcony, creating an exciting array of shapes, sizes, and directions of space.

Another house in this group is "Rock-Ridge," of 1890. Built of stone like "Turtle-Point," this house is more regular in plan with an almost symmetrical facade. Situated high above the lake, it is an enormous structure, its size defeating any opportunity for the kind of success that Price achieved in other designs. Eclectic detail and half-timbering are reminiscent of Norman Shaw and the "Queen Anne" style.[53]

During the next ten years Price grew away from his strong, megalithical mode and worked in other styles at Tuxedo, some approaching the Queen Anne, others more Georgian. In 1892 the Cammack House done for Addison Cammack, inventor and patentee of the famous bay window parlor car of the Pennsylvania and Boston & Albany railroads, was vaguely reminiscent of the Romanesque. The imposing structure, high on a hill overlooking the lake, was built of brick instead of stone with much of the detail in terra-cotta, a material Price was to use effectively in many formal designs.[54] After part of the house was destroyed by fire, some of the structure was incorporated into the Tuckerman House built on the site.

A late house at Tuxedo, the George St. George House of 1900, is in a formal Georgian style with features similar to Kingscote, the house Price is accredited with designing a few years later at

This rendering of "Turtle-Point" shows the house as viewed from Tuxedo Lake. *American Architect and Building News*

The George St. George House of 1900. Price's handling of the brick quoins, the upper lights of the double-hung windows, and the overall Georgian character of the house result in a stylistic affinity with the Georgian Court buildings. *Photo by the author*

Lakewood for George Gould's son. The Tuxedo house, though, is of different materials—red brick, decorated with white brick quoins, while the Lakewood house is stucco with white terra-cotta quoins. When the St. George House was built, it was well known for the commodious servant's quarters and the kitchen and pantry on the first floor. Price was one of the first architects to bring these rooms out of the basement in larger houses.

Aside from his work in the commercial field, Price's lasting significance in the States comes from the early work at Tuxedo. His later buildings were more derivative of past styles, but were handsome designs, carefully studied examples of an artist's devotion to beauty and a craftsman's concern with quality workmanship.

To this day descendants of the original owners continue to use Tuxedo Park as a vacation spot or place of permanent residence. However, with vanishing fortunes and rising taxes, many of the early pretentious homes have disappeared. Some have been moved, or altered, or converted to institutional use, others destroyed by neglect or fire. Only five of Price's original cottages are extant. The Clubhouse and Bachelor's Annex have been replaced by a more modern structure. New buildings accommodate numerous newcomers, not necessarily members of the Tuxedo Club. But the high standard of taste set by Price and Lorillard, and the unique character of their architecture, have never been equaled by subsequent building there.

Over the years Tuxedo Park has become more like other communities, being incorporated as the village of Tuxedo Park with an elected mayor. Although domestic service is scant and the pattern of life less formal, many of the social and sports attractions continue on a modified scale. But an aura of exclusiveness still clings to the park as the strictly guarded, great iron entrance gate bars the way to the stranger and protects the inhabitants from an influx of prying tourists. Created by an ebullient millionaire and a talented architect, this little world of Tuxedo has its own special place in American social history and in the development of late nineteenth-century architecture.

Buildings in Canada

While at work on the Tuxedo Park designs, Price was also engaged in work for patrons elsewhere, including the directors of the railroads. In 1885 he designed a bay window parlor car for the Pennsylvania Railroad. The interior, conceived as an elegant private parlor, was as close to a permanent residence in feeling as space would allow. An even more elegant car was designed for the Boston and Albany Railroad—a combined parlor and sleeping car. Shortly afterward Price came to the attention of Sir George Stephen, president of the Canadian Pacific Railway, possibly as a result of the railroad work or through an introduction arranged by Pierre Lorillard. It is also conceivable that his earlier progress was followed by William Van Horne, the company's vice-president, general manager, and an ardent architectural amateur.

By the mid-1880s the Canadian Pacific Railway was in an extraordinary state of expansion. New railway stations for the urban and rural areas as well as hotels to attract tourists to the scenic sites were needed for its continued growth. The involvement of William Van Horne with the expansion of the hotel system has been noted by his biographer, William Vaughn:

It has been aptly said that Van Horne "capitalized the scenery." But sight-seers could not be attracted to the mountains and rivers of British Columbia unless suitable accommodations were provided for them. The company's charter permitted it to operate hotels, and Van Horne now began to realize a long-held dream by starting a system of picturesque hotels commanding the choicest views in the Rockies and Selkirks. He

found recreation and delight in sketching, suggesting, or modifying the elevations and plans of these structures.[55]

It seems plausible that Van Horne admired Price's work and considered him capable of expressing what was needed in Canada at that time. During 1886 the directors of the Canadian Pacific Railway, involved in plans for a western access route to Montreal with a railroad station and cen-

View of one bay of a parlor car that Price designed for the Pennsylvania Railroad Company. *American Architect and Building News*

tral office building for that city, awarded the commission to Bruce Price.

In October of that year Price presented his first design for the new Windsor Station, but economic concerns necessitated revisions toward simplification. Finally, early in 1888 his fourth design was approved. Construction began in the spring and was completed by February 1889 at a cost of about two million dollars. The impatient patrons advocated speed and the builders, William Davis and Sons of Ottawa, with their newly-devised six-derrick system, certainly hastened the completion.[56] Omar Lavallée states that William Van Horne, proud of the accomplishment, shocked the inhabitants of Montreal with a sign proclaiming in six-foot high letters: "Beats all Creation—the New C.P.R. Station."[57]

Built of cut stone in an arch-and-spandrel system, Windsor Station is a creative and bold expression of the Romanesque Revival. It recalls Henry Hobson Richardson's work of the 1870s in the use of Romanesque details—the clustered piers of the facade, the textured masonry, the cornice detail, the polygonal turrets and pointed dormers, and the column capitals in the waiting room. It also parallels developments in Chicago. Similarities can be noted in the Chicago Art Institute (1886–87) by Burnham and Root, and in the Auditorium Building of the Art Institute by Adler and Sullivan. Although the station has been considerably enlarged, the original part is intact and still dominates the city center skyline. Unfortunately, as Harold D. Kalman maintains, later additions are not fully integrated with Price's design.[58]

The Windsor Street Station in Montreal was an original and bold expression of the Romanesque style. *Architectural Record*

In 1886, soon after Price had received the commission for Windsor Station, he was also asked to prepare designs for a resort hotel on the eastern slope of the Rockies, near Banff. Earlier in 1885, surveyors for the Canadian Pacific had discovered hot springs in that area and the company quickly realized the advantages of a deluxe hotel on the site, an area combining beautiful scenery with the medicinal springs. The townsite was named "Banff" after the Scottish birthplace of the president of the Canadian Pacific, Sir George Stephen. The environment may have been viewed by Van Horne and the others as similar to the Scottish Highlands. As it happened, Price's hotel, ready for vacationers and invalids by June of 1888, gave evidence of Scottish or Rhenish castle derivation, which in turn was largely inspired by the châteaux of the Loire valley. He used steep hipped roofs, pointed finialed dormers, corner turrets, and oriels—all descendants of these styles.

Unfortunately destroyed in 1925, Price's design also closely approximated that of his earlier hotels in the States and was likewise shingled. Nestled in the mountains, its relationship to the site offered a somewhat analogous situation to that of his houses at Tuxedo. The five-story frame structure was in the shape of an H, with an additional wing jutting out from the long side toward the scenic Bow River. Tiered verandas at the ends of the wings gave visual access to the spectacular scenery. Far removed from civilization, the hotel became an exotic resort along the railway route. Having thus established his reputation in Canada with these two buildings, Price was later to be recalled for other important commissions.

The next step in the creation of a railway hotel system occurred in the city of Quebec. In 1892, not the Canadian Pacific Railway Company itself but a group of private citizens wishing to stimulate tourist trade formed the Château Frontenac Company. Most of the gentlemen were actually connected with the Canadian Pacific Railway. In fact, the head of the company was William Van Horne, the new president of the railway. Having acquired a magnificent site for a hotel overlooking the Saint Lawrence River, they quickly raised sufficient capital to begin construction. Bruce Price was selected as the architect. Work was begun in May 1892, and the Château Frontenac had its formal opening nineteen months later, on December 18, 1893.[60]

Externally, the composition is compact and robust. For the walls Price selected bright orange-red Glenboig brick, brought from Scotland, with ashlar trim as his principal building materials. For the high-peaked roofs he chose oxidized green copper. Perched on Dufferin Terrace like a medieval

Price's rendering shows the original appearance of the Château Frontenac. *Architectural Record*

Plan of the Chateau Frontenac. *Architectural Record*

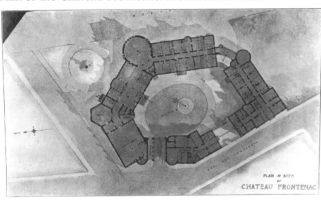

fortress, it is colorful and attractive against the blue sky and water. The irregularity of the terrain suggested to Price a complex of connecting wings adapted to the different heights. This allowed for an asymmetrical placement of towers and turrets, of gates and entrances, of chimneys and windows. Four wings of unequal length resulted in a horseshoe-shaped plan. Like Frank Lloyd Wright years later, Price insisted upon an intimate relationship between design and site, and succeeded admirably in this instance.

In its pre-Renaissance French design it follows the traditional style of the surrounding ramparts, which were built on the site of the Château Louis, the governor's residence during the French and early English regimes.[61] The historical importance of the site, as well as its actual appearance, strongly influenced the architect in his selection of the picturesque old style. The architect, Russell Sturgis, was impressed by Price's design and considered the choice of the French style most advantageous. Noting that it was the only historical style that could accommodate innumerable windows without appearing foolish and distorted, he added praise for the architect's skill in using nineteenth-

century window styles in a medieval type of structure.[62] The medieval châteaux would have been well-known to Price, both through his travels in Europe and by illustrations in contemporary books. One publication, Victor Petit's *Châteaux de la Vallée de la Loire*, contained many illustrations of pre-Renaissance French designs. One of these, the Château de Jaligny, rebuilt in the fifteenth century, may have provided inspiration for the Château Frontenac. Kalman notes, "similar are the strong flat wall surfaces horizontally articulated and covered by steep, unbroken roofs; the robust towers with conical roofs and canted eaves; and the triangular dormers with three finials."[63] As at Windsor Station, Price's style also showed the influence of Richardson's work of the 1870s and early 1880s. Among the examples, Richardson's N. L. Anderson House in Washington, D.C., had much the same feeling for mass as the Frontenac. In an interview with Barr Ferree in 1899, Bruce Price acknowledged his dual indebtedness to both medieval and contemporary architecture when he described the motif of the Château Frontenac as "the early French chateau adapted to modern requirements."[64]

While the design for the Château Frontenac is undoubtedly the work of Bruce Price, William Van Horne was in part responsible for its character. Writing to Sir George Stephen, his predecessor as president of the Canadian Pacific Railway, Van Horne shared his ideas for the proposed hotel, stating that he would not throw money away on "marble and frills" but would

> depend on broad effects, rather than ornamentation and details. . . . I am planning to retain the old fortifications and to keep the old guns in place, setting the hotel well back from the face of the hill so as to afford ample room for a promenade, and I think it will be the most talked-about hotel on this continent.[65]

He apparently watched the progress of the construction and kept abreast of its every aspect. John M. Gibbon relates, "Van Horne took particular pride in this hotel, and went out one day with Bruce Price on a little boat on the St. Lawrence River to convince himself that the elevation as seen from the river was sufficiently majestic."[66]

The bulk of the interior space on the first two floors is devoted to public lounges and dining area. The one hundred and seventy bedrooms were furnished with sturdy oak furniture in sixteenth-century style. Price located the best bedrooms in the main wing facing the Saint Lawrence River, and filled the towers with the choicest suites. Decorated in various national styles, they were furnished with valuable antiques. All of the interior design was the work of the Messrs. Edward and William S. Maxwell of Montreal.

Price, with his wife, Josephine, attended the official opening of the Château Frontenac and was honored as the American architect who had already contributed so much to Canadian architectural style. He had a host of friends in the Province of Quebec and had been put up for membership in Montreal's most exclusive clubs. Since the rules of these clubs excluded foreigners, he was proposed as an honorary member. Then someone discovered that only members of the royal family were eligible for honorary membership. Then, as his daughter Emily Post remembers with delight, a new rank was created to solve the dilemma, namely, that of Perpetual Guest. And this rank had only one member: Bruce Price.[67]

Emily also loved to recount an experience of the 1890s that exemplified the esteem her father enjoyed. The duke of Connaught, later governor general of Canada, was touring the Dominion with his duchess, and Price, his friend, was invited to travel on the royal train. At a whistle stop in Alberta the ranchers had gathered for a glimpse of their queen's youngest son. A band was waiting to play "God Save the Queen." As the train halted, several railroad officials stepped off and were greeted by the local station master. Then came Bruce Price, tall, handsome, smiling. The band struck up the national anthem and a little child came forward and thrust a bouquet into Price's hand. At the same moment His Royal Highness the duke of Connaught appeared on the platform of his car. Later, as Bruce Price expressed his embarrassment, the duke chuckled and said, "Never mind, Bruce. It isn't your fault that God made you the perfect image of a duke."[68]

During the 1890s Price spent half of his time working for Canadian clients. His prestige and popularity grew in Canada as well as in the United States. Shortly after the opening of the Frontenac, Sir Donald Smith, one of the founders of the Canadian Pacific Railway, commissioned him to design Royal Victoria Academy, on the campus of McGill University, Montreal. Built in 1895, it was named for Queen Victoria and graced with a statue of the queen at its center. Constructed of cut stone, the structure is classic in its symmetry but reminiscent of the medieval in its turreted decoration and its roof treatment. It is, in fact, a simple combination of a three-part mass with a pediment accenting the central doorway. The central section of the facade is recessed to form a covered porch with seven large, arched openings.

Another direct commission from the Canadian Pacific Railway followed the McGill building. In 1895 Price was asked to prepare plans for a combined hotel and railroad station in Montreal. Construction began in May 1896, and the Place Viger Hotel and Station were opened for use in August 1898. In full-blown French château style, the structure relates stylistically to the Frontenac but lacks its vigorous solidity. Instead, it exhibits a lighter, more romantic, fairy-tale-castle style. The bright orange-red brick building with its green copper roof created a cheerful exterior for this miniature city with the very latest accommodations. The first floor performed the functions of a station, including a ballroom and dining rooms. Above, eighty-eight bedrooms were luxuriously furnished. The Place Viger Hotel enjoyed brisk business and social prestige until declining patronage forced its closing in 1933. In 1951 the city of Montreal bought the building for use as office space and extensively altered its appearance.[69]

Meanwhile the Château Frontenac had become so popular that it became a national symbol for luxurious hotel designs in Canada, as well as for federal buildings, railway stations, and apartment houses. The growing patronage of the hotel demanded an addition, which Price designed in 1897—the Citadel wing and Pavilion, which joined the open ends of the original horseshoe-shaped plan. This wing, thinner and lighter, distinctly vertical in composition with a more attenuated round tower, more directly influenced twentieth-century architects in their adaptation of the château style. In 1908–9 W. S. Painter added the Mount Carmel Wing, an extension toward the north of Price's Citadel Wing. In 1920–24 massive extensions by Edward and W. S. Maxwell, including the seventeen-story Tower block, doubled the hotel's capacity, bringing its total number of guest rooms to 658, in contrast to the 170 of the original building.[70]

The Place Viger Hotel and Railroad Station was opened for use in 1898. *Architectural Record*

Price's last design in Canada was the James Ross House at 3544 Peel Street, Montreal. It was constructed in 1900 by Ross himself, a contractor who had served on the Board of the Château Frontenac Company and was one of the builders of the railway. Built of cut stone in the French château style, it is a smaller and gracious adaptation of that mode. Purchased later by J. W. McConnell, it was given to McGill University. Now known as "Chancellor Day Hall," it serves as an administration building for the faculty of the Law School. These buildings in Canada must have occupied half of Price's time from the mid-1880s through the 1890s, but they added considerably to his prestige as an architect.

Other Work, 1885–1892

Price's other work was divided during the critical years 1885–1892. Reflecting the influence of the widely disparate Tuxedo and Canadian commissions, it covered a broad geographical area. His personal creativity had reached a peak at Tuxedo Park, but his accomplishments elsewhere were varied in quality as well as style. The French character of his work in Canada followed him back to the States where, although used with moderate success, it was received with less enthusiasm in a milieu lacking the Canadian archaeological precedent.

In 1885 his growing reputation won him recognition in Cincinnati, Ohio, and a commission for a group of semi-detached houses at Mount Auburn, a section of the city at the corner of Highland Avenue and MacMillan Street. The one house that still stands gives an indication of the original, impressive, planned-community group. One of the striking features of this house is the startling intensity of the color combination—red brick, gray stone, green shingles, and cream stucco—not unusual in Price's work at the time. That same year in Cincinnati he competed against, among others, Burnham and Root, Wheelwright and Everett, and Henry Hobson Richardson for the design of the Chamber of Commerce Building. Price's design was similar to municipal buildings of early sixteenth-century French Renaissance style. Its historical evocations were evidently unacceptable to the judges, for Richardson was awarded the competition.[71]

Price was filled with ideas during these productive years of his life, but often deeply frustrated by circumstances that either modified his original intentions or prevented the execution of his designs. A case in point is the Sterling House in Stratford, Connecticut. Built in 1886 from a Price design, there is evidence that an amateur architect and friend of the client, Cordelia Sterling—namely, Rufus W. Bunnell of Stratford—was given freer reign than Price in the actual execution and was permitted to make unfortunate changes.[72] A design of 1886 of a Japanese style house for the San Francisco area received great popularity but was never built. It is thought to be the first published drawing in the United States of a house in Japanese style.[73] Another famous design of 1886, a variation on the Japanese design, apparently met a similar fate. It was planned for Colonel W. H. Howard at San Mateo, California, but there is no record of its construction there.

Although these and other interesting designs were never executed, others were completed that greatly expanded Price's creative range. In 1887 a city house for his brother-in-law Mr. Morton at 36 West Fifty-sixth Street in New York was praised by a contemporary critic. Russell Sturgis said, "the general effect of the picturesque and spirited front to enliven the dull street is most delightful."[74] This house, which no longer stands, was of red brick with a stone first floor, and terra-cotta and stone detail. Price's design depended partially on the fact that the floor levels did not coincide with those of the houses on either side of it. The projection of its bays on the second and third stories added variety to the rather monotonous row of 1870 houses that flanked it. The organization of the windows on three floors in groups of five was bold and original, and had a quality similar to early works of Frank Lloyd Wright. The false gable gave the house added distinction. Unlike its neighbors, the basement story was lower, so that the entrance was closer to the street. Hidden under a great stone arch, it was a sheltered retreat from the noisy street. The decoration of the house—modified classic pilasters and bands of geometric patterning in the brick—indicated Price's continuing interest in picturesque medieval and Renaissance styles.

The F. H. Levey House of 1887 located in Elizabeth, New Jersey, now destroyed, was somewhat French in appearance. Although the architect was still working in basic shapes grouped simply together, the detail of the house was more elaborate. The steep pitched roof and high chimneys, the decorative corner turrets, and the flamboyant terra-cotta details reflected his work in Canada. However, two other designs of that same year, a cottage in Rye, New York, and a house for Tacoma, Washington, are similar to the sturdy, simple Tuxedo designs.

The house built for Mrs. A. L. Loomis at Ringwood, New Jersey, that same year is even closer to the vigor of the Tuxedo work, with its bold gambrel roof, large irregular stones, projecting porches, and circular terrace on the right side. The more important features are made dominant by the subordination of the lesser elements, resulting in a design of classic proportions and quiet elegance.

In 1889 a similar house, Carisbrooke, set high on a hill above Schroon Lake in the Adirondacks, was built for J. D. Platt. Certainly Price must have known Andrew Jackson Downing's comments about the Carisbrooke in England, for which this house quite likely was named.[75] The curved shingle walls, the battered tower, and the reverse curve on the tower roof were all reminiscent of Tuxedo. During recent years the house was used as an inn and unfortunately was demolished in 1955.

Two other houses of the same year were decidedly more eclectic. One "Springhurst" in Black Rock, Connecticut, hinted of English half-timbered style. The other, the J. C. Pumpelly House in Morristown, New Jersey, in its general treatment suggests American Colonial and Georgian styles combined with the high-pitched roof of the French château style.

Although Price was largely involved with domestic architectural commissions, he accomplished some forceful work in other areas. In 1889 he designed the Church of Our Savior in Salem, Ohio.[76] Of simple Romanesque Revival style it recalls early English churches, with its large, square tower incorporated in the front facade and occupying the full width of the nave. The broad roof encloses both nave and aisles with its low double pitch. The result is an integrated, powerful design.

Another nondomestic commission was the Second National Bank of Cumberland, Maryland, 1890. Situated on a major corner in the town, this little bank, though now overpowered by larger buildings, is still impressive through the force of its strong design. The decorative elements have been grouped into strong shapes within the basic, simple geometry of the whole mass. Until August 1954 the red-brick and brownstone exterior provided a warm and dignified contrast to the shiny contemporary facades. Then extensive alterations included a new red granite covering of the brownstone.[77]

Two buildings done for Yale University were noteworthy during this period and influenced other college architects. In 1889 Osborn Hall was constructed. It was named after its benefactor, Mr. Osborn, a New York broker who had handled the accounts of the wealthy, including William H. Vanderbilt, J. P. Morgan, Jay Gould, and William Rockefeller. Designed in a kind of Richardsonian Romanesque, it formed a strong corner for the fortresslike Old Campus. Constructed of gray Stony Creek granite and trimmed with red Long Meadow sandstone, it was roofed with orange-red tile. The curved facade was approached by encircling stairs leading to its five large entrance arches supported by triple columns. This imposing portal was flanked by two circular towers. The heavy stone plus the bold treatment resulted in an impressive entrance to the university. By the early twentieth century interest in the Romanesque style on the part of both architects and patrons was waning. Whether this change in attitude was stylistic or

Osborn Hall at Yale, built in 1889, was a striking derivation of Richardson's Romanesque style. *Architectural Record*

purely a matter of accommodation, the building suffered premature destruction in favor of a more spacious contemporary structure, Bingham Hall. Commenting on the building Montgomery Schuyler said, "Mr. Bruce Price's building seems to me in itself one of the best things in its kind that Richardson's work inspired, in spite of some obvious faults, such as the apparent weakness of the triple columns that carry the entrance arches, than which no fault could be less Richardsonian."[78] Schuyler then makes a comparison between Osborn Hall and Alexander Hall at Princeton University, the latter designed by William A. Potter. He noted such a similarity between the two that he wondered which came first. Actually Osborn Hall by Price preceded the Potter design by at least two years.[79] Potter must have been familiar with Osborn Hall and used it as a model for his building. John Massey Rhind, who did the sculpture for Price's American Surety Building, did the sculpture for the facade of Alexander Hall.

The second building at Yale was Welch Hall of 1891. The simple design, the construction of rusticated stone, and the many arched windows indicate the Romanesque style, while the high-pitched roof, tall chimneys, and peaked fourth-floor dormers suggest a French Canadian influence. Three entryways provide access to the three vertical divisions of the building. Originally entirely a residence, the first floor is now rearranged for office space. Viewed from New Haven Green, this solid, functional building is still impressive.

Many of these undertakings were not generally congenial to Price's spirit. Although his financial and professional status grew spectacularly during this period, his commissions became increasingly incongruous, in the light of his personality and ability. As Graybill sums it up, "The kind of work

Welch Hall at Yale, built in 1891, is a simpler adaptation of the Romanesque style. *Architectural Record*

he did best was already out of fashion, to be replaced by conscious efforts to impress the world; self-conscious efforts required by America's growing world importance and cultural inferiority."[80]

Price became increasingly eclectic in his choice of building styles. Although basically conservative, he could, it seems, assume any stylistic direction that best suited his taste or that of his patron. Like other select architects of the time, he was deluged with an enormous amount of work. Although no records remain from Price's office, it must have been large. He employed as many as fifty assistants, who occupied the entire top floor of the St. James Building.[81] Beset with numerous diverse commissions and attempting to live up to the expectations of his patrons, the obliging Price found little time for original thinking.

Tall Buildings in New York

By the 1890s Bruce Price's reputation enabled him to function over a wide geographical area in the United States as well as in Canada. At the same time he occupied himself with the problem of the tall commercial building in New York, and was one of the leaders in its development. Although he cannot be credited with the first so-called skyscraper, he did design the prototype tall building "tower," which was widely copied by other architects. This design, which became almost a formula, was Renaissance in style. Although Chicago was the site of initial progress in tall-building design, the buildings there were more volumetric and have little to do with the later development of a different aesthetic in New York. Chicago was the site of the most progressive building in the last phases of masonry construction. Richardson's great Marshall Field Warehouse in Chicago (1885–87), a seven-story structure constructed of stone, strongly influenced commercial building development. When the first skeleton buildings were done there, they tended to conform to the masonry style.

Price must have known of developments in Chicago, not only from publications, but certainly from George A. Fuller, the New York engineer who was the builder of many of Price's buildings. Fuller constructed the Tacoma Building in Chicago in 1886, which was the design of William Holabird and Martin Roche. Twelve stories in height, it was the first to have a riveted-metal frame construction. Yet this building, like later examples in Chicago, was more volumetric than Price's work in New York. Price's attention was focused primarily on the aesthetic considerations connected with skele-ton construction and he expressed himself clearly on these matters:

> The fact is the tower idea is the only artistic solution of the problem of high building design. The great defect of most high buildings is the hideous back wall and the utter lack of care by the architect or the owner to make the interior sides, as they rise up beyond the surrounding roofs, architectural entities of any sort whatever. Our commercial buildings are, almost without exception, designed wholly with reference to their relation to the street, while, as a matter of fact, they have no such relation at all, their aerial aspect being of more value to the city as a whole than the distorted partial views that, as a rule, are all we can obtain from the street.[82]

Other architects, notably Garnier, Perret, Le Corbusier and Wright, shared Price's concept, with variations. They were all concerned with the total visual effect of their buildings. However, crowded cities' building codes often prevented the exercise of their aesthetic freedom. In recent years the United Nations buildings, Lever House, the Seagram Building, the Empire State Building, and others, exemplify the ideal that Price envisioned.

Possibly Price's increasing interest in classical forms at this stage in his career affected his concept of tall building design. He must have reasoned, as so many others had done before him, that classicism implies a beginning, a middle, and an end, or, in architectural terms—a base, a mid-section, and a top. His first important design, which took into consideration this total visual effect, was the Sun Building, planned for City Hall Square, New York.

Although never constructed because the site proved unsatisfactory, it influenced his subsequent tall building commissions and became the prototype for tall buildings all over the country.[83] Conceived as an isolated tower, all four sides of the structure received equal treatment, with the exception of the street-side entrance porch. This three-story porch was ornately decorated against the severely simple main section of the building above it. A gradually increasing ornamentation near the top terminated in an elaborate cornice. The heaviness of the higher decoration was intended to make it visible and coherent from the street below. A pyramidal roof completed the vertical thrust of the proposed thirty-four stories.[84]

In 1894 Price's first and most important executed tall building was constructed for the American Surety Company. He won the competition over an impressive list of New York's most important architects, including McKim, Mead and White, George B. Post, Carrère and Hastings, N. LeBrun and Sons, R. W. Gibson, W. Wheeler Smith, George Martin Huss, and John R. Thomas. Located on the southeast corner of Broadway and Pine in lower Manhattan, it created a sensation. The erection of New York's "first real skyscraper" aroused

Constructed in 1894, Price's American Surety Building was an early example of the tower concept. *Architectural Record*

considerable interest in the city.[85] Every day the yard of Trinity Church, across the street, was filled with interested and anxious onlookers. No one thought it could really stand up when it reached its height of twenty stories. Upon completion, it became a fully tenanted and popular building. Its preeminence in height lasted until 1899, when George B. Post's edifice known as the St. Paul's Building topped New York's skyline and became the tallest in the world.[86]

Price's skyscraper rested on concrete and brick caissons sunk seventy-two feet to bed rock. The steel framework superstructure was sheathed with Maine granite. Its design followed the "tower" concept. The fronts on Broadway and Pine were repeated on the south and east faces of the building, which rose above the roofs of adjoining structures. Because the site is irregular, the plan is not perfectly square. The elevation follows the concept of the Sun Building design, in that the simple central mass of eleven stories is topped by heavier decoration near the top. The three lower floors are set off by colossal Ionic columns backed by piers. At the top of the piers are sculptured figures executed by Price's friend, the sculptor John Massey Rhind. These symbolic caryatids and other sculptural adornment help tie the various parts of the building together, thus permitting the realization of the classic ideal in both structure and decoration.[87] Because of its great height, in early views of New York Price's building was a landmark. Now, however, twentieth-century skyscrapers dwarf it and hide two of the sides. Moreover, it has been considerably enlarged in width and thus looks more cumbersome and less like a tower. It is now the Bank of Tokyo.

The St. James Building of 1896, located on Broadway and West Twenty-sixth Street, was a less-expensive version of the American Surety Building. In this case, the steel framework was covered with warm red brick with quoins and other decoration in cool yellow terra-cotta. The designs for this building and for the mansion at Georgian Court, in each of which Price used terra-cotta in much the same way, were exhibited at the Architectural League Exhibition of 1897.[88] He was obviously fascinated, like Louis Sullivan, his great contemporary, with the decorative effects inherent in the shape of the material.

This building, sixteen stories high, was denied the isolated "tower" concept. Perhaps in the interest of economy, only the facades on Broadway and Twenty-sixth Street were given full decorative treatment. Evidently the practical mercantile world sometimes hindered the realization of Price's ideas. However, as in the Sun and American Surety designs, he accents the upper and lower

Detail of the northeast portion of the "Canterbury Pilgrims" frieze by Robert Van Vorst Sewell. *Photo by Douglas L. McIlvain*

The music room of the mansion is decorated in dainty French rococo style. Each piece of the carved and gilded furniture bears the owner's monogram. *Photo by Douglas L. McIlvain*

In the mansion library dark mahogany columns flank the fireplace of black African marble. *Photo by Douglas L. McIlvain*

Detail of the sea horses and cherubs. *Photo by Sister Mary Theresa McCarthy*

In his design for the St. James Building of 1896, Price used terra-cotta quoins in much the same way as on the mansion at Georgian Court. *American Architect and Building News*

sections of the building. The middle section of ten stories is a simple, unified arrangement of windows in groups of two, divided by brick piers. By contrast, the heavier uppermost mass of four stories, largely of terra-cotta, is topped by a handsome classical cornice. Five huge arches, separated by modified Ionic engaged columns, flank three floors of windows grouped in three's. The rhythm of the arches is repeated in the lower floors of the building—round-arched coupled windows on the second floor, and a restrained, arched entrance flanked by Ionic engaged columns.

In 1899 Price designed several buildings on narrow corner lots. The International Banking and Trust company building at Broadway and Cedar Street is L-shaped in plan, with a wing extended behind the small buildings on Broadway. The first two floors are sheathed with gray limestone, the other twelve stories in white brick and terra-cotta with red brick used decoratively in the voussoirs of the round-headed windows and other detail. The general treatment resembles that of the American Surety and St. James buildings, with simplification in ornamentation. A similar Price design of 1902 was that of the Bank of the Metropolis, at Sixteenth Street and Union Square. It was built by the George A. Fuller Company and owned by the Bank

of Manhattan. With its bowed Ionic portico, slender shaft, and elaborate cornice, it is a fine example of the Beaux-Arts influenced commercial style.

A design for a "proposed office building" later became, with appropriate changes, the Hudson Terminal Building on lower Broadway, built about 1900. Price's very solid design with massive projections at the four corners was weakened by later modifications.

Other large buildings of the early 1900s indicate the variety of Price's involvement. In 1900, in collaboration with A. M. Darroch, an associate at the time, Price designed a dormitory building at Barnard College in New York. As in the earlier designs, color plays an important role in the visual effect. The building is constructed on a steel frame covered with red brick with gray stone trim; the patterning of the brick gives added texture. Built on the edge of the campus of Columbia University, facing Amsterdam Avenue at 120–121st streets, the building called Plimpton Hall resembles Price's more medieval domestic work.

During the early 1900s Price was the consulting architect to Marvin & David for the Hotel Knickerbocker completed in 1906 and located at the corner of Broadway and Forty-Second Street. Although it is impossible to determine the extent of Price's influence in this project, the hotel was built in his favored "modern Renaissance" style and of his favorite materials of this period—red brick, stone, and terra-cotta. The Knickerbocker was an extremely fashionable and popular hotel from 1906 until 1920. At the latter date, it assumed its later role as an office building.[89]

Price's last two executed tall building designs were done in collaboration with Jules Henri de Sibour. After graduation from Yale in 1896, this talented young architect had joined Price's New York office. In 1898, at Price's suggestion, he sailed for Paris for a period of training at the École des Beaux-Arts. Upon his return he rejoined Price, who made him a partner in 1902. Henceforth, the firm became known as Price & de Sibour. That year they designed the Century Building at 72–74 Broadway in New York. Constructed by the George A. Fuller Company for the Century Publishing Company, it included faint echoes of Price's American Surety Building just a short distance away. The building and others adjacent to it have since been replaced by a larger building. The other structure of 1902, the Law Building at 259 Fifth Avenue, a strikingly simple design with undecorated surfaces and enormous plate glass windows, has also been replaced. It was closer to later twentieth-century styles except for the elaborate cornice characteristic of so much of Price's later work.

Late Work, 1892–1903

Concurrent with work in the design of sky-scrapers, other disparate demands were made upon Price and his staff. In collaboration with the firm of McKim, Mead and White and the architects James B. Lord and Clarence S. Luce, he designed the King Model Houses of 1891.[90] This block of houses, located at 138–139th streets between Seventh and Eighth avenues in Manhattan, was intended for people of moderate wealth. The project was an effort to increase the value of the property by attracting wealthy tenants from downtown. Constructed of light brick with stone and terra-cotta trim, the general effect is that of Renaissance town houses, with freely adapted details of quoins and window arches. Although the project eventually became a kind of low-cost housing development, it is still considered desirable and attractive.

Another Price design of 1892 was the Hotchkiss School in Lakeville, Connecticut.[91] The architect planned a self-sufficient complex with tall central section and two lower wings. Price's intention was to bring everything close together, rather than place buildings picturesquely around a large area. Russell Sturgis complimented the design for its quality and plan: "The great colleges which have been rearranging their buildings lately would have been wise had they considered the convenience of pupils and teachers as thoroughly as have the managers of this school."[92] The size of the original part is now inadequate and forms only the heart of a more extended campus. The yellow brick of the old buildings contrasts violently with the red brick of the newer Georgian additions.

That same year Price designed the Railroad Station in Elizabeth, New Jersey. The well-organized, stone structure was Romanesque in style. A tall tower anchored the building to the ground in a positive way. The arcade motif of the windows permitted extraordinary interior light. Unfortunately, a purely functional structure has now replaced the fine building.

Price returned to New Haven in 1892 to design a building for the New Haven Colony Historical Society. It was, as he described it, to be "modeled after the Italian 'renaissance,' sometimes called the colonial style, but with such modifications as are made necessary by a climate more rigid than that of southern France."[93] Completed in September 1893, it was used by the Society until November 1930, after which it became Yale University's Bureau of

"The Turrets," a summer home at Bar Barbor, Maine, was a great and dramatic design. *Stately Homes in America*

134

Appointments. In 1940 it was destroyed to make room for the new part of Silliman College. By an interesting twist of fate, the architects were Eggers & Higgins, successors to Price's pupil John Russell Pope.

The best of Price's later domestic architecture was a summer home built in 1893 for John J. Emery of Cincinnati. Located at Bar Harbor, Maine, "The Turrets," as it was called, was a great and dramatic design.[94] Built of sandy-pink stone, its general robustness suggests Tuxedo, although its many turrets also link it with the French château style. The plan is extraordinarily open. To the right of the main entrance, one large room fills the entire half of the house and opens onto the porch that links it to the sea. Its casual informality marks it as perhaps the climax of the seaside houses of the nineteenth century.

The simple geometry of Price's earlier work was also apparent in Saint Mary-by-the-Sea, an Episcopal Chapel at Black Rock, Connecticut, constructed in 1893. The exterior walls were built of logs brought from Canada. A large covering roof protected the exterior porch as well as the interior of the chapel. This simple, restrained building, unfortunately destroyed in the 1920s, was used for its brief life span by wealthy yachtsmen who cruised in the area.

Price's work seems to alternate between simplicity and extravagance. That same year a design was made for Daniel Baird Wesson of Springfield, Massachusetts, a well-known inventor who had developed the Smith and Wesson revolver and thereby amassed a fortune. Since he wanted his house to be lavish and pretentious, he decided in favor of the French château style.[95] In fact, by 1893, this style was so popular with wealthy clients that architects often were not free to choose their own form of eclecticism. Possibly Price was too busy to oversee the commission himself, for he entrusted an able young associate, Edwin J. Parlett, with the completion of the project. It is therefore difficult to determine the extent of Price's involvement in the work.

Built of red Maine granite, most of which is left rough, the Wesson House looks monumental and impressive on the gently sloping site. The carriage entrance to the house is on one side, but the main entrance facing the street is flanked by two circular towers with green copper roofs; the garden façade is even more ornate, with its rounded stairway projection and ornamental ironwork on the balconies. The interior is supposedly Louis XIV but contains a Colonial library, a Louis XV salon, and a magnificent entrance hall similar to those in English Georgian houses.

The French influence continued in Price's work but was often accompanied by a classic simplicity and directness. The Henry R. English House at 38 Hillhouse Avenue in New Haven, Connecticut, is an excellent example of this style tendency. Built in 1895 it is a striking, compact, neoclassic design, which indicated a new development in house planning for the wealthy. Social prestige in the "gay nineties" demanded spacious areas for the entertainment of numerous guests. An open interior plan with many first-floor rooms centering around a large entrance hall became the vogue.

While Price was working in a classic style, he did a proposed addition to the White House in Washington, D.C. His tremendous respect for the original design prompted his plan to enlarge the house from either end. The tripartite plan was intended to separate the private, social, and public functions of the president's house.[96] But the commission for the addition was given to his worthy competitors, the firm of McKim, Mead and White.

Undoubtedly Price's disappointment over the loss of the commission was overshadowed by his next interesting challenge. It was at that time, early in 1896, that George Jay Gould asked him to design buildings for him at Lakewood. Work at the estate that became known as Georgian Court occupied the architect over a period of five or more years. The Gould commission was an example of another trend of 1890s when more and more wealthy Americans were building country homes for year-round habitation and using their city dwellings for only a few months of the year.

During this period of his life, Bruce Price was an important and highly respected member of his profession and held many offices in architectural societies and on architectural committees. He served as a member of the Legislative Committee on Government Architecture and helped formulate rules for the standardization of fees, ownership of designs, and architectural plagiarism. In 1896 he was one of the judges for the Sherman Monument, the competition being awarded to the celebrated sculptor Augustus Saint-Gaudens. In 1896 and 1898 he judged the competitions for the Traveling Scholarship of the University of Pennsylvania. In 1898 he was elected president of the Architectural League of New York.[97] Architectural journals published his ideas and suggestions, as well as his constant stream of designs.

His work included a number of monuments. One of the best known is the memorial to the architect Richard Morris Hunt, situated along the edge of Central Park between Seventieth and Seventy-first streets on Fifth Avenue in New York. This memorial, designed in 1897, was a coveted commission in the architectural profession because of Hunt's prestige. Daniel Chester French was the sculptor for the bronze bust of Hunt as well as for the two flanking decorative figures. Price's design is derived from the classic style. A central niche flanked by two pilasters and carrying an entablature terminating in two piers serves as a background to the high pedestal upon which is placed the bust of Hunt. Six Ionic columns of dark marble support the entablature, which is decorated with classic motifs. The Municipal Art Society of New York sponsored the project from its own resources and from the contributions of other associations, whose names are carved on the marble slabs between the columns.[98]

Another important design was the monument for George A. Fuller, the contractor who had so often worked on buildings for Price. Done in 1901 in Oakwoods Cemetery, Chicago, it has a grand Greek pergola of extraordinary simplicity. Simple Doric columns that support the almost square pergola entablature are incorporated at their bases into the stone seats that flank each side. It may have suggested the style for a "Pergola" at the Pan American Exposition in Buffalo, by Carrère and Hastings.[99] Price's own monument is a simpler version of the Fuller Monument. Placed in the family plot in Hollenbeck Cemetery in Wilkes-Barre, Pennsylvania, it contains his grave as well as that of his wife and infant son.

During the early 1900s Price returned to his birthplace, Cumberland, Maryland, and designed the Parish House of Emmanuel Episcopal Church. It is a small stone building that fits into the architectural scheme of the adjacent, older church, the successor to the one in which Price was baptized. The tall, central, pointed window repeats the large window of the church, but seems to emphasize it rather than detract from it. The three small windows on the opposite end also repeat the motif of the other end of the church. In this strong, simple mass of stone Price recaptured the power of the early Tuxedo designs. He presented this small building to the congregation as a remembrance of his affection.[100]

No records remain to clarify how much work Price's office was doing during these years around 1900. He lost a number of important commissions to illustrious competitors, including: a design for Mount Sinai Hospital, New York (1899), to Arnold W. Brunner; one for the Wilkes-Barre Court House (1900), to Carrère and Hastings; and designs for the New York Customs House and the New York Stock Exchange (1900), to Cass Gilbert. He exhibited drawings for other projects of which there is no proof of construction.

Price's last major work was the Miriam Osborn Memorial Home in Harrison, New York. It was a benefaction of Mr. Osborn who had financed Osborn Hall at Yale. After the death of Mr. Osborn in 1885 and Mrs. Osborn in 1891, the home was planned in accordance with her will. Price had published a rendering for the commission in 1900, but the building was not completed until 1907, four years after his death. The drawing is very similar to the executed design, but the latter is somewhat enlarged and heightened. The red-brick building with white terra-cotta trim is of classic design, with two powerful, handsome towers placed equidistant on the main facade. Obviously, Price's firm, and particularly de Sibour, had to complete the job.

In 1928 an Infirmary Wing was added to this Home, which was strikingly similar to a Price design published in 1899—a Home for Aged Gentlemen in Westchester County, New York. This wing was dedicated to the wife of Sir George Stephen and to the mother and wife of Sir Donald Smith. These were the two men who had built the Canadian Pacific Railway. Mr. John W. Sterling, friend and attorney of Mrs. Osborn and entrusted with the matter of the Home, donated the money in memory of the families of two of his best clients. Thus, in Price's wide circle of clients, there was an interesting complex of friendships.[101]

Another late project pointed up the esteem enjoyed by Price. In 1901 he exhibited drawings for a palace for His Royal Highness the crown prince of Japan.[102] Tokuma Katayama of Tokyo was the architect.[103] From all accounts Price worked hard on the designs which, in fact, reflected the exchange of Japanese and American stylistic influence during the late nineteenth century. Although Katayama eventually built a palace for the crown prince presumably incorporating Price's ideas, Price did not live to see it. He became ill in the winter of 1902–3, and family and friends urged rest and a change of scenery. According to his daughter Emily, on some days when he could no longer go to his office his young associate John Russell Pope would come down to Tenth Street to confer with him.[104] Yet, as he confided to Emily, who always shared his interests and satisfactions, he was not himself when he was not working. In March 1903 he was operated on by Dr. McBurney in New York Hospital for a "disease of the stomach." In May he went to Europe for a holiday. The sea voyage proved too much for him and he landed at Le Havre a very sick man. Emily got him to Paris to the Hotel de la Tremoille, where within a week he died on 29 May 1903.[105] Emily Post later recalled that she gave his papers and drawings to John Russell Pope, whom Price "had in a sense made his heir, recognizing the genius in the younger man which was to place him in the foremost ranks of the country's architects."[106]

A view of the estate taken from the stable tower, showing the mansion, the formal garden, and the lagoon that connects with Lake Carasaljo. *Moss Archives, Pach photo*

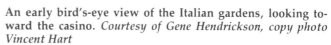

An early bird's-eye view of the Italian gardens, looking toward the casino. *Courtesy of Gene Hendrickson, copy photo Vincent Hart*

Bruce Price was an artist-executive with an artist's devotion to beauty, best known for the design of private homes. Like many of his great contemporaries in the architectural profession, he also enjoyed high status in society. The wealthy and the powerful were his friends as well as his clients. With the exception of Pierre Lorillard IV, they usually wanted their houses to be re-creations of European cultural traditions. He satisfied them with well-constructed buildings in wood or stone and, in the process, became a key figure in the synthesis of the wooden domestic architecture that has since influenced much of the western world. His houses, particularly at Tuxedo, provided a basis for subsequent eclecticisms as well as inspiration for Frank Lloyd Wright. In his handling of structures built of stone, he was a link between Richardson and Wright.

Price's most lavish and extensive domestic commission was that of Georgian Court. He threw all his creative energies into the design of the buildings and the landscaping of the estate and thoroughly enjoyed the challenge with which George Gould presented him. During the years 1896 through 1902, the pine forest on the banks of Lake Carasaljo became one of the showplaces of the nation.

In its general design, Georgian Court sums up much of his preceding work in a classical mode. Emphasis upon axial planning is realized in the design not only of the buildings, but of the gardens as well. In addition, his recurrent concern for open planning and an easy flow of interior space is at the heart of the plan of the buildings. Always partial to terra-cotta as a decorative material, he used it with great taste on the buildings, the entrance gate piers, and the posts of the encircling fence. Finally, the adaptation of building to site was a paramount concern to Price. However, unlike Tuxedo, for example, where he designed dwellings to blend with the woods, or at Quebec where he perched the Frontenac appropriately on the high bluff, at Lakewood he had to transform the site to accomodate his proposed designs. He had to ready a pine forest for classic adornment and Georgian architecture. The result was a splendid contribution to the Gilded Age architectural style.

Part III

Special Artistic
Features at
Georgian Court

The Gardens Designed by Bruce Price

The Italian or Classic Gardens, extending for almost a quarter of a mile between the Casino and Lake Carasaljo, lend a touch of the old world to Georgian Court. They were designed by the architect Bruce Price so that all would be in harmony—the buildings, the natural surroundings, and the gardens. In fact, the natural surroundings determined the form of the gardens. The proximity of Lake Carasaljo suggested the construction of a natural inlet, thereafter known as the sunken garden or lagoon. In an unpublished description of the gardens in the college archives, entitled "The Classic Gardens at Georgian Court," Price explains his intent: "To carry out this plan it became necessary, from the very first, to give the garden design much of the character of the famous formal gardens of Italy."

The initial concept of a lagoon was followed by a plan for a large electric fountain to be set at a suitable distance from the water sources. Its circular area became the dominant focal point of the gardens. From this point three roads were constructed radiating from it and extending to the Casino. From the roads, pathways that were originally bordered by arbor vitae lead to smaller, circular, focal areas, thereby creating a classic, axial pattern not unlike that of formal European gardens, notably those of Versailles.[1]

George Gould's art collectors, notably Sir Joseph Duveen, searched the gardens of Europe for objects of adornment. Several countries and centuries were drawn upon, thus rendering the statuary and other pieces priceless by their rarity: small marble fountains, superbly carved, date from fifteenth-century Italy; life-size stone statues of Greek gods and goddesses, and figures symbolizing the sea-

Carpo, fair goddess of the harvest, graces a corner of the garden. *Photo by Vincent Hart*

A marble pergola at the north end of the Italian Gardens encloses a secluded, sunny spot. *Photo by Vincent Hart*

Ornate marble chair in the Italian Garden. *Photo by Vincent Hart*

sons found in Kent, England, are dated seventeenth century, floral urns mounted on brick and marble pedestals are skillful copies of French originals. Near the north end of the gardens two large semicircular marble pergolas with Tuscan columns, marble benches, and statuary emphasize the classic character. Here and there are Price-designed wrought-iron lamp standards mounted on marble bases.

At the south end near the lake, the sunken garden with lagoon is the most lavish classic recreation. The huge space surrounding the water is walled and paved with red brick trimmed with white marble. There are carved marble benches, copies of originals in the Vatican Garden. Wherever neither money nor influence could bring rare objects from Europe, Gould had to content himself with copies. In order to unite the low level near the water with the much higher bank of land, Price designed a sumptuous architectural adjunct with balustraded double marble staircase leading to the higher terrain. Marble lions flank the staircases of the multi-level esplanade.

A superb example of late Renaissance design. *Photo by Vincent Hart*

Wrought-iron lamp standards designed by Bruce Price are found throughout the estate. *Photo by Vincent Hart*

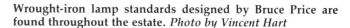

Near the entrance to the sunken garden are four marble urns, eight feet in height, which date from the sixteenth century. They are arranged in pairs on either side of the adjacent roadway. Their carved details are of mythological significance. My theory as to the meaning of the carvings is that the pair on the right is dedicated to Demeter, or Ceres, the goddess of the harvest; the creatures flanking the base of this pair are sphinxes. The other pair is dedicated to Bacchus, or Dionysus, the god of wine and vegetation; the supporting creatures are griffins. Judging from the appearance and arrangement of the figures, those on one side of the Demeter urn depict Pluto's abduction of Persephone, and on the other, Demeter's subsequent search for her daughter. Unlike the Demeter urns, which tell a story, the other two vases seem to be decorated with figures traditionally associated with the worshipers of Bacchus. The dancing poses of the figures call to mind the wildness of the Bacchanalian festivals. This pairing is not only logical from a thematic standpoint, because both divinities control similar domains; it is also consistent from a mythological angle, for Demeter and Bacchus were worshiped together by the Greeks and Romans.

The "mighty lion" is a recurring symbol throughout the estate:
    on the main entrance gate piers
    at the entrance to the sunken garden
    at the foot of the lagoon stairways. *Photos by Vincent Hart*

A view of the marble stairways and lagoon area soon after
completion in the early 1900s. *Moss Archives, Pach photo*

Furthermore, certain motifs, or symbols, are inter-
changeable to signify either deity, and thus can be
used identically on both sets of urns.[2] Seen from
the main entrance on Seventh Street, these gleam-
ing white urns appropriately frame the majestic
Apollo Fountain grandly situated nearby.

The focal point on the first level of the esplanade
is a superb seventeenth-century marble fountain,
over twenty feet in height, taken from a garden in
southern France.[3] Rising from the center of a circular basin twenty feet in diameter, a shaft that sup-
ports two more basins at different heights is surmounted by a classic male figure holding a
dolphin. When the fountain is in operation, the
water flows from the mouth of the fish and trickles
down to the three basins.

In order to connect the beautiful curved lagoon
of the water level with the lake and still give access
to public passage, Price designed an arched road
bridge to cross the fifty-foot expanse. Constructed

An eight-foot marble urn near the entrance to the sunken
garden. *Photo by Vincent Hart*

A huge wrought-iron piece, an eagle perched on a dragon, was purchased from the Paris Exposition of 1900. *Photo by Vincent Hart*

The majestic dolphin fountain rises to a height of more than twenty feet. *Photo by Davis Studios*

The sunken garden looking west, as it appeared during the Gould residency. *Moss Archives, Pach photo*

of red brick and terra-cotta in continuation of the sunken-garden design, it is supported by ornamental brick piers corresponding with the post design of the enclosing fence of the estate. The effect is impressive whether viewed from the lagoon side or from across the lake.

In 1901 a nonclassic feature was added to the gardens—a unique and interesting piece that now seems originally planned. An immense wrought-iron eagle perched on a dragon, purchased for Gould by Duveen through Tiffany and Company from the Japanese Section of the Paris Exposition of 1900, stands as a focal point midway on the center road of the garden. The sculpture was made for the Japanese government by the German firm the Brothers Armbruesler, of Frankfurt.[4] Disassembled for shipping, it was reassembled here and mounted on a huge base of boulders.

The general artistic theme of the Italian Gardens is appropriately echoed here and there throughout the estate. Near building entrances and garden paths, similar white floral urns, wrought-iron lamp standards mounted on marble bases, and marble benches continue the classic spirit.

Detail of the marble-decorated red-brick wall that surrounds the lagoon area. *Photo by Vincent Hart*

An early view of the elliptical Formal Garden slightly north of the mansion. *Moss Archives, Pach photo*

The Formal Garden

Midway between the mansion and the stables, Bruce Price planned a large elliptical flower garden, familiarly known as the Formal Garden. Flower beds placed with mathematical precision and bordered with boxwood and mazelike paths hold lovely annuals or perennials. Over the years a wide variety of blooms have delighted the passers-by.

Supporting a sundial at the center of the garden is a bronze sculptured group of three interlocking satyrs. This handsome piece, which is the focal point of the garden, is raised above the ground level on a marble-bordered plot of lawn. Marble benches nearby and along the paths invite a tranquil pause. At the east and west, groups of decorative floral urns formally enframe the edges. On the periphery tall pines, holly trees, Japanese maples, and copper beeches add notes of casual informality.

As a visitor enters the main gate of the estate, the garden is directly ahead. Looking beyond the garden he sees the Apollo Fountain in the distance. The result is a striking vista, purposely and cleverly created by the architect.

In the center of the Formal Garden playful bronze satyrs support a bronze and marble sundial. *Photo by Vincent Hart*

The Apollo Fountain Sculpted by John Massey Rhind

Bruce Price's original plan for the Italian Gardens included a large circular lawn area at the termination of the three long roads. In due time this spot was to have at its center an elaborate electrically powered fountain. Early in 1900 George Gould commissioned the friend and sometime collaborator of Price, John Massey Rhind, to design and execute the central group of the fountain as a birthday gift for his wife. When the superb gift was unveiled at Edith's birthday party in 1902, Westbrook Pegler of the New York *Journal* is reputed to have commented, "Coming generations will not see the like of this again."[5] He added that no other man of his day would build a fountain such as this with his own money.

Rhind chose the Apollo theme for the mythological symbolism of the fountain. Having studied under the French sculptor Dalou, and having spent several years in Paris under other instructors, he was undoubtedly somewhat influenced by French prototypes. Wayne Craven, in mentioning the Gould commission, indicates that it is "very much in the 'French flavor' of Versailles."[6] In fact, the Apollo fountain in the gardens at Versailles seems to have been a strong influence upon Rhind's selection of theme. In this fountain, which occupies a place of honor along the main promenade of the palace, Apollo, the sun god symbolizing Louis XIV, is shown in his chariot being drawn from the depths of the sea by four fiery steeds so that he may illuminate the heavens. However, Rhind's fountain is not a copy of that of Versailles but an original arrangement of the same figural motifs. In both fountains are to be found the Apollo figure, the chariot, sea horses, cherubs, fish, and figures with conch shells. But Rhind's pyramidal design, with the main forms not half submerged but placed higher above the water, is more compact and graceful.

The outer brim of the great basin of the Georgian Court fountain is a circle of white marble sixty feet in diameter. The central group is bronze and white Istrian marble. A colossal nautilus shell of bronze with a large octopus on its foremost part forms a chariot on which stands the bronze figure of Apollo driving a pair of marble seahorses. Apollo's powerful body is partially clothed with a sweeping drape, which appears to be carried by the wind as the god rides the sea. With head erect and piercing glance he seems to be scanning the realms. Rhind gave this figure a firm chin and determined expression, befitting a god worshiped by the ancients as conqueror, guardian, and deliverer. The seahorses are bridled by heavy ropes of bronze, hung with simulated sea moss cast in bronze. With his left hand Apollo holds the governing reins; his right hand projected toward the sky wields a threatening whip. His legs in a striding position are planted firmly in the basin of the shell-like chariot.

The manes of the charging, winged sea horses appear unruly and disheveled as they swirl down and around the heavy necks of the animals, whose flared nostrils and open mouths indicate excitement. Each steed strains forward with one foreleg resting on a short pedestal in front of him, the other raised with the hoof arched back. The hind

Front view of the Apollo Fountain, designed by John Massey Rhind. *Photo by Vincent Hart*

quarters of each horse are conventionalized into scaly, curled, taillike forms that extend along the outer sides of the chariot. The triumphant approach of Apollo seems to be heralded by two flanking mermaids, each blowing into a large conch shell to announce his arrival. Their tails intertwine with those of the horses and all terminate in large, graceful fins.

Placed between the sea horses at the front base of the chariot are two charming cherubs. Although made of marble, they seem almost pink-cheeked. Their small, round bodies add to their realistic appearance. The little boy supporting a large fish is holding open the mouth of the fish. The little girl presents a rather timid appearance as she holds her right hand to her mouth and rests the other hand on the fish. A swaddling drape gracefully unfolds across the backs of these figures so that both seem enframed by the wings of the sea horses.

Plausible reasons for Rhind's handling of the

Apollo theme may be found in ancient myths. According to the most popular accounts, Apollo's principal duty was to drive the sun chariot back and forth across the sky. Other myths glorify him as a god of healing, a prophetic figure, or as a savior from shipwreck, while some writers maintain that Apollo was a divine guardian of navigation. This function seems to have had its root, not in any special lordship over the sea, but in the wide diffusion of his cult in all Hellenic settlements. He exercised control not so much over the sea as over those elements and physiographical features which made for the convenience and safety of voyages—trade winds, harbors, estuaries, and the like.

Despite seeming incongruities of theme, Rhind's fountain is artistically impressive. Its pump mechanism, located underneath the esplanade leading to the sunken garden, draws water from Lake Carasaljo and throws upward twenty-five thousand gallons per hour. The flow of water is cleverly designed. The two sea horses appear to be

A view of the fountain from the rear shows Apollo astride the bronze nautilus-shell chariot. *Photo by Vincent Hart*

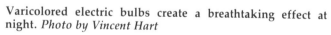

Detail of mermaid draped with seaweed. *Photo by Vincent Hart*

Varicolored electric bulbs create a breathtaking effect at night. *Photo by Vincent Hart*

snorting as swirling streams spray from their nostrils. The sprays from the conch shells held by the mermaids suggest melody being blown out. A spray issues from the mouth of the fish held by the cherubs, while from the mouth of the octopus, at the top of the chariot, two powerful sprays rise to a height of thirty feet. In a circular arrangement between the centerpiece and the rim of the basin, eight cylindrical forms mount water nearly twenty-five feet into the air. At the top of these forms many small openings emit thin but powerful streams of water. The streams twist upward slightly and fall at their peak, suggesting sheaves of windblown wheat. For this reason, the fountain is also known as the Wheat Fountain.

During the daylight hours when the fountain is in full play, crowds gather to delight in the gently blowing mist, to take innumerable photos, or simply to sit and admire. The lighting of the fountain at night is achieved by means of varicolored electric bulbs placed under glass at the top of the eight cylindrical forms. The effect is truly breath-taking. As the sun sinks in the west, Apollo is silhouetted against the indigo sky. With the lights playing on the water as the first star appears, everyone agrees that the fountain is the crowning glory of the Court.

According to J. Walker McSpadden, author of *Famous Sculptors of America*, Rhind discussed his elaborate preparation for the sculpture group as follows:

> I first made a full-size plaster model of the whole thing, and set it up in the exact spot; for that is the only way I could tell about the proper dimensions. The dwarf trees in the background did not admit of too large a fountain.[7]

Accordingly, when the sculptor's models for the marbles were ready, they were sent to Italy, where the artist Pietro Faitini carved them to order.[8] The bronze figures were cast by the John Williams, Inc., Bronze Foundry of New York City.[9] The marvelous pump mechanism, which simultaneously operates this fountain and a smaller dolphin fountain nearby, was manufactured by the H. & R. Roots Company of Indianapolis.

The Sculptor John Massey Rhind

The creator of the unique Apollo Fountain, John Massey Rhind, born on 8 July 1868 in Edinburgh, Scotland, came from a family of sculptors, of whom grandfather, father, and brothers were all engaged in that art. His father, John Rhind, R.S.A., was a prominent decorative sculptor also noted for statues of public figures. According to a biographer of Rhind in *Munsey's Magazine*, "two of the best local monuments are the work of his father." This same writer regards the elder Rhind's reclining figure of the marquis of Montrose in St. Giles as "a remarkable piece of classic art" and the colossal statue of William Chambers, the publisher, as "one of the landmarks of the Scottish capital."[10] John's wife was also of a highly artistic nature. As a result, some of the finest artists of Edinburgh were attracted to their home, where conversation centered on the arts.

This artistic milieu nourished the creativity of young John, who from earliest childhood modeled in clay and played with the sculptor's tools. While serving as an apprentice in his father's studio, he attended art classes at the Royal Scottish Academy. As a youth he was sent by his father to an art school in Lambeth, where he became a pupil of Jules Dalou, a clever sculptor and one of the leaders of the Commune who had been forced to flee from France. This teacher had much to do with the formation of the brilliant style that later characterized Rhind's work. Then always in contact with the artistic happenings of his country, Dalou sent a

John Massey Rhind (1868–1936). *Museum of the City of New York, photo by Davis & Sanford*

152

design to a competition in Paris. After it was judged the best of the entries, the government pardoned the exile, who returned to his homeland.

After Dalou's departure Rhind enrolled at the Royal Academy in London, where his skill and training won him three gold medals in one year. He was the first student who ever scored such a success. Sir Frederick Leighton, president of the Royal Academy, took a particular interest in this most promising student. Upon learning of Rhind's training under Dalou, he awarded the young sculptor a Traveling Scholarship to Paris and advised him to learn whatever else this master could teach him. Rhind's subsequent tutelage at the Parisian capital gave his future work the unmistakable imprint of the École des Beaux-Arts and its satellites. He studied and made sketches of the sculptural adornment in the gardens of Versailles, in the collections of the Louvre, and on the façades of many of the public buildings. But his own style during these early years was ruggedly realistic.

After two years in Paris, Rhind returned to England, where he soon received promising commissions. His interest in architecture as an art allied to sculpture resulted in a commission for a series of figures for a large building in Glasgow designed by the architect Hugh Barclay. While at work there, he fell in love with and married the architect's daughter Agnes. Optimistic with the taste of success, he looked longingly toward America. In 1889, despite parental misgivings, John and his bride left Scotland for the United States, where he set up a studio on Fourteenth Street in New York City. It was exactly the right moment. Until that time a decorative sculptor had been able to find scant employment in this country. However, increasing industrial wealth and the influence of European art forms upon American taste were bringing about a change. Architects of both public buildings and private mansions were seeking talents like those possessed by Rhind. Wayne Craven writes, "American architects, following the Beaux-Arts style, were beginning to incorporate decorative sculpture into their architectural designs, and John Massey Rhind was soon to become one of the leading carvers of such ornamentation."[11]

Since Rhind was an extroverted, genial person and a hard worker, before long he received his first commission from Dean Hoffman, a request for chapel decorations for the Episcopal Seminary on West Twenty-first Street and Ninth Avenue, this area known as. Chelsea Square. This work, when completed, established his reputation in New York City. Soon afterward a competition was sponsored by William Waldorf Astor for three bronze-paneled doors for Trinity Church, to be placed in commemoration of his father. Of the three winners of the competition, Rhind was one, along with Karl Bitter and Charles Niehaus. Rhind's beautifully modeled competition panel depicted the expulsion of Adam and Eve from Paradise. The fine design and skillful modeling of nude and clothed figures indicated the promise of a successful career. Being a rapid worker, Rhind completed his door within a two-year period.

His next accomplishment was a memorial fountain in Washington Park in Albany dedicated to the memory of Senator Rufus King, for which Rhind had been recommended to the city fathers by the venerable John Quincy Adams Ward. The resultant work is one of the most successful examples of its type in America. The theme is that of Moses as savior of his people. Centered within a circular basin is a hill of immense boulders. At its summit a large bronze figure of Moses stands with arms outstretched as if in supplication, a staff in his right hand. Three other bronze figures arranged equidistantly around the boulders—an old man, a woman with a water jar, and a mother and child—are in the act of drinking the water he has caused to gush from the rock. Commendable are the expressions and appropriate gestures of these figures as well as their excellent anatomical portrayal and graceful draperies.

In the early 1890s Rhind became acquainted with the architect Bruce Price, who was one of the pioneers in tall building design in New York City. Price engaged Rhind to make decorative figures for the front facade of the American Surety Building at Broadway and Pine street. For the space above the grand Ionic colonnade, the sculptor designed and executed six robed, female figures representing Peace, Truth, Honesty, Fortitude, Self-denial, and Fidelity. The way in which these graceful figures continued the vertical thrust of the colonnade proved Rhind's unique ability to make sculpture an integral part of architectural design. Another proof of this ability is the large mural complex in Italian Gothic style on the elaborate front of Alexander Commencement Hall at Princeton, upon which he worked for a period of three years during the mid 1890s. The theme of this design was that of the arts and sciences as taught at the university. The central seated figure of Learning is flanked by other life-size personifications representing Language, Theology, Law, History, Philosophy, Architecture, Painting, Poetry, Music, and Geometry. Rhind's harmony of line and figure delighted the architect, William A. Potter, and was the first of many similar collaborations.

In 1896 in his Closter, New Jersey, studio, Rhind completed the model of one of his most outstanding commissions, a huge bronze statue of John C. Calhoun for the city of Charleston, South Carolina.

Rhind at work on his heroic statue of Calhoun. *Courtesy of the Frick Art Reference Library, photo by C. Bilordeaux*

About 1860 the people of South Carolina gathered a fund of about sixty thousand dollars to erect a worthy monument of their great statesman. A charming story is told that Calhoun's early sweetheart took charge of the fund, guarded it safely through the Civil War years, and lived till her late nineties to see her hero safely aloft. The statue, weighing nearly three tons and cast in ten pieces, stands twelve feet eight inches tall and rests on a forty-foot shaft. The commanding figure of Calhoun, clad in street attire and flowing cape, appears to stride, left foot slightly forward, left hand on his hip and the right holding a rolled parchment. The pedestal shaft contains two bronze bas reliefs, each ten by six feet, showing Calhoun in his great debates in the Senate and in the War Department.

During that same decade Rhind created the impressive bronze portrait statue of Stephen Girard, the Philadelphia merchant philanthropist, which stands in the City Hall Plaza of Philadelphia. It is a gift of Girard College, which he founded. Rhind related a humorous story about his difficulties in correctly costuming Girard, whose manner of dressing was rather unusual. While at Girard Col-

lege one day, searching for a suitable picture, Rhind and the caretaker found a bag of clothing in a large wardrobe. To the sculptor's delight he had happened upon the exact pair of trousers, an embroidered waistcoat, and other articles of clothing, including a beaver hat, a pair of spectacles, and a pair of carpet slippers, all actually worn by Girard. This gave him not only the style but also the proportions of the man himself.

During the first quarter of the twentieth century Rhind's studios in New York City and near the Palisades in Alpine, New Jersey, were the scenes of an intense pace of production. By 1900 he had already become famous for both public monuments and decorative sculpture. Around the turn of the century two years were spent on four bronze figures of Henry Hudson, General Wolfe, Peter Stuyvesant, and DeWitt Clinton for the Exchange Court Building in New York City. These idealized portraits of men who had played an important part in the historical development of the city were each about ten feet high. For Bushnell Park, Hartford, Connecticut, he created the Corning Fountain, a decorative work of historical theme. A large circular basin topped by a bronze hart suggesting the name of the city is surrounded by four kneeling Indians, illustrating four epochs of Indian history. One, dressed in a skin robe, is spearing fish; another, shading his eyes with one hand, is on the lookout; while a third, tomahawk in hand, is on the warpath; the fourth and finest figure depicts an Indian making signs of friendship by sitting on a war hatchet and raising the pipe of peace. About this time, too, Rhind was beginning to work on the totally different commission of the Georgian Court Apollo Fountain.

John Massey Rhind was also active in the Philadelphia area. Commissioned about 1895 and completed several years later was his bronze statue of Henry Howard Houston (1820–95), a great benefactor of the city. Among Houston's benefactions was Wissahickon Heights, which he gave to Fairmount Park, where his statue now stands on a site selected by the commission the year of his death. In May 1900 the payment of $11,000 for the bronze and granite monument was made to Rhind. Shortly afterward Rhind began another work for the Wissahickon Valley, which he completed in 1902, a limestone statue of a Delaware chief of Tedyuscung (ca. 1700–1763) mounted on a natural rock base. During the 1750s and 1760s this chief represented the grievances of his people at conferences with the white authorities. In 1976 the Fairmount Park Art Association described the monument as follows:

A wooden statue "dear to the heart of every Germantown boy" crowned a height in the Wissashickon. When it began to decay (it is now preserved in the Germantown Historical Society), Mr. and Mrs. Charles W. Henry commissioned Rhind to replace it, and his majestic Indian has long been a noted Wissahickon landmark.[12]

Rhind's reputation spread to other important cities. For Schenley Park in Pittsburgh he did a bronze statue of the poet Robert Burns; for Jersey City, New Jersey, a Peter Stuyvesant; for Albany, New York, a heroic figure of General Philip J. Schuyler; for Muskegon, Michigan, Generals Ulysses S. Grant and William T. Sherman; for Clermont, Iowa, statues of ex-speaker David B. Henderson and General Grenville Dodge. At the St. Louis Fair in 1904 the Dodge statue took a gold medal.[13]

Rhind was also achieving fame for large-scale sculptural decoration, which he labored to make an integral part of the architectural design. During the early 1900s he executed two notable works for the city of Pittsburgh: for the Farmer's Bank of Pittsburgh, eighteen figures, each ten feet high and carved from a solid block of marble, and for Carnegie Institute an elaborate bronze figural decoration. For the entrance to Macy's department store in New York City he carved four charming female figures from pink Tennessee marble. For Memphis, Tennessee, he modeled figures for bronzes to be placed on the top of the courthouse. As related by J. Walker McSpadden, Rhind made the following comment on this commission:

> In modeling these figures, I had to stop and consider how they would be viewed. In the first place, they would only be seen at a considerable height—nearly a hundred feet; and secondly they would be viewed at any angle.[14]

Consequently, the figures were made following correctly foreshortened drawings.

The millionaire Henry Clay Frick became friendly with Rhind and, recognizing his abilities, commissioned a bust of the banker and philanthropist George Fisher Baker (1840–1931), who had helped found the First National Bank of New York and served in turn as teller, bookkeeper, director, and chairman of the board. Since Baker gave Harvard University a gift of $6 million for the foundation and endowment of the Graduate School of Business Administration, the University has placed Rhind's bust in the Baker Library named after the philanthropist.

During the second decade of the twentieth century Rhind completed two impressive equestrian statues for the city of Newark, New Jersey. The "Washington," a heroic-size bronze and a most original conception, is located in Washington Park on Broad Street. The site selected for the group was a raised, grassy mound along the street where Washington must have passed during the dark days of the Revolutionary War. The general, depicted as commander-in-chief of the Continental Army, is not mounted but stands beside his horse, one hand resting lightly on its mane. The sculptor shows Washington in the act of taking formal leave of his soldiers at Rocky Hill near Princeton, New Jersey, after the signing of the articles that terminated the war in 1783. In historical accuracy of costume the work is unimpeachable. At its dedication on 2 November 1912 President William Howard Taft was expected to be the guest of honor and make the presentation speech. Prevented, however, by the death of Vice-President Sherman, his substitute was the Reverend Dr. William J. Dawson, pastor of the First Presbyterian Church, who delivered an eloquent address. Dr. Dawson praised both the generosity of the donor, Amos H. Van Horn, an Essex businessman who bequeathed the memorial to the city, and also the talent of its sculptor, John Massey Rhind.[15]

The other monument in Newark is a full-size copy of the famous bronze "Colleoni" by the fifteenth-century Italian sculptor Verrocchio, which stands in the Campo dei Santi Giovanni e Paolo, Venice. Rhind had spent considerable time in Venice studying the masterpiece and its pedestal and making careful studies and photographs. When his friend Christian W. Feigenspan, another

Rhind's statue of George Washington, located in Washington Park, Newark. *Courtesy of the Newark Public Library*

The bronze "Colleoni" by Rhind in Clinton Park, Newark.
Courtesy of the Newark Public Library

public-spirited businessman, learned about the Van Horn bequest of the "Washington," he resolved to do something similar to beautify the city and to commemorate the 250th anniversary of its founding. His choice of subject was prompted by Rhind's enthusiastic suggestion of a "Colleoni" copy as a marvelous symbol of civic pride. The sculptor made a piece mold of a fine cast of this statue in the collection of the Chicago Art Institute and a full-size plaster model of the Venetian pedestal. He then carefully supervised the casting of the group and the carving of the pedestal. The site selected for the forty-foot work, Clinton Park, was considered to simulate as appropriately as possible the setting of the original, with the figures facing southeast to receive the best possible daylight. The unveiling and the presentation to the city took place on 26 July 1916.[16]

A second time the city of Philadelphia gained the services of Rhind for a large monument on the campus of Girard College. This Soldiers and Sailors Civil War Monument honored the memory of all the former students of the College known to have served in the Civil War. Nine-foot bronze figures of a soldier and a sailor standing in defense of the flag of the Union are mounted on a nine-foot granite base. The memorial was unveiled with appropriate

ceremonies on 20 May 1914, the address being delivered by Major Moses Veale, a veteran of the Civil War and long a popular chapel speaker at Girard College.

Other works of Rhind included such varied creations as the following: the decorations on General Grant's Tomb on Riverside Drive, New York; a recumbent figure of Father Thomas McKee Brown for the church of Saint Mary the Virgin, New York; and a statue of General Samuel Colt (1814–62), the inventor of the revolver, for Hartford, Connecticut. In addition, Rhind's friend and admirer Henry Clay Frick commissioned a memorial to Joseph Hodges Choate, a Salem, Massachusetts boy who became a great lawyer, patriot, statesman, and ambassador to the Court of Saint James. The Choate Memorial, or "The Spirit of Salem," as it was called, was erected at the junction of Essex and Boston streets in Salem. Since Frick did not live to see its completion, its actual presentation to the city was made by U.S. Senator George Wharton Pepper of Philadelphia, an intimate friend of both Frick and Choate. The memorial typifies the spirit of patriotism: a helmeted female figure in bronze holds a shield in the left hand with the raised right hand grasping a sheaf of bay leaves. This figure, sixteen feet high and weighing thirty-one tons, is seated on a base of pink marble. The estimated cost of the memorial was $75,000. The inscription on the base reads: "Joseph Hodges Choate, January 24, 1832–May 14, 1917, patriot, statesman and loyal defender of American ideals." In his presentation speech, Senator Pepper paid the following tribute:

I would speak of Choate, the patriot, were it not that the genius of the sculptor has made words of mine unnecessary. I might have chronicled the loving acts of service which Choate rendered to his country, but Mr. Rhind has done a better thing. By the magic of his art he has personified Patriotism; he has accorded to her the beauty of face and form which are hers by right and he has represented her in the very act of rewarding this son of Salem by extending to him the crown of bay.[17]

Early in 1923 the Wanamaker Memorial Committee commissioned Rhind to do a statue of John Wanamaker. Completed by 29 November of that same year, it was presented by the committee as a gift to the city and was placed at the base of the east side of City Hall in Philadelphia. It is a life-size figure in bronze mounted on a seven-foot-high granite base. A fine character study, the merchant prince stands there in everyday pose—his hat and coat over one arm, and the other hand resting by its thumb in a trouser pocket. According to J. Walker McSpadden, Rhind gave the following explanation of this matter-of-fact representation:

Mr. Wanamaker often stood that way. I couldn't do a "stagey" portrait of such a man, even if I wanted to. As he stands there, he is both at rest and in action. I have tried to show him just ready to walk out of his office and stopping to say, "Well, how big an order shall we place for those goods to-day?"[18]

Later in Rhind's career, at the request of the state of Georgia, he modeled a full-length portrait statue of Dr. Crawford W. Long. When finished in marble in 1926, it was placed in Statuary Hall in the U.S. Capitol. Also completed about this time was the sculpture for the McKinley Memorial in Niles, Ohio, the president's birthplace. This figure, carved from Georgia marble, stands in the center of an open Doric court in the exquisite classic building designed by McKim, Mead and White. Rhind portrays the president as if he had just risen from his chair. The simplicity of the portrait against the stately columns strikes a new note in American memorial art. In addition Rhind modeled forty por- trait busts, eventually cast in bronze, of McKinley's close friends and fellow statesmen. Among them are Warren G. Harding, Sir Henry Bessemer, John Hay, Theodore Roosevelt, Elihu Root, William Howard Taft, George Westinghouse, and Joseph Green Butler, the man primarily responsible for the creating of the McKinley Memorial.

John Massey Rhind, a warm human being— ruddy of face and sturdy of body, with friendly smile and Scottish accent—was an artist for his time, prolific and successful. As a sculptor of ar- chitectural decoration and public monuments, he was widely acclaimed by patrons as well as by fel- low sculptors. He was active in the National Sculp- ture Society, the Municipal Art Society and the Ar- chitectural League of New York. In the Player's Club and National Arts Club, on Gramercy Park and at the Salamagundi on lower Fifth Avenue, he was regarded as an essential part of the evening's entertainment. His happy and full life came to an end on 22 October 1936.[19]

The Japanese Garden Designed by Takeo Shiota

The lovely Japanese Garden on the Georgian Court estate was also planned by George as a birthday gift for Edith. The idea occurred to him while on a trip to Japan with his family. Completed between 1909 and 1910, it afforded his wife happy hours of quiet retreat from the formality of the mansion. There she could entertain a guest or two in the little teahouse, or simply enjoy the tranquil solitude.

Accustomed to doing everything in grand style, George chose the best talent available for the commission, the noted garden designer Takeo Shiota (1881–1946). Having come from Japan in 1907, Shiota was well known for his garden designs along the eastern seaboard.

A one-acre area west of the Italian Gardens marks the location of this garden, which is set back at some distance from the west road. A curving path leads to a small wooden footbridge that crosses a dry-stone stream. In springtime flowering rhododendrons create a striking approach, in autumn the Japanese maples are brilliant masses of color, and in winter the gray branches of the trees form lace against the dark evergreens. A rustic wall that shuts out noise and distraction encloses the front and right side of the garden; the entrance is through a hooded gateway or portico called the *machiai*.

A garden path or *roji* leads to the little square teahouse close by the gateway. It is a genuine *Sukiya* with low-pitched roof and *shoji* along the sides toward the garden. The ceiling of the teahouse is less than six feet high. True to Japanese custom, the interior accommodates no more than five persons. The teahouse has an interesting history. It was displayed at the Anglo-Japanese Exhibition in London in 1900. One of Gould's art collectors purchased it and had it disassembled and shipped to Georgian Court. Years later, when the garden was under construction, the house was reassembled and placed correctly in the garden enclosure.

Shiota designed an authentic tea garden, a *Chaniwa* a series of little hills, planted with effectively grouped low trees and appropriate shrubbery. In the center of the garden on a small hilly island is one tall pine, which is the center of this little universe. At the right water enters through a little waterfall and meanders as a stream through pebble-cemented banks, crossed here and there by wooden bridges or stepping stones. The bridges provide places from which to view the garden. Stepping stones are placed with studied irregularity to induce the visitor to walk slowly and enjoy the vistas, which are made even more beautiful by the streams of water that mirror the sky. Rocks, pebbles, and sand form the bed of a dry stream that winds out in front of the enclosing wall. The roughly circular course of the garden path is bordered with low cedar posts that match the bridges. Many little detours eventually lead back to the teahouse. Variform stone lanterns are the only garden accessories—pedestal lanterns for lighting effects, and "snow-viewing lanterns," called thus because on their broad tops can rest beautiful mounds of snow. On the borders and in the background the East and West mingle—Japanese cherry trees and Jersey pines—but enough of old

A wooden footbridge leads to the hooded gateway of the Japanese Garden. *Photo by Vincent Hart*

Close by the gateway is an authentic teahouse. *Photo by Vincent Hart*

A little stream meanders through pebble-cemented banks.
Photo by Vincent Hart

A secluded spot near the enclosing wall of the Japanese Garden. The residence Maria Hall is seen in the background.
Photo by Vincent Hart

Artists delight in capturing the beautiful features of the garden. *Photo by Vincent Hart*

Japan is here to give a spirit of tranquillity in which one would linger.

The years have dealt kindly with the lovely garden. The cherry trees nearby have grown old and gnarled, the rhododendron higher and more flower-filled, and the maples serenely mature. Long after the days of the Goulds, students, faculty, and countless visitors have come to linger in this secluded spot, perhaps to re-create a tea party, to charm viewers with Oriental dancing, or to memorialize the beautiful scene in a yearbook photograph. Artists have come to sketch or paint its ever changing beauty, hour by hour or season by season. Takeo Shiota himself notes similar changes in a typical Japanese garden:

It is delightful in the daytime. It becomes quiet and poetic at night. Even in midwinter its beauty never departs. The older a Japanese garden, the more natural it looks, and added years serve only to increase its glories.[20]

The Garden Designer Takeo Shiota

In 1881, in a little village forty miles east of Tokyo, was born Takeo Shiota, the son of a well-to-do farmer. In a charming monograph he describes his birthplace as follows: "Near my home are many beautiful streams, and wild scenery with old historical castles, tranquil shrines and large temples." He also recounts his boyhood explorations in these natural surroundings and his awakening love of nature: "In my school days I was known as a rough mischief-maker; but when, as I grew older, I decided to take up the profession of landscape gardener, my character changed and I became quiet and thoughtful."[21]

After graduation from high school Shiota traveled on foot through half of Japan in order to study its famous scenery, architecture, and gardens. He gradually came to two important conclusions—"the one, a garden reflects the work of a mediocre or skillful landscape gardener, and second, gardening is like the art of painting, infinite."[22] His decision to become a landscape gardener took him to Tokyo for instruction. There, several years of study under different masters made him realize that only nature herself could teach him what he wished to know. For five more years the scenery of Japan was his true teacher.

After becoming thoroughly acquainted with his native land, both the wild, uncultivated terrain and the lovely established gardens, Shiota decided to cross the Pacific to the United States and seek his fulfillment there. Arriving in 1907, he made his headquarters in New York City. After eight successful years in this country he summed up his professional and personal aspirations with the following statement:

My greatest ambition is to design a garden more beautiful than all others in the world, and thus to prove the truth of the saying "Japanese landscape gardening is the Queen of all the Arts." My greatest enjoyment is in nature and the contemplation of natural things, landscape and the actions of animals or fishes. For that reason I go hunting. I go to the deep woods of North Carolina and Virginia to hunt deer, to shoot ducks and quail, for at least three months of the year.

To go far from the noise of civilization, to live the simple country life and breathe deeply of pure air—that is the cleanser of life.[23]

Thus did Shiota indicate the depth of his dedication to his art and its spirit.

In addition to his work at Georgian Court, Shiota is famous for the design of the Japanese Garden of the Brooklyn Botanic Gardens, considered to be his masterpiece. This fine Hill-and-Pond Garden, covering an area of two acres, the gift of the late Alfred T. White, was opened to the public on 6 June 1915. At its center is a small lake shaped like the Chinese character for "heart" or "mind." Standing in the water is a fine *torii* or gateway, which is dedicated to the Shinto god of the harvest. It is inscribed with the Japanese words *dai myo jin,* meaning "great illuminating deity." The Harvest Shrine itself stands on a hill nearby. On the far shore a pavilion built over the water and an adjacent waiting-bench offer a fine view of the lake. A little drum bridge crosses to a tiny island on which stands a snow-viewing lantern. A more elaborate bridge spans an inlet near a rocky precipice and waterfall. Planted along the shores of the lake are Japanese iris, weeping cherry trees, pine trees, and a variety of shrubs.

According to Clay Lancaster in his book *The Japanese Influence in America*, Shiota created several other gardens in the metropolitan district. One of these was that in Plainfield, New Jersey, on the grounds of the home of P. D. Saklatvala. In this garden a wide stream is crossed by a long, gently arched bridge. Near the edge of the water on the far side a small shrine houses a hammered-copper bust of the owner's mother, a member of the Tata family of India. Farther upstream and a little inland, a two-storied pavilion overlooks a pool shaped like the state of New Jersey. A second was a tea garden adjoining Scofield House in Tuxedo Park, New York. Like the garden at Georgian Court, it is enclosed by a board fence and an even larger gateway. Its teahouse, an authentic *cha-seki*, is especially noted for its size and completeness.[24] Shiota himself lists several other gardens in his monograph, which Lancaster states are now either in poor condition or extinct, namely, a tea garden on the Hoyt property at Oyster Bay, Long Island, a garden on the Salisbury estate in Plainfield, New Jersey, and one built for C. Brown on Emerson Hill, Staten Island.[25]

Lancaster also states that in the 1920s Shiota formed a partnership, that of Rockrise and Shiota, which operated at 366 Fifth Avenue, New York. In the 1930s he became a floral designer at the Astor Hotel, no longer standing, where he was responsible for the North Garden on the roof. He died in 1946.[26]

The Canterbury Pilgrims Frieze Painted by Robert Van Vorst Sewell

The frieze "The Canterbury Pilgrims" dominates the upper portion of the west, north, and east walls of the great hall of the mansion. Commissioned by Gould shortly before the actual construction had begun, the artist Robert Van Vorst Sewell painted it on canvas in his New York studio according to measurements given by the architect Price. As a result it is beautifully adapted to the various entablatures and moldings of the room; its size is seven feet in height and eighty-four feet in length. Upon completion of the building in December 1897, the frieze was mounted on the walls. This unique masterpiece is a tribute to the interpretative genius of the artist and the crowning glory of a room which provides it with a perfect setting.

The selection of the theme was made to the satisfaction of both patron and artist. As a sportsman, George Gould delighted in a subject that would allow for many steeds. Robert Sewell, a student of the early English writers, had a particular fondness for the works of Geoffrey Chaucer. In the frieze twenty-four of the cast of Chaucer's immortal characters as described in the Prologue to *The Canterbury Tales* are riding on a pilgrimage to England's most famous shrine: that of Saint Thomas à Becket at Canterbury. In Chaucer's day the pilgrimage was a popular religious devotion sanctioned and encouraged by the Church. Nevertheless, while some pilgrimages were undertaken to do penance for sins or to obtain a favor, many like this one described by Chaucer were merely the occasion for an enjoyable journey, especially in the pleasant month of April. Along the way these pilgrims tell stories that are powerful and subtle comments on the social milieu of the time.

Drawing upon his experience with people from all walks of life, Chaucer creates characters who are a cross-section of fourteenth-century English society. With a few apt phrases or comments he describes not only their outward appearance but also their pretensions and affectations, their vices or their admirable qualities. Consequently, his characters have a universal significance.

In Sewell's painted procession the figures are rendered with minute fidelity to Chaucer's text but arranged in a different sequence in order, no doubt to emphasize the most important characters. Following is the order chosen by the artist, beginning with the rearmost pilgrim on the west wall panel of the great hall.[27] Accompanying the listing of the figures are short excerpts that he selected from the Prologue as his own inspiration for each character. Apparently in order to aid the reader, Sewell alters the Middle English text by substituting modern English words for those of Chaucer. For the purpose of clarification I have given the original text, along with my own comments on the characters. Where appropriate, I have included descriptions of the costumes as Sewell painted them.

Portion of Sewell's frieze showing, *left to right:* the Reeve, the Country Parson, the Prioress, the Second Nun, the Monk, the Miller, the Pardoner, and the Summoner. *Photo by Vincent Hart*

WEST WALL

THE REEVE

The Reve was a sclendre colerik man.
. . . .
Ful longe were his legges and ful lene, ·
Ylyk a staf, ther was no calf ysene.
Wel koude he kepe a gerner and a bynne;
Ther was noon auditour koude on him wynne.
. . . .
Tukked he was as is a frere aboute,
And evere he rood the hyndreste of oure route.

Clad in greenish blue, Osewold the Reeve rides straight and proud upon his dappled gray stallion. His hair is close-cropped, his face is beardless, and at his side hangs a sword in scabbard. Once a carpenter, he is now an overseer of a manor house where he shrewdly controls all the accounts. No one can outwit, and everyone fears this clever, conniving, hot-tempered man.

THE COUNTRY PARSON

A good man was ther of religioun,
And was a povre Persoun of a town,
But rich he was of holy thought and werk.
He was also a lerned man, a clerk.
. . . .
To drawen folk to hevene by fairnesse,
By good ensample, this was his bisynesse.

The learned country Parson is a prime example of holiness in the Church and the most sincere churchman on the pilgrimage. He is portrayed seated on a brown mare in humble monk's garb, symbols of the poverty that he lived as well as preached.

THE PRIORESS

Ther was also a Nonne, a Prioresse,
That of hir smylyng was ful symple and coy;
Hir gretteste ooth was but by Seinte Loy;
And she was cleped madame Eglentyne.
Ful wel she soong the service dyvyne,
Entuned in hir nose ful semely.
And Frenssh she spak ful faire and fetisly,
After the scole of Stratford atte Bowe,
For Frenssh of Parys was to hire unknowe.

Sewell gives center prominence to Madame Eglentyne, Chaucer's most ambiguous figure. Riding upon a white horse with red trappings, she is simultaneously described as nun and courtly lady. Though her white habit and brown cloak identify her religious consecration, her coy glance and affected gesture, the rich coral beads hanging on her left arm, and the red stockings and shiny slippers suggest her worldliness. Furthermore, her tale in which she sings the praises of the Mother of God is anti-Semitic in content and makes the reader wonder about the depth of her spirituality.

THE SECOND NUN

Another Nonne with hire hadde she,
That was her chapeleyne.

Similarly garbed, this gentle unassuming nun behind Madame Eglentyne is her companion and secretary. She recounts the tale of Saint Cecilia and inveighs against the vice of idleness.

THE MONK

A Monk ther was, a fair for the maistrie,
An outridere, that loved venerie,
A manly man, to benn an abbot able.
Ful many a deyntee hors hadde he in stable.
. . . .
I seigh his sleves purfiled at the hond
With grys, and that the fyneste of a lond;
And, for to festne his hood under his chyn,
He hadde of gold wroght a ful curious pyn.

This athletic monk with bald head shining like glass is garbed in a black cloak trimmed with fur and clasped with a gold brooch. He is mounted on a black, richly bridled stallion, and is gesturing toward Madame Eglentyne. Although talented enough to be an abbot and entrusted with the estates of the monastery, he neglects his monastic duties for the pursuit of the hunt and fleshly pleasures.

On the gate wall behind this monk the imprint of a black hand symbolizes that the Black Plague has touched this inn. Sewell may have painted it here as a subtle reference to punishment for clerical infidelity.

THE MILLER

The Miller was a stout carl for the nones;
Ful byg he was of brawn, and eek of bones.
. . . .
A baggepipe wel koude he blowe and sowne,
And therwithal he broghte us out of towne.

Leading the pilgrims on this west wall is Robin the Miller, who pipes the band out of Southwark. This red-bearded, swinish, drunken man is garbed in a white and greenish-blue jerkin and bright red stockings. Weighed down with bagpipes, he travels along on a white donkey.

Perhaps Sewell has placed the Miller in this panel rather than at the head of the entire procession to emphasize the running antagonism Chaucer seems to create between him and the Reeve nearby. The Miller tells a story about a carpenter who is deceived by a rival. A carpenter by trade, the Reeve recounts a tale about a crooked miller who is outwitted by his victims.

NORTH WALL

THE PARDONER

. . . ther rode a gentil Pardoner
. . . .
He hadde a croys of latoun ful of stones,
And in a glas he hadde pigges bones.
But with thise relikes, whan that he fond
A povre person dwellyng upon lond,
Upon a day he gat hym moore moneye
Than that the person gat in monthes tweye.

A depraved character, the Pardoner goes around the countryside selling indulgences, fake relics, and computations for a penance. Sewell portrays him carrying a glass of pig bones in one hand and a gold cross in the other. A bag, presumably of relics, is slung over the saddle of his white mount. Garbed in scarlet robe and hat, with thin blonde hair hanging to his shoulders, he is effeminate in appearance.

THE SUMMONER

A Somonour was ther with us in that place,
That hadde a fyre-reed cherubynnes face,
For sauce fleem he was, with eyen narwe.
As hoot he was and lecherous as a sparwe,
With scalled browes blake and piled berd.
Of his visage children were aferd.

This Summoner, himself a rascal and a thief, calls delinquents to the ecclesiastical court. Clad in white surplice, black hood, and cloak, he presents a somber, morose appearance with his stringy white hair and scabby face.

THE FRIAR

A Frere ther was, a wantowne and a merye,
A lymytour, a ful solempne man
. . . .

A detail of the north wall panel, *left to right:* the Friar, the Wife of Bath, the Squire, the Knight, the Yeoman, and the Humble Wayfarer. *Photo by Vincent Hart*

Ful swetely herde he confessioun,
And plesaunt was his absolucioun:
He was an esy man to yeve penaunce,
Ther as he wiste to have a good pitaunce.

Appropriately tonsured and garbed in black, Huberd the Friar rides on a white mount. This lustful, scandalous man, a frequenter of taverns where he dallies with the barmaids, is licensed to hear confessions throughout the countryside. For a fee he grants absolution and administers slight penances.

THE WIFE OF BATH

A good Wif was ther of biside Bathe,
But she was somdel deef, and that was scathe
. . . .
Upon an amblere esily she sat,
Ywympled wel, and on hir heed an hat
As brood as is a bokeler or a targe;
A foot-mantel aboute hir hipes large,
And on hir feet a paire of spores sharpe.
In felaweshipe wel koude she laughe and carpe.
Of remedies of love she knew per chaunce,
Foe she koude of that art the olde daunce.

Dame Alice, the Wife of Bath, is the most memorable of Chaucer's characters. Knowing all the arts of love, she has lured five men into marriage. Accustomed to pilgrim journeys, she rides easily on her black saddle horse. On her head she wears a white kerchief topped by a large black hat. Her gown is rose colored and white with large, puffed sleeves, over which a deep rose cloak is draped around her full hips. Bright red stockings and shoes fitted with spurs complete her costume. Animatedly chatting, she gestures toward the squire who rides ahead of her.

THE SQUIRE

With hym ther was his sone, a yong Squier,
A lovere and a lusty bacheler
. . . .
Embrouded was he, as it were a meede
Al ful of fresshe floures, whyte and reede.
Syngynge he was, or floytynge, al the day;
He was as fressh as is the month of May.
Short was his gowne, with sleves longe and wyde.
Wel koude he sitte on hors and faire ryde.

Next rides the Knight's son, the curly-headed Squire who is garbed in the station of one learning the arts of war and love. He is seated on a white horse bridled with red trappings. His short, embroidered green tunic, red stockings, and red cap provide a striking contrast to the raiment of Dame Alice, at whom he throws a backward glance.

THE KNIGHT

A Knyght ther was and that a worthy man,
That fro the tyme that he first bigan
To riden out, he loved chivalrie,
Trouthe and honour fredom and curteisie
. . . .
And everemoore he hadde a sovereyn prys;
And though that he were worthy, he was wys,
And of his port as meeke as is a mayde.
He nevere yet no vileynye ne sayde
In al his lyf unto no maner wight.
He was a verray, parfit, gentil knyght.

The loftiest character in the group of pilgrims, both in social status and in moral fiber, is the Knight. Recently returned from war, he undertakes the pilgrimage in order to give thanks for success in battle. Sewell centers him in the north wall panel and portrays him in a brown tunic spattered with the rust left by his coat of mail. His profound philosophical tale about two knights and a maiden is the first and the longest story of them all.

THE YEOMAN

A Yeman hadde he and servantz namo
At that tyme, for hym liste ride so;
And he was clad in cote and hood of grene.
A sheef of pecok arwes, bright and kene,
Under his belt he bar ful thriftily,
Wel koude he dresse his takel yemanly:
His arwes drouped noghte with fetheres lowe
And in his hand he baar a myghty bowe.

The Yeoman, a forester and the only attendant of the Knight, is portrayed in a green coat and hood. On his breast is "a Christophe," the image of Saint Christopher, the patron saint of foresters. Attached to his belt is a sheef of peacock arrows as well as a sword and dagger. A huge bow rests on his shoulder.

THE HUMBLE WAYFARER

Portrayed next to the Yeoman and clad in a green coat and hood is a figure identified by Sewell as a humble wayfarer. Because this character does not exist in Chaucer, the artist may have identified him with the Canon's Yeoman, mentioned in the "Prologue" but not elsewhere depicted on the frieze.

THE DOCTOR OF PHYSIC

With us ther was a Doctour of Phisik;
In al this world ne was ther noon hym lik,
To speke of phisik and of surgerye,
For he was grounded in astronomye.
He kepte his pacient a ful greet deel
In houres by his magik natureel.
. . . .
Ful redy hadde he his apothecaries
To sende hym drogges and his letuaries.
For ech of hem made oother for to wynne—
His friendshipe nas nat newe to bigynne.

Trained in astrology, this learned physician claims to know the cause of every disease. By means of natural magic or astrology he cares for the patient during the stages or "houres" of an illness. Having determined the malady, he prescribes a remedy from his well-stocked collection. But as a healer he cares more for money than for the patient. Garbed in a red ermine-trimmed coat and fancy black hood, he carries a green vial in his left hand while his money bag hangs from his belt.

THE SHIPMAN

A Shipman was ther, wonynge fer by weste;
For aught I woot, he was of Dertemouth.
. . . .
Ful many a draughte of wyn had he drawe
Fro Burdeux-ward, whil that the chapman sleep.
Of nyce conscience took he no keep.
If that he faught, and hadde the hyer hond,
By water he sente hem hoom to every lond.

Conversing with the physician, the heavily bearded Shipman rides upon his nag as well as he can, evidently more at ease in a sailing vessel than on land. Heavily tanned, he wears a coarse brown gown with sleeves rolled to the elbows. A dagger hangs from a cord around his neck. Although undoubtedly a wise and capable sailor, he does not scruple to tap the wine casks while the merchants are asleep, or to make his enemies walk the plank.

THE MERCHANT

A Marchant was ther with a forked berd,
In motlee, and hye on a horse he sat;
Upon his heed a Flaundryssh bevere hat,
His bootes clasped faire and fetisly.
His resons he spak ful solempnely,
Sownynge alwey th' encrees of his wynnyng.
This worthy man ful wel his wit bisette;
Ther wiste no wight that he was in dette.

This worthy Merchant, who represents the rising mercantile class of the fourteenth century, is clever in all bargainings and dealings and knows how to keep his counsel. Portrayed with forked beard and clad in figured red and green coat and soft beaver cap, he rides erect and proud upon his horse.

THE HABERDASHER

And they were clothed alle in o lyveree
Of a solempne and a greet fraternitee.

(By "they" Chaucer is referring to the Haberdasher, Carpenter, Weaver, Dyer, and Tapestry Weaver. Sewell includes only the Haberdasher.) The Haberdasher represents the guildsmen in Chaucer's group of pilgrims. As a contrast with the Merchant beside him, Sewell portrays this man with a high hat on his head. He also wears a coat of red and green, though of larger figured pattern. High boots edged in fur complete his rich attire. Of all the pilgrims he is the only one whom the artist portrays as jerking back a rearing horse. Sewell may have done this in order to give more interest to this corner figure and lead in to the next panel.

East Wall

THE SERGEANT AT LAW

A Sergeant of the Lawe, war and wys,
That often hadde been at the Parvys,
Ther was also, ful riche of excellence.
Discreet he was and of greet reverence—
He semed swich, his wordes weren so wise.
Justice he was ful often in assise,
By patente and by pleyn commissioun.
For his science and for his heigh renown,
Of fees and robes hadde he many oon.

Wise and discreet, and well-practiced in legal matters, the Lawyer is one of the king's advisers. His large fees enable him to dress handsomely. Sewell portrays him garbed in a red ermine-trimmed cloak and white cap, with his right hand gesturing as if in discourse.

THE CLERK OF OXENFORD

A Clerk ther was of Oxenford also,
That unto logyk hadde longe ygo,
As leene was his hors as is a rake,
And he was nat right fat, I undertake,
But looked holwe, and therto sobrely.
Full thredbare was his overeste courtepy;
For he hadde geten hym yet no benefice,
Ne was so worldly for to have office.
For hym was levere have at his beddes heed
Twenty bookes, clad in blak or reed,
Of Aristotle and his philosophie
Than robes riche, or fithele, or gay sautrie.

The poor, thin-looking Clerk, a student of philosophy, rides with eyes cast down. Dressed in plain black, he carries under his right arm a red book symbolizing his greatest concern—the pursuit of knowledge.

HARRY BAILEY THE HOST

A semely man oure Hooste was withale
For to been a marchal in an halle.
A large man he was with eyen stepe—
A fairer burgeys was ther noon in Chepe—
Boold of his speche, and wys, and wel ytaught,
And of manhod hym lakkede naught.
Eek thereto he was right a myrie man.

Sewell gives Harry Bailey, the genial Host of the Tabard Inn, center prominence on the east wall. Portrayed as a heavy-set man, he is dressed in a light brown short-sleeved tunic with long red inner sleeves, dark brown hose, and high brown boots. Astride a dappled gray stallion bridled in red trappings, he raises his right hand in a beckoning gesture. In the Prologue he is the character who suggests that each pilgrim tell two tales along each way to make the time seem shorter. He guarantees that upon the return from Canterbury the one who has recounted the most morally valuable and entertaining story shall be given a supper at the expense of all—at his inn, of course!

THE POET CHAUCER

Since Chaucer did not describe himself, when Sewell comes to his portrait he uses his own imagination. A dignified, unassuming figure simply clad in a dark brown robe, Chaucer is portrayed riding to the left and a little forward of Harry Bailey. In his right hand he holds a white flower, the symbol of spring.

THE MANCIPLE

A gentil Maunciple was ther of a temple,
Of which achatours myghte take exemple
For to be wise in byynge of vitaille;
For wheither that he payde or took by taille,
Algate he wayted so in his achaat
That he was ay biforn and in good staat.

The Manciple is the purchasing agent for one of the Inns of Court, or law schools. Evidently a friendly yet shrewd man, he doubtless could make fools of all the lawyers whom he served. Sewell portrays him as a confident-looking, smiling figure holding a flask of red wine high in his right hand as he rides a dark brown steed. He is garbed in a loose

Visible here toward the northeast are, *left to right:* the Merchant, the Haberdasher, the Sergeant at Law, the Clerk of Oxenford, Harry Bailey the Host, the Poet Chaucer, the Manciple, and the Cook. *Photo by Vincent Hart*

green coat trimmed in red and wears a brimmed white hat decorated with red ribbons.

THE COOK

A Cook they hadde with hem for the nones
To boille the chiknes with the marybones.
. . . .
He koude rooste, and sethe, and broille, and frye,
Maken mortreux, and wel bake a pye.
But greet harm was it, as it thoughte me,
That on his shyne a mormal hadde he,
For blankmanger, that made he with the beste.

The humble Cook rides a donkey instead of a noble steed. The artist depicts him clad in a red undertunic, with sleeves and red hose rolled up, over which he wears a white apron. On his head is a small red cap. Sewell depicts the sore on his skin as mentioned by Chaucer. It has been interpreted as a symbol of inner corruption—a frequent theme in Chaucer's poem. Incidentally, the fact that the Guildsmen brought along their own cook would

seem to be an affront to Harry Bailey, the generous host and provider.

Sewell achieves a continuity of movement in the painting that produces a living quality and carries the eye in one unbroken sweep from beginning to end. In addition, he displays his genius as a draftsman and a master of anatomy in the rendering of the forms. The variety of poses and expressions and the skillful overlapping of figures complement the lively naturalness of Chaucer's narrative.

In writing about the production of this work, Sewell describes his indebtedness to the new direction in French painting:

I have endeavored to portray a mediaeval scene in a modern way, and to apply the principles of the "plein-air" school to the production of a decoration.

The full range of tone from black to white and the entire gamut of pigment have been used. I have eschewed producing by any conventionalities of tone or color the qualities commonly called "mural," as I am of the opinion that the real mural quality is a matter of design, and that in the enrichment of design it is legitimate to employ, if we wish, the full resources which these enlightened times afford, chief among which I hold to be "plein-airism," the most important contribution of this cycle to art.

In taking this stand I anticipate and desire to face the criticism which my attitude will be sure to provoke. The theory has been advanced, and by many accepted, that extreme modern naturalism, though legitimate and even necessary in pictorial art, is out of place in decorative work—a theory with which I cannot concur.[28]

Lamenting the lack of receptivity on the part of contemporary artists who, failing to recognize the merits of a new approach to decorative painting, cling to their old ways, Sewell continues:

The history of decoration points to the fact that, in the past, any new discovery in the direction of naturalism was quickly adopted by the men who left their mark upon their period as decorators. Before the discovery of perspective its laws were continually violated by artists who, notwithstanding, produced very beautiful works. For us to affect their ignorance in order to produce an appearance of archaism or primitive "naïfté," would be not only to stultify our own age, but to furnish a strong argument to those who desire to prove that civilization has in this century developed the germ of degeneration and decline.

The artists of the early Renaissance were not so wedded to the stiff and flat portrayal of the human figure that they were unable to quickly profit by the examples of grace and naturalism afforded by the discovery of the Greek statues. Had they been as great admirers of pre-Raphaelism, primitivism, and archaic conventionality as many are today, we may be quite safe in saying that there would have been no Renaissance in art; and had the same indifference to new thought extended to all other branches of knowledge, the dark ages would still be with us.[29]

Thus, disregarding the prevailing academic conception that a mural should be characterized by a certain lack of pictorial depth and lean more toward the flat and decorative, Sewell renders his subject in a natural "plein-air" style that is most effective. He has produced the illusion of an optical depth of several feet, within which the pilgrims ride in procession in front of a low wall broken here and there by gates. Since Sewell is illustrating the Prologue to the *Canterbury Tales*, perhaps he here intends to depict the courtyard of the Tabard Inn in order to indicate that the pilgrims are just starting out on their journey. The suggestion of a wooded area behind the wall adds further depth to the perspective.

The artist uses a complete palette of many colors. However, because the color scheme of red, light grays, and gold predominates in the interior decoration of the hall, comparable tones of reds, gray whites, and ochers prevail in the frieze. The scheme is not exaggerated, but merely complies, as a mural should, with existing architectural elements. The rich panoply of colors and forms delights the eye of the visitor to the mansion and makes Chaucer's famous poem live again.

Like other masters before him, Sewell was careful about the exact physiognomy of the characters he depicted. He searched for modern models for the pilgrims, who might appropriately pictorialize Chaucer's verbal images. An interesting experience of a faculty member of Georgian Court College testifies to the artist's practice. Some years ago Sister M. Consolata Carroll, professor of English, welcomed to the mansion an elderly gentleman who wanted to see the frieze. Introducing himself as Mr. Edward Newton, the son of an Anglican clergyman, he explained that he had posed for one of the characters. As he gazed at the frieze he exclaimed, "There I am," and pointed to the young Squire riding near the Wife of Bath. "I had that sketch made when I was sixteen and have never seen myself accoutered as the Squire." He then pointed out the Monk, riding near the Prioress, for whom his brother Richard had posed.

Sister Consolata also related another personal experience, decidedly humorous in nature. While she was attending a lecture on drama delivered at Columbia University by John Mason Brown, a gentleman sitting next to her struck up a conversation. When he learned that Sister was a professor at Georgian Court College, he told her that he was a dramatist and had often visited Georgian Court in the days of the Goulds. He particularly recalled the time when the beautiful, fashionably attired lady accompanying him made a terrible faux-pas. As she entered the great hall she gazed in awe at the painting. Edith Gould, sweeping into the room, said, "My dear, how do you like the frieze?" "Marvelous," replied the beauty. "Christ entering Jerusalem on a donkey!" Edith was speechless, the dramatist was thoroughly embarrassed, and the young beauty moved serenely on to the next encounter. Sister Consolata, who retold this story to Professor James Tobin of Fordham, relates his reaction. "It's precious," Tobin said. "It's a perfect picture of the Gilded Age!"

This huge masterpiece always impresses countless other visitors, if not more informed, at least more circumspect. And to the students of Georgian Court College it serves as a continual reminder of the literary masterpiece of Geoffrey Chaucer.

The Muralist Robert Van Vorst Sewell

Robert Van Vorst Sewell, the painter of the frieze of "The Canterbury Pilgrims," was born in 1860 in a brownstone house on Forty-fifth Street, New York City. His father, Robert Sewell, was a noted lawyer, and his mother, Sarah Van Vorst, was a descendant of one of the earliest Dutch families in this country. In 1883 he graduated from Columbia University with a degree of Bachelor of Arts. In 1885 Princeton University conferred an honorary degree of Master of Arts upon him, which indicates the acclaim with which his early works were received. Driven by a keen interest in painting, he went to Paris in 1886, where he studied with the masters Jules Lefebvre and Gustave Randolph Boulanger. Lefebvre was noted for his brilliant portraiture and excellent anatomical form. Boulanger had been a student and an "alter ego" of Jean Léon Gérôme, who influenced French art by his paintings of Oriental, Greek, and Roman subjects. Sewell's work shows the influence of both masters.

While studying in Paris, Sewell met Lydia Amanda Brewster of Plattsburg, New York, who was a student under Carolus Duran. She was the daughter of Benjamin Thomas Brewster, a descendant of elder William Brewster, who came to this land on the Mayflower. Her mother was Julia Amy Washburne. As a child, Lydia, or Amanda as she preferred to be called, was stimulated by the mountain scenery around her home and attained considerable facility in the use of color. After formal training at the Art Students League and at Cooper Union in New York City, she traveled to Paris in 1886 and enrolled at the Julian Academy.

The young couple were married on 12 April 1888 and built a home and studio at Oyster Bay, Long Island. They had two sons, Robert Brewster and William Joyce. As an idealist and a portraitist of note, Amanda inspired and profoundly influenced her husband's success. She was the recipient of many awards and achieved international recognition.

While Sewell was studying in Paris he became aware of the diversity of styles that prevailed there. Academic Romanticism was continuing in the works of Jean Gigoux, Charles Jacque, and Nicolas Cabat. Rosa Bonheur was acclaimed as a painter of animals. The paintings of historical genre by Alexandre Cabanel and the symbolical and allegorical subjects of Adolphe William Bouguereau established themselves as the core of French academic art. Among the avant-garde painters, Impressionism and its various offshoots were popularly acclaimed. The established schools continued their influence but reflected the changing tastes in art. As · a result there emerged three fundamental schools of artistic thought. First, there was the imaginative school, which renewed the impulse toward large-scale decorative work exemplified in the mural style of Puvis de Chavannes. Next, the school of nature study, an outgrowth of the Barbizon school, fostered the growth of landscape painting. Third, the school of Impressionism, with its new approach to color handling, exerted a profound influence upon French art.

Of the three, Sewell preferred the imaginative, decorative school, as is evidenced in his murals. Nevertheless he absorbed the ideals of the nature school and was attracted by the brush technique of the Impressionists. His major works are murals and landscapes that reflect all three influences. He tended toward the representation of literary and mythological themes using a natural setting and often an Impressionist approach.[30]

A student of the early English writers, Sewell made paintings that closely followed their texts, as is exemplified in the Georgian Court frieze of Chaucer's pilgrims. He also took inspiration from Tennyson, and painted a series of lunettes depicting the life of King Arthur, now the property of Choate Rosemary Hall, Wallingford, Connecticut. This series, originally twelve in number, is characterized by a strong sense of design, excellent handling of anatomy and backgrounds, and fine spatial control. The depiction of the human figures and of the settings gives evidence of the artist's fidelity to Tennyson's text as well as his intimate knowledge of medieval costumes and customs. The general handling and the colors—predominating reds, greens, and blues—recall the style of the English Pre-Raphaelites. Incorporated into the design of each painting is a scroll bearing its title in Old English lettering.

One painting, entitled *The Passing of Arthur*, a circular canvas five feet in diameter, is located above the fireplace in the main dining hall. Inscribed around its circumference are Arthur's parting words to his loyal knight Sir Bedivere, from Tennyson's poem: "The Old Order Changeth Yielding Place to the New and God Fulfills Himself in Many Ways." Another canvas, almost five feet square, entitled *The Last Tournament*, hangs in an administrative office. The remaining eight noted in the Archives are triangular in shape, with a base span of seven feet and an apex height of a little over two feet depicting the following subjects: *Merlin Takes the Child Arthur, Excalibur the Sword, Arthur Draws the Sword from the Anvil, Geraint and Enid, Gawaine and Lady Ettard, Flight of Lancelot and Guinevere, Arthur's Last Fight,* and a second *The Passing of Arthur.*

In a letter to George St. John, headmaster of the school from 1908 to 1947, Sewell describes the importance of the theme of the series, saying:

> They represent two and a half years of work during the most ripened period of my life, after long study of the Arthurian cycle which has always interested me so keenly.
>
> The period of the laying of the foundation of Christian knighthood is one which has always appealed to me and which should stir the heroic impulses of the youth of today.

To these stories in picture form I have devoted my later years.[31]

Sewell also refers to his gift of the circular painting in the main dining hall, and expresses his hope that the school may be interested in the purchase of the others in the series. Since the artist does not mention an exact date of execution and no dates appear on the canvasses, they are thought to have been done during the early 1900s, around the time when his sons attended the school. Robert Brewster Sewell was a member of the Class of 1914 and William Joyce Sewell was a student there from 1912 to 1914. Subsequent correspondence indicates that the series was purchased by the school. In one letter found in the Choate archives, St. John describes his feeling about the paintings saying:

> and I believe every one who comes to the School, whether he knows it or not, is made happier and stronger by their being here! . . . I hope you realize what they stand for in my mind, of beauty and inspiration and chivalry and all the intangible things that I should like these youngsters to remember as more lasting gifts from the School than the Latin and Algebra that we put into them more definitely.

In this same letter to Sewell's son he continues:

> My recollections of your father are clear and happy ones: his was not a personality that would ever be forgotten! I remember best of all his coming when the large painting in the dining room was put in place: the breathless anxiety as it was unrolled, and the mechanical details of its mounting attended to, and then his climbing on to the shelf to paint in some of the gulls that are flying over the rocks, to touch a high light on a wave, and, at my request, to sign his name.[32]

For many years these paintings adorned the wood-paneled interiors of Hill House and the Memorial House Common Room.

Other works inspired by literature formerly hung in the South Kent School, South Kent, Connecticut. Receiving wide acclaim was his careful representation of the story of Siegfried, entitled *The Life of Everyman*. His series of lunettes, entitled *The Story of Psyche*, hung for many years in the Palm Room of the St. Regis Hotel, New York City. Other works in this vein are the easel paintings *Bacchante* and *Aerial Nymphs*, painted in 1891, now in private collections. Sewell is also noted for his fine paintings of Alaskan scenery, now presumably in the family collection. Some of them are briefly described in letters from the son Robert Brewster Sewell, addressed to George St. John, now in the Choate archives.

A number of awards came to the artist—the first

Hallgarten prize at the National Academy in 1889, a silver medal at Boston in 1891, the silver medal at the Pan-American Exposition in Buffalo in 1901, and in 1904 the silver medal at the Saint Louis exhibition. From 1889 to 1901 he was active in the Architectural League of New York and in 1901 was elected an Associate of the National Academy of Design. He held membership in the Society of Mural Painters, the Century Association, and the Union League Club of New York.

His numerous exhibitions in the New York area familiarized the public with his work. Among his friends and admirers was the architect Bruce Price. Hence, in 1897, when George Gould was looking for a master painter to adorn the upper walls of the great hall of the mansion, Price suggested Sewell as the artist most capable of executing a huge decorative frieze.

Always seeking fresh inspiration for their work, Robert and Amanda traveled in various parts of the world. They lived for many years in Florence, Italy, their most loved city. Compatible in their personalities and mutual love of art, they enjoyed a rich and happy life. Robert died quite suddenly on 18 November 1924, while engaged in work on a painting. Amanda followed two years later. They are buried side by side in the ancient cemetery of the Laurels near Florence.[33]

Epilogue

With the stock market crash of 1929 and its fateful aftermath, Lakewood's reputation as a winter resort began to decline. One by one the beautiful mansions were sold and were converted to apartment houses or institutional use. The lavish hotels fell into decay and were finally demolished. By the 1940s the town was approaching the end of one era and the beginning of another. Little by little it became a pleasant suburban refuge for city folk as well as a haven for refugees from Central and Eastern Europe. Poultry farms became the thriving business while alert citizens campaigned for and attracted an influx of light technical industries. By the 1960s Lakewood had also become famous as a retirement community.

As the town develops and expands, the metamorphosis continues with an architectural character quite different from that of the Gilded Age. Nevertheless, its enduring natural beauty provides seasonal enjoyment for the citizens. Over toward the east the John D. Rockefeller Estate is now the beautiful Ocean County Park, with its acres of evergreens planted at the millionaire's direction. Toward the west the former Arthur B. Claflin estate is now called Pine Park. On the eastern banks of Lake Carasaljo one of the few reminders of a fashionable past remains intact—the lavish estate of George Jay Gould. Since 1924, above its wrought-iron entrance gate, a similarly wrought-iron arch enframes the words *Georgian Court College*.

While Gould was building Georgian Court, he had no foreknowledge of the far-reaching consequences of his achievement. When after his death his heirs decided to sell the estate to the Sisters, they undoubtedly realized the worthiness of their decision and perhaps sensed the good that would result from it. But neither the Gould heirs, nor anyone for that matter, can estimate the value of the educational apostolate that continues at Georgian Court College under the Sisters of Mercy, nor the delight that the beauty of the estate and its treasures have afforded an endless stream of visitors. Since 1924 graduates of many faiths, fortified with noble principles, have left its gates and entered many walks of life to influence, to nurture, and to educate still others. Visitors who come to gaze in disbelief at this Gilded Age splendor take away the remembrance of delightful, enriching moments. While other millionaires have knowingly left their fortunes for a host of purposes, some worthy, some not, George Gould unwittingly left a marvelous legacy.

Several years after the transition from estate to college campus, Arthur Brisbane, the editor who first lived in Kingscote and later also purchased Hamilton House, published an editorial in which he wrote:

> Mr. Gould started out to build, in the pine forests of Lakewood, most healthful region within easy reach of New York City, the most comfortable and magnificent home that money could provide for his wife and his seven children, and he succeeded.
>
> Undoubtedly many, as they saw all this luxury and magnificence, looking through the high gold-tipped fence that cost enough to build half a dozen comfortable homes, said to themselves, "What terrific ex-

The wrought-iron arch above the Seventh Street entrance gate enframes the words Georgian Court College. *Photo by Vincent Hart*

In June 1924, although the students had finished their academic year at the College of Mount Saint Mary's in North Plainfield, their graduation was held at Georgian Court. *Archives of Mount Saint Mary's*

travagance," and some perhaps added, "That's enough to make a man into a Socialist." It is not however, a thing to make a sensible man into anything but a sensible man.

What was built for a few children will provide a splendid college home year after year for ambitious young women, studying under the best of health con-

ditions, in the centre of a great estate, in the mild air of the Lakewood pine forests.

Nothing really done well in this world is wasted. Time and history prove it.[1]

Time and history have indeed proved the worth of George Gould's "extravagance." Georgian Court College has grown and prospered. Its reputation for academic excellence and its dedicated faculty attract more and more students to its gates.

Soon after the purchase of the estate, the original buildings were adapted for college use. The mansion became a residence for students and faculty. In its plush great hall and first-floor rooms visitors attend concerts, receptions, and honor-society inductions. The marble staircase and fireplace are elegant settings for yearbook and wedding photos. At Christmas time the administration and faculty gather for festive cheer before the annual banquet and caroling.

The Sisters recognized that the floral conservatory at the west end would be the ideal place for a chapel. In due time stained-glass windows designed by the F. Mayer Studios in Munich replaced the frosted glass. In jeweled colors of predominating blues and reds, the mysteries of the Rosary were beautifully depicted. The windows and

The mansion conservatory is now a lovely chapel. *Photo by Vincent Hart*

On May 15, 1932, the stable tower was destroyed by fire. *Courtesy of Gene L. Hendrickson, copy photo Vincent Hart*

chapel appointments were the gift of Marie Heide, sister of the candy manufacturer. The bronze Stations of the Cross were donated by the Costello family of Perth Amboy, New Jersey. At the right of the conservatory a grotto formerly used for fern culture became the Lourdes shrine of Our Lady. Through the intervening years countless faculty members, students, and friends have worshiped in this most beautiful of chapels.[2]

The interior space of the stables was radically altered by the architect Robert J. Reiley of New York City. It then became the dining hall, kitchens, classrooms, offices, resident and music rooms—in other words, the hub of college life. The exterior remained unchanged until 1932, when on Sunday, 15 May, about eleven in the morning, a fire broke out in the tower while all the students were rehearsing in the Casino for the annual Musicale. Thought to have begun in the electrical wiring, the fire destroyed the tower and the central section of

Detail of Raymond Hall (former stable) as reconstructed after the fire. *Photo by Davis Studio*

The tanbark pony ring is now an auditorium-gymnasium. *Photo by Vincent Hart*

the building. By September of that year, though, the structure was restored to something like its original appearance by the architect Thomas E. McMullen of New York City. Among the changes that he made were the alteration of the entrance area and the elimination of the tower.

As for the Casino, it made an excellent college sports and general purpose building. The huge tanbark ring is now an auditorium-gymnasium, with a floor of highly polished wood. Since the first graduation in 1924, the vast space has been the setting for many college events: graduations and convocations, proms and parties, games and tournaments, musicales and art exhibits, and countless other affairs. Above the ring, on three sides of the building the original guest rooms provide student recreation rooms and offices. The original sports facilities are used daily by the students; the sports lounge is now a snack bar, and the ballroom a truly elegant Student Club.

On 14 May 1939 a deep stage constructed at the west end of the auditorium was dedicated under the patronage of Saint Cecilia to the famous soprano and alumna Jessica Dragonette. For many years Jessica, called "America's sweetheart of the airwaves," returned each May as guest artist of the Musicale.

The first Catholic church in Lakewood was moved to the campus in 1924. *Courtesy of Mary Hurlburt, photo by Richard Steele*

The church was connected to the north wings of the original stable by a classic peristyle. *Photo by Vincent Hart*

In addition to the conversion of the original buildings for college use, many more have been added through benefactors, purchase, or construction. In the fall of 1924 a lovely little chapel was annexed to the stables complex. Its history is unique. It was not constructed at the site but in the center of Lakewood about two miles from the campus. Built in 1890, it originally was the first Catholic church in Lakewood.[3] Anticipating the early completion of a new parish Church of Saint Mary of the Lake, Monsignor R. Spillane, the pastor and generous friend of the Sisters, decided to give the old church to the college rather than to sell or demolish it. It was then moved from Main Street to its present location.

The feat of moving the church, which took about two weeks, was recorded in *Believe It or Not* by Robert Ripley. From miles around people came to watch. On a series of broad treaded wheels ten teams of horses dragged the building along North Lake Drive, the inclined grade of which required constant readjustment of the cradle to prevent slipping or straining. When the church reached the tall iron fence along Lakewood Avenue, an opening was made to allow passage of the building.

After being set in place on its new foundation at the north end of the former stable yard, it was buttressed, stuccoed, and provided with appropriate trim in order to conform stylistically with the original Georgian stables. In place of its Gothic tower, a small bell tower and sacristy were added on the north end.[4] At the front, facing south, a white wooden peristyle in classic style was constructed to connect the building with the existing wings, thereby forming a lovely quadrangle that has become the heart of the campus.

In 1929 a local resident, inspired by the pastor's generosity, gave the Sisters a house that also was moved to its present location, west of the chapel.

A view showing the rear of the chapel; Mercedes Hall is to the right. *Davis Studio*

Hamilton House on Seventh Street, now a college residence hall, was built ca. 1906 for Mary Lillian Hamilton, a relative of Edith Gould. *Photo by Davis Studios*

Kingscote as it is today. After the fire of 1908, the interior and the third floor were modified by the architect Horace Trumbauer. *Photo by Davis Studios*

Through modification and addition, it was made to conform as closely as possible to the architectural character of the original buildings. Named Mercedes Hall after Sister Mary Mercedes, one of the pioneers of the Mercy Congregation, it serves as a faculty and student residence.

The next year the Sisters made two more additions for student housing. They purchased Hamilton House, the lovely Georgian mansion nearby on Seventh Street, which had been built by Edith Gould for her aunt Mrs. Mary Lillian Hamilton. They also acquired Kingscote on Lakewood Avenue. For some years these two mansions had been the property of Arthur Brisbane, who had bought them from the Goulds in the early 1920s.

Kingscote now serves as the administration building of the college. Enclosing the grounds is a marble-topped gray stucco wall with several ornate wrought-iron gates, thirteen feet high. When his daughter Marjorie Gould Drexel came to live there, George had the wall constructed as a protection for

The Henry S. Kearny mansion, acquired in 1940, is now the Music Center of the college. *Photo by Darue Studios*

In 1951 Farley Memorial Library was built east of the Italian Gardens. *Photo by Vincent Hart*

The Saint Joseph residence hall was completed in 1961. *Photo by Vincent Hart*

The Arts and Science Center, constructed in 1964, is located on the former Gould golf course site. *Photo by Vincent Hart*

her children from the horsemen riding to and fro in the streets surrounding his estate. Inside these walls today, rows of forsythia bushes create yellow masses of color in April and greenery thereafter. Outside, ivy vines creep up the sides. In springtime azaleas and flowering trees make the grounds a "fairyland"; in autumn the foliage, fiery red and yellow, makes patterns on the soft gray walls.

In 1940 the Henry S. Kearny mansion on Lakewood Avenue just east of the Court fence was acquired. First a Campus Club and then residence hall, it is now the Music Center. In 1944, a house on North Lake Drive, the onetime home of Madame de Cuevas, daughter of John D. Rockefeller, became the residence called Lake House. In 1967 this house was sold to the local parish of Christ Methodist Church.

Continued growth and expansion of the college have necessitated new construction. In 1951 Farley Memorial Library was built east of the Italian Gardens. Ten years later Saint Joseph Hall replaced the wooded area to the northwest of the Gardens. By this time the college needed further academic facilities. In 1964, on the north end of the property, the site of the original polo fields and golf course, the Arts and Science Center housing classrooms, laboratories, offices, and learning centers was constructed, as in 1967 was another residence, Maria Hall, overlooking the lovely Japanese Garden. Surrounded by the luxuriant foliage of aging trees, these newer structures coexist happily with Price's Georgian buildings.

Undergraduate and graduate students walk back and forth across the garden paths and find quiet study places in classic pergolas.[5] Local residents and visitors from afar enjoy the cultural offerings of the college and share its facilities.

On 20 December 1978 Georgian Court, the George Jay Gould Estate, was entered in the National Register of Historic Places. Earlier included in the New Jersey State Register, it enjoys renown as a place of special artistic and architectural significance. Thus the magnificent conception of Gould and his artists lives on in the public interest.

The end of the story of this estate of the Gilded Age is yet to be told. It is the fervent hope of the present occupants that its use as a fine Catholic liberal arts institution will continue for many years to come.

Maria Hall, a comfortable residence, was built just north of the Japanese Garden. *Photo by Vincent Hart*

Notes

PROLOGUE

1. By the 1920s the railroad was renamed the Jersey Central Railroad. One of the most interesting of the privately operated coaches was that of James Hazen Hyde, son of the founder of the Equitable Life Assurance Society. For six weeks in the spring of 1903, he ran a coach, the *Liberty*, from the Holland House, Fifth Avenue, New York City, to Laurel-in-the-Pines, using changes of eleven teams of horses. These expeditions were recorded by the German artist Max Klepper in charming watercolors, property of the New York Historical Society.

2. Gustave Kobbé, *The New Jersey Coast and Pines* (1889; reprint ed., Baltimore, Md.: Gateway Press, 1970), p. 86.

3. Several unpublished sources were utilized for the history of Lakewood: *Know Your Township—Lakewood*, prepared by the Lakewood League of Women Voters, September 1959; a cassette tape recorded by the Reverend Marshall Sewell entitled "Lakewood—a Fifty Year Perspective," 26 October 1978; and Paul Axel-Lute, "Lakewood-in-the-Pines: A History of Lakewood, N.J.," Lakewood, 1975.

PART I

1. Margherita Hamm, *Famous Families of New York* (New York: Putnam, 1901), p. 237.

2. *Arms and Pedigree of Kingdon Gould of New York and Georgian Court, Lakewood, New Jersey* (New York, 1906). The booklet is in the collection of the New York Genealogical Society.

3. The exact day of birth cannot be ascertained.

4. *New York Times*, 15 September 1886, p. 1.

5. *New York Telegram*, 11 August 1930, part two, p. 1.

6. Ibid.

7. The date of birth of these children are as follows: Jay, 1 September 1888; Marjorie, 11 September 1890; Vivien, 2 May 1892; George, Jr., 28 March 1896.

8. *New York Evening Journal*, 14 November 1921, p. 3.

9. Ibid., 23 March 1925, p. 13.

10. The church built in 1884 still stands on the corner of Madison Avenue and Second Street.

11. *New Jersey Courier*, 14 April 1898, p. 1.

12. As told by Mary Hurlburt, Lakewood historian.

13. The total cost of the mansion has been estimated at approximately $1,000,000.

14. Barr Ferree, "A Talk with Bruce Price," Great American Architect Series, no. 5, *Architectural Record* (June 1899), p. 70.

15. Ibid., p. 66.

16. Ibid., p. 74.

17. Technical Department, "The Builder," Great American Architect Series, no. 5, *Architectural Record* (June 1899), p. 131.

18. Ferree, "Talk", p. 73.

19. "The Architect as Artist," Great American Architect Series, no. 5, *Architectural Record* (June 1899), p. 114.

20. As told by Sister M. Consolata Carroll, R.S.M.

21. It is not known which parts of these murals and decorations were actually painted by each artist. George W. Maynard was a popular decorator at the turn of the century, who painted murals in the Waldorf Hotel and Plaza Hotel, New York; Sherry's New York ballroom; Congressional Library ceiling and entrance hall wall. Charles M. Shean painted landscape decorations in the Manhattan Hotel, New York. Irving Ramsay Wiles, N.A., was a noted painter and muralist, winner of numerous awards. He was represented in the collections of the Metropolitan Museum, New York; National Gallery of Art and Corcoran Gallery, Washington, D.C.; Butler Art Institute, Youngstown, Ohio; and numerous galleries in the United States.

22. *New Jersey Courier*, 30 December 1897, p. 1.

23. During a six-day sale from 28 April to 4 May, 1924, most of the original pieces of furniture, specially designed by the firm of Theodore Hofstater & Co., New York, together with other furnishings of the estate, were sold at auction by the Gould heirs under the auspices of Samuel Marx, Inc., Auctioneers and Appraisers, 24 West 58th Street, New York City.

24. Katherine Hoffman, "George Gould's Home at Lakewood," *Munsey's Magazine* 23 (June 1900): 305–7.

25. Ibid., p. 302.

26. This recognition and identification was first made by Cheryl Stoeber, Georgian Court College, Class of 1979.

27. Elizabeth Meriwether Gilmer, "The Goulds," *Cosmopolitan Magazine* 46 (May 1909): 606.

28. *New York Evening Journal*, 14 November 1921, p. 3.

29. Bruce Price, "A Georgian House for Seven Thousand Dollars," *Ladies' Home Journal* 17 (October 1900), p. 15.

30. This information about Horace Trumbauer was supplied by Frederick Platt of Elkins Park, Pennsylvania.

31. *New York Evening Journal*, 24 March 1925, p. 12.

32. Ibid.

33. *New York Times,* 10 December 1899, p. 23.

34. These statements are included in a hand-lettered testimonial found in the Georgian Court College archives.

35. George Jay Gould, "Polo and the Business Man," *The Independent* 56 (June 1904): 1232.

36. John Allen Krout, *Annals of American Sport.* Pageant of America, 15 vols. (New Haven, Conn.: Yale University Press, 1929), 15: 220.

37. Allison Danzig, *The Racquet Game* (New York: Macmillan Co., 1930), p. 60.

38. Ibid., p. 69.

39. Robert N. Burnett, "George Jay Gould," *Cosmopolitan Magazine* 35 (May 1903): 60.

40. C. M. Keys, "The Overlords of Railroad Traffic," *World's Work* 12 (January 1907): 8437–38.

41. Burton J. Hendrick, "The Passing of a Great Railroad Dynasty," *McClure's Magazine* 38, no. 5 (March 1912): 487.

42. Keys, "Overlords", p. 8441.

43. Ernest Howard, *Wall Street Fifty Years after Erie* (Boston: Sratford, 1923), pp. 42–43.

44. Ibid., p. 46.

45. Ibid., p. 49.

46. Ibid., p. 55.

47. Ibid., p. 85n.

48. See frontispiece and illustrations in Ralph Pulitzer, *New York Society on Parade,* (1910; reprint ed., Leisure Class in America Series, New York: Arno, 1975).

49. *New York Evening Journal,* 6 March 1925, p. 11.

50. Ibid., 11 April 1925, p. 9.

51. *New York Times,* 14 November 1921, p. 1.

52. *New York Evening Journal,* 1 May 1925, p. 23.

53. *New York Times,* 15 July 1922, p. 1.

54. Ibid., 17 May 1923, p. 1.

55. *New York Evening Journal,* 23 April 1925, p. 17.

56. The date of indenture was 19 May 1924, witnessed by the executors of the George Jay Gould estate, Kingdon Gould and Schuyler Neilson Rice and by Mother Mary Cecilia Scully, President, and Mother Mary John Considine, Secretary, of Mount Saint Mary's College, North Plainfield, New Jersey.

PART II

1. Vincent J. Scully, *The Shingle Style* (New Haven, Conn.: Yale University Press, 1955) p. 77.

2. Henry-Russell Hitchcock, *Architecture: Nineteenth and Twentieth Centuries,* The Pelican History of Art Series (Baltimore, Md.: Penguin Books, 1958), p. 362.

3. Scully, *Shingle Style,* p. 4.

4. Ibid., pp. 28-31.

5. Hitchcock, *Architecture: Nineteenth,* p. 365.

6. Ibid., pp. 278–79.

7. J. Thomas Scharf, *History of Western Maryland,* 2 vols. (1882; reprint ed., Baltimore: Regional Publishing Co., 1968), 2: 1118–20.

8. Ibid.

9. The most complete record of their work is in Richard H. Howland and Eleanor P. Spencer, *The Architecture of Baltimore,* ed. Wilbur Harvey Hunter, Jr. (Baltimore, Md.: Johns Hopkins Press, 1953).

10. Price's first important design in Baltimore is thought to be Saint Paul's Evangelical Lutheran Church, at the corner of W. Saratoga and Fremont streets, built in 1866.

11. The firm of Baldwin and Price was listed in *The Baltimore City Directory,* 1870.

12. *Vestry Records,* 6 April 1871.

13. Edwin Post, *Truly Emily Post* (New York: Funk and Wagnalls, 1961), pp. 6–7.

14. This cabinet was given to the Museum of the City of New York in July 1954 by Emily Post. The accession number is 54.115.1; for the jewelry, 54.115.26.

15. The records of the Wilkes-Barre Historical Society give the date of construction as 1876. The building, now known as Bedford Hall, is on the campus of Wilkes College.

16. *American Architect and Building News,* 8 September 1877, p. 288.

17. Countess Priscilla Venerosi Pesciolini of Florence, Italy, the daughter of Josephine Lee Price's small brother who accompanied the Prices on their wedding trip, told Graybill that Price brought back crates of tiles from Italy.

18. *American Architect and Building News,* 22 December 1877, p. 410. This probably refers to Wilkes-Barre.

19. Ibid., 28 July 1877, p. 241.

20. Ibid., 17 August 1878, p. 57.

21. Post, *Truly Emily,* pp. 32–33.

22. *American Architect and Building News,* 4 May 1878. See also *Record of New Building, 1878* (January), p. 20.

23. Scully, *Shingle Style,* p. 77.

24. Ibid., p. 78.

25. *American Architect and Building News,* 5 June 1880, p. 254.

26. The handsome structure followed the general plan invented by Lewis Miller, and encouraged by Bishop Vincent, after its first use in the First Methodist Episcopal Church of Akron, Ohio, in 1868. The unusual two-story semi-octagonal space is surrounded by radiating rooms on two different floors, which can be separated from the large room by sliding doors. The plan and its purpose is described by Ellwood Hendrick in *Lewis Miller* (New York: Putnam, 1925), p. 147. A symbolic interpretation can be found in Thomas E. Tallmadge's *Architecture in Old Chicago* (Chicago: University of Chicago Press, 1941), pp. 171–73.

27. For example, Wright's Willitts House, Highland Park, Illinois, of 1902. According to Graybill, the Neff house was presumably completed by June 1882, because, for the first time, the Neff address is published at this location in *Williams' Cincinnati Directory.*

28. Freeman was never original. By 1888 he was copying from Price's work at Tuxedo. For example, see a Freeman design illustrated in *American Architect and Building News,* 2 June 1888.

29. Ibid., 6 January 1883, p. 12.

30. The house became the parsonage in 1924, when it was given to the church by Kate Pettebone Dickson.

31, Cleveland Amory, *The Last Resorts* (New York: Harper & Bros., 1952), p. 112.

32. Ibid., p. 108.

33. Illustrated in *American Architect and Building News,* 13 March 1886. The address is incorrectly given as Fifth Avenue. The house is dated 1884 on the facade. It is listed in the *Record of New Building, 1884-85* (July), p. 13.

34. Talbot E. Hamlin, *The American Spirit in Architecture,* Pageant of America, 13 vols. (New Haven, Conn.: Yale University Press, 1926), 13:169.

35. *American Architect and Building News,* 3 May 1884, p. 216.

36. Post, *Truly Emily,* p. 8.

37. For a complete account, see Teobert Maler, "Researches in the Central Portion of the Usumatsintla Valley," *Memoirs of the Peabody Museum of American Archaeology and Ethnology, Harvard University,* vol. 2, no. 2 (Cambridge, Mass.: Harvard University Press, 1903). For an account of the interaction between Charnay and Lorillard, see *American Architect and Building News,* 27 January 1883, pp. 44–45. See also Désiré Charnay, *The Ancient Cities of the New World* (New York: Harper & Bros., 1887).

38. Emily Post, "Tuxedo Park, an American Rural Community," *The Century Magazine* 82, no. 6 (October 1911): 796.

39. Ibid., p. 798.

40. *Harper's Weekly,* 18 December 1886, p. 827.

41. Amory, *Last Resorts,* pp. 83–84.

42. Ibid., p. 89.

43. George Sheldon, *Artistic Country Seats,* 5 vols. (1886–87; reprint ed., New York: Da Capo, 1978), 2: 47–49.

44. Frank Kintrea, "Tuxedo Park," *American Heritage* 29, no. 5 (August/September 1978): 71.

45. Sheldon, *Artistic Seats*, p. 41. According to Sheldon, the house was originally occupied by J. L. Breese, later by Pierre Lorillard. Scully, *Shingle Style*, calls it the Lorillard house.

46. Scully, *Shingle Style*, p. 126.

47. Ibid., illustrations 155 and 156, the Wright and Chandler houses. The street side of the Chandler house has since been altered.

48. Sheldon, *Artistic Seats*, p. 35.

49. Scully, Shingle Style, illustrations 142 and 143.

50. "A Review of the Third Annual Exhibition of the Architectural League," *Building*, 31 December 1887, p. 219.

51. Hartwig Frischel, "Das Moderne Amerikanische Wohnhaus," *Kunst und Kunsthandwerk* 14 (1911): 519.

52. Russell Sturgis, "The Works of Bruce Price," Great American Architect Series, no. 5, *Architectural Record* (June 1899), illustration, p. 49.

53. Ibid., illustration.

54. Ibid., illustration, p. 48.

55. Harold D. Kalman, *The Railway Hotels and the Development of the Chateau Style in Canada*, University of Victoria Maltwood Museum, Studies in Architectural History Number One, 1968, pp. 7–8.

56. Ibid., p. 8.

57. Omar Lavallée, "Windsor Station 1889–1964," *Canadian Rail* 152 (February 1964): 27.

58. Kalman, *Railway Hotels*, pp. 8–9. See also *American Architect and Building News*, 16 June 1888, p. 282, and 17 November 1888, p. 229.

59. Kalman, *Railway Hotels*, pp. 9–10.

60. Ibid., p. 11.

61. See Joan E. Morgan, *Castle at Quebec* (Toronto: J. M. Dent & Sons, 1949) for a detailed study of the history of the Château.

62. Sturgis, "Works of Price," pp. 27–34. Illustrations pp. 28–33.

63. Kalman, *Railway Hotels*, p. 13.

64. Barr Ferree, "A Talk with Bruce Price," Great American Architect Series, no. 5, *Architectural Record* (June 1899): 82.

65. Walter Vaughan, *The Life and Work of Sir William Van Horne* (New York: Century, 1920), p. 199.

66. John M. Gibbon, *Steel of Empire: The Romantic History of the Canadian Pacific, the Northwest Passage of Today* (Indianapolis, Ind.,: Bobbs, 1935), p. 336.

67. Post, *Truly Emily*, p. 120.

68. Ibid., pp. 65–66.

69. Kalman, *Railway Hotels*, p. 16.

70. Ibid., pp. 16–17.

71. Mrs. Schuyler Van Rensselaer, *Henry Hobson Richardson and His Works* (Boston and New York: Houghton Mifflin Co., 1888), pp. 97–99.

72. This information was given to Graybill by Mrs. Frank Samanis of Stratford, Connecticut, who was born in 1858.

73. See drawing in *American Architect and Building News*, 1 January 1887.

74. Sturgis, "Works of Price," p. 38.

75. Comments about this style may be found in Andrew Jackson Downing, *Rural Essays* (New York: Leavitt and Allen, 1857).

76. The date is indicated in the church records.

77. James W. Thomas and T. J. C. Williams, *History of Allegheny County, Maryland* (Cumberland, Md.: Titsworth & Co., 1924), p. 425.

78. "A Review of the Works of Charles C. Haight," Great American Architect Series, no. 6, *Architectural Record* (July 1899), p. 6.

79. Potter's drawings were done in 1891, but the building was apparently not completed until 1896. See *American Architect and Building News*, 12 December 1891.

80. Samuel H. Graybill, Jr., "Bruce Price, American Architect, 1845—1903," Ph.D. diss., Yale University, 1957, p. 147.

81. As told to Graybill by Mr. Fred J. Mack, architect of Wilkes-Barre, who worked briefly for Price as a draftsman.

82. Sturgis, "Works of Price," p. 76.

83. Among the more important buildings that were similar to the Sun Building were LeBrun's Metropolitan Life Insurance Company Building in New York, 1909, and the United States Custom House in Boston, by Peabody and Stearns, 1915.

84. The drawing is dated 25 December 1890.

85. Lloyd Morris gives the American Surety Building this distinction in *Incredible New York* (New York: Random House, 1951), p. 199.

86. Francisco Mujica, *History of the Skyscraper* (New York: Helburn, 1930), plate 28.

87. Sturgis, "Works of Price," pp. 4–12.

88. The drawings were first exhibited at the Architectural League, New York, in 1897. a photograph indicating the completion of the St. James Building first appeared in the *Inland Architect and News Record* (February 1898). See also Sturgis, "Works of Price," pp. 12–18, illustration p. 13.

89. Jefferson Williamson, *The American Hotel* (New York: Alfred A. Knopf, 1930), p. 261.

90. For a complete description, see Montgomery Schuyler, "The Small City House in New York," *Architectural Record* 8 (April–June 1899): 379.

91. *The Hotchkiss Annual* (Lakeville, Conn., 1893), p. 13.

92. Sturgis, "Works of Price," p. 55.

93. *Proceedings at the Public Opening of the New Society Building, New Haven Colony Historical Society*, (New Haven, Conn., 1893), p. 8.

94. Bruce Price, "Suburban House," *Homes in City and Country* (New York: Charles Scribner's Sons, 1893), p. 75.

95. Described in Juliette Tomlinson's *Ten Famous Houses of Springfield* (Springfield, Mass., n.p., 1952).

96. *Harper's Weekly*, 28 November 1896, pp. 1174–76.

97. *American Architect and Building News*, 12 November 1898, p. 55.

98. Sturgis, "Works of Price," pp. 25–26.

99. Illustrated in *American Architect and Building News*, 24 May 1902.

100. *Emmanuel Episcopal Parish Register*, vol. 1, 15 November 1900 and 27 February 1902.

101. This information is contained in a mimeographed brochure, available at the Home, entitled "Summary of the Osborn Home."

102. *Catalogue of the Sixteenth Annual Exhibition of the Architectural League of New York* (New York, 1901), p. 42.

103. This information on Katayama is from Graybill's correspondence with K. Abe, Tokyo, Japan.

104. Post, *Truly Emily*, p. 116.

105. *New York Times*, 31 May 1923, p. 7.

106. Post, *Truly Emily*, p. 163.

PART III

1. Many of the bushes died during the 1940s. All of the arbor vitae was removed.

2. These conclusions are supported by the careful research of Nancy Morse, Class of 1979, Georgian Court College.

3. Noted in the Georgian Court College Archives.

4. From a letter in the Georgian Court College Archives addressed to Mother Mary John, dated 25 October 1927, from Duveen Brothers, Inc., 720 Fifth Avenue, New York City. The letter states that the sum paid for the piece was $20,000.

5. From a typed paper in the Georgian Court College Archives.

6. Wayne Craven, *Sculpture in America* (New York: T. Y. Crowell Co., 1968), p. 487.

7. J. Walker McSpadden, *Famous Sculptors of America* (New York: Dodd, Mead & Co., 1924), p. 268.

8. From a letter from Duveen Brothers, Inc., then located at 18 East 79th Street, New York City, dated 19 October 1953. The letter is in the Georgian Court College Archives.

9. I am indebted for some of this research material about the fountain to June MacMillan, "An Expository and Descriptive Work on the Fountain of Apollo" (B.A. thesis, Georgian Court College, 1954).

10. N. MacDonald, "A Genius of the Chisel," *Munsey's Magazine* 14 (March 1896): 671.

11. Craven, *Sculpture*, p. 486.

12. Fairmount Park Art Association, *Sculpture of a City: Philadelphia's Treasures in Bronze and Stone* (New York: Walker & Co., 1976), p. 212.

13. Archives of American Art, New York City, from a folder on J. Massey Rhind.

14. McSpadden, *Famous Sculptors*, p. 257.

15. "Ceremonies at the Unveiling of the Washington Monument, Van Horn Bequest, Newark, New Jersey, 2 November 1912." Commemorative booklet.

16. "Ceremonies at the Unveiling of a copy of the Colleoni Equestrian Statue by Verrocchio Executed by J. Massey Rhind, Sculptor, Newark, New Jersey, 26, July 1916." Commemorative booklet.

17. *Boston Sunday Advertiser,* 21 October 1923, p. 1.

18. McSpadden, *Famous Sculptors,* p. 261.

19. *New York Times,* 22 October 1936, p. 23.

20. Takeo Shiota, *The Japanese Landscape* (Newark: Newark Museum Association, 1915), p. 11.

21. Ibid., p. 12.

22. Ibid.

23. Exhibition Booklet for the Japan Society, Brooklyn Botanic Garden, New York, 1 August 1915.

24. Clay Lancaster, *The Japanese Influence in America* (New York: W. H. Rawls, 1963), p. 200. See also illustration of the P.D. Saklatvala garden, p. 202.

25. Shiota, *Japanese Landscape,* p 13.

26. Lancaster, *Japanese Influence,* p. 205.

27. Robert Van Vorst Sewell, "The Canterbury Pilgrimage: a Decorative Frieze," New York, n.d., p. 5. This little booklet, which is in the Georgian Court College Archives, was printed for American Art Galleries by J. J. Little and Company, Astor Place, but apparently never formally published.

28. Ibid., p. 3.

29. Ibid., p. 4.

30. I am indebted for some of the facts regarding Sewell's background and style to Helen Reid Cole, "Robert Van Vorst Sewell, Muralist, 1860–1924" (B.A. thesis, Georgian Court College, 1943).

31. From a letter to Mr. George St. John, Headmaster, 18 March 1924, Choate Rosemary Hall Archives, Wallingford, Conn.

32. From a letter to Robert Brewster Sewell, 7 January 1925, Choate Rosemary Hall Archives, Wallingford, Conn.

33. The information about Sewell's death and burial is taken from a letter to Mr. George St. John, Headmaster, 28 November 1924, Choate Rosemary Hall, Wallingford, Conn.

EPILOGUE

1. *New York Evening Journal,* 4 April 1925, p. 14.

2. On 20 January 1978 during a severe snowstorm, the original inner and outer glass and metal roofs collapsed under the weight of the snow. By the spring of 1980, with the use of contemporary materials, the roofs were restored to their original appearance by the Edward J. Byrne Studio, Doylestown, Pa.

3. The first parish Church of Saint Mary of the Lake was built by the first pastor, the Reverend Thomas B. Healy. The cornerstone was laid on 15 August 1890; the dedication took place 29 April 1891. Before that time Mass was celebrated in private homes or in small temporary chapels in Lakewood.

4. The interior of the chapel is of modified Gothic style. It is wood-paneled and painted in light tones. The large lancet window over the altar was a gift of the Reverend Thomas B. Healy. The lancet windows along the side walls, made by the F. Mayer Company of Munich and New York, were donated by friends and relatives of the Sisters of Mercy.

5. In 1976 the first graduate students arrived on campus (men and women) to begin work toward M.A.'s in education. In 1979 a coeducational undergraduate evening program was initiated.

Bibliography

PROLOGUE and PART I

Books

Danzig, Allison. *The Racquet Game.* New York: Macmillan Co., 1930.

Hamm, Margherita A. *Famous Families of New York.* 2 vols. New York: Putnam, 1901.

Howard, Ernest. *Wall Street Fifty Years after Erie.* Boston: Stratford, 1923.

Hoyt, Edwin P. *The Goulds.* New York: Weybright & Talley, 1969.

Kobbé, Gustave. *The New Jersey Coast and Pines.* 1889. Reprint. Baltimore: Gateway Press, 1970.

Krout, John Allen. *Annals of American Sport.* Pageant of America, vol. 15. New Haven, Conn.: Yale University Press, 1929.

McMahon, William. *South Jersey Towns.* New Brunswick, N.J.: Rutgers University Press, 1973.

O'Connor, Richard. *Gould's Millions.* New York: Doubleday, 1962.

Articles and Periodicals

Burnett, Robert N. "George Jay Gould." *Cosmopolitan Magazine* 35 (1903): 59–61.

Eaton, Percival R. "Lakewood, a Famous Winter Resort." *New England Magazine* 33 (1906): 604–19.

Ferree, Barr. "A Talk with Bruce Price." Great American Architect Series, no. 5. *Architectural Record* (June 1899), pp. 65–112.

Gilmer, Elizabeth Meriwether. "The Goulds." *Cosmopolitan Magazine* 46 (1909): 603–15.

Gould, George Jay. "Polo and the Business Man." *The Independent* 56 (1904): 1231–34.

Hendrick, Burton J. "The Passing of a Great Railroad Dynasty." *McClure's Magazine* 38, no. 5 (1912): 483–501.

Hoffman, Katherine. "George Gould's Home at Lakewood." *Munsey's Magazine* 23 (1900): 301–9.

Keys, C. M. "The Overlords of Railroad Traffic." *World's Work* 12 (1907): 8437–45.

Price, Bruce. "A Georgian House for Seven Thousand Dollars." *Ladies' Home Journal* 17 (1900): 15.

Sturgis, Russell. "The Works of Bruce Price." Great American Architect Series, no. 5. *Architectural Record* (June 1899): 1–64.

———. "The Builder." Great American Architect Series, no. 5. *Architectural Record* (June 1899), pp. 131–33.

Treadwell, Prentice, "The Architect as Artist." "Great American Architect Series, no. 5." *Architectural Record* (June 1899), pp. 13–14.

Unpublished Material

Arms and Pedigree of Kingdon Gould of New York and Georgian Court, Lakewood, New Jersey. New York, 1906. Booklet.

Axel-Lute, Paul. "Lakewood-in-the-Pines: a History of Lakewood, N.J." Mimeographed. Lakewood, N.J., 1975.

Know Your Township—Lakewood. Booklet prepared by the Lakewood League of Women voters, Lakewood, N.J. September 1959.

Other Sources

Newspapers have been useful for information about the Goulds. Particularly helpful was the series entitled "Edith Gould's Own Story of the Life of a Rich Girl," written by Edith Gould Wainwright, daughter of

George and Edith Gould. This series of forty chapters appeared in the *New York Evening Journal* from 23 March to 7 May 1925.

Taped interviews prepared by: Mother M. Patrick McCallion, Mount Saint Mary's Motherhouse, North Plainfield, N.J., 1979; Sister M. Consolata Carroll, Georgian Court College, Lakewood, N.J., 1978; Reverend Marshall Sewell, Lakewood, N.J., 1978.

PART II

Books

Amory, Cleveland. *The Last Resorts.* New York: Harper & Bros., 1952.

Charnay, Désiré. *The Ancient Cities of the New World.* New York: Harper & Bros., 1887.

Downing, Andrew Jackson. *Rural Essays.* New York: Leavitt and Allen, 1857.

Gibbon, John M. *Steel of Empire: The Romantic History of the Canadian Pacific, the Northwest Passage of Today.* Indianapolis, Ind.: Bobbs, 1935.

Hamlin, Talbot F. *The American Spirit in Architecture.* Pageant of America, vol. 13. New Haven, Conn.: Yale University Press, 1926.

Hitchcock, Henry-Russell. *Architecture: Nineteenth and Twentieth Centuries.* The Pelican History of Art Series. Baltimore, Md.: Penguin Books, 1958.

Kalman, Harold D. *The Railway Hotels and the Development of the Château Style in Canada.* University of Victoria Maltwood Museum, Studies in Architectural History, Number One, 1968.

Maler, Teobert. "Researches in the Central Portion of the Usumatsintla Valley." *Memoirs of the Peabody Museum of American Archaeology and Ethnology, Harvard University.* Vol. 2, no. 2. Cambridge, Mass., 1903.

Morgan, Joan E. *Castle at Quebec.* Toronto: J. M. Dent & Sons, 1949.

Morris, Lloyd. *Incredible New York.* New York: Random House, 1951.

Mujica, Francisco. *History of the Skyscraper.* New York: Helburn, 1930.

Post, Edwin. *Truly Emily Post.* New York: Funk & Wagnalls, 1961.

Price, Bruce. "The Suburban House." *Homes in City and Country.* New York: Charles Scribner's Sons, 1893.

Scharf, J. Thomas. *History of Western Maryland.* 1882. Reprint. Baltimore, Md.: Regional Publishing Co., 1968.

Scully, Vincent J. *The Shingle Style.* New Haven, Conn.: Yale University Press, 1955.

Sheldon, George. *Artistic Country Seats.* Vol. 2. 1886–87. Reprint. New York: Da Capo, 1978.

Van Rensselaer, Mrs. Schuyler. *Henry Hobson Richardson and His Works.* Boston & New York: Houghton Mifflin Co., 1888.

Vaughan, Walter. *The Life and Work of Sir William Van Horne.* New York: Century, 1920.

Williamson, Jefferson. *The American Hotel.* New York: Alfred A. Knopf, 1930.

Articles and Periodicals

American Architect and Building News is useful for many references to Bruce Price's works. The magazine began publication in 1876, just one year before Price moved to New York. For the rest of his life, he was one of the major contributors to the magazine. The 2 August 1903 issue was a posthumous memorial to his late works.

Kintrea, Frank. "Tuxedo Park." *American Heritage* 29 (1978): 69–77.

Post, Emily. "Tuxedo Park, an American Rural Community." *The Century Magazine* 82 (1911): 795–98.

"A Review of the Third Annual Exhibition of the Architectural League." *Building* 7 (1887): 219.

PART III

Books

Craven, Wayne. *Sculpture in America.* New York: T. Y. Crowell Co., 1968.

Fairmount Park Art Association. *Sculpture of a City: Philadelphia's Treasures in Bronze and Stone.* New York: Walker & Co., 1976.

Ferree, Barr. *American Estates and Gardens.* New York: Munn & Co., 1904.

Lancaster, Clay. *The Japanese Influence in America.* New York: W. H. Rawls, 1963.

McSpadden, J. Walker. *Famous Sculptors of America.* New York: Dodd, Mead & Co., 1924.

Shiota, Takeo. *The Japanese Landscape.* Newark: Newark Museum Association, 1915.

Taft, Lorado. *The History of American Sculpture.* New York: Macmillan Co., 1930.

Articles and Periodicals

Á Beckett, John J. "A Scotch American Sculptor." *Art Interchange* 48 (1902): 84–86.

MacDonald, N. "A Genius of the Chisel." *Munsey's Magazine* 14 (1896): 671–79.

Payne, Frank Owen. "The American Indian in Sculpture." *Munsey's Magazine* 60 (1917): 41–50.

Unpublished Material

Cole, Helen Reid. "Robert Van Vorst Sewell, Muralist, 1860–1924." B.A. thesis, Georgian Court College, 1943.

MacMillan, June. "An Expository and Descriptive Work on the Fountain of Apollo." B.A. thesis, Georgian Court College, 1954.

Price, Bruce. "The Classic Gardens at Georgian Court." Georgian Court College Archives. Typed paper.

Sewell, Robert Van Vorst. "The Canterbury Pilgrimage: a Decorative Frieze." New York, n.d.

Index

References to illustrations are printed in italics.